From Simple Input
to Complex Grammar

LD
&CC **The MIT Press Series in Learning, Development, and Conceptual Change**
Lila Gleitman, Susan Carey, Elissa Newport, and Elizabeth Spelke, editors

Names for Things: A Study in Human Learning, John Macnamara, 1982

Conceptual Change in Childhood, Susan Carey, 1985

"Gavagai!" or the Future History of the Animal Language Controversy, David Premack, 1986

Systems That Learn: An Introduction to Learning Theory for Cognitive and Computer Scientists, Daniel N. Osherson, Michael Stob, and Scott Weinstein, 1986

From Simple Input to Complex Grammar, James L. Morgan, 1986

From Simple Input to Complex Grammar

James L. Morgan

The MIT Press
Cambridge, Massachusetts
London, England

This book was set in VIP Times by Village Typographers, Inc., and printed and bound by Halliday Lithograph in the United States of America.

Library of Congress Cataloging-in-Publication Data

Morgan, James L.
  From simple input to complex grammar.

  (The MIT Press series in learning, development, and conceptual change)
  Bibliography: p.
  Includes index.
  1. Language acquisition. 2. Learning ability.
I. Title. II. Series.
P118.M68   1986   401'.9   86-2988
ISBN 0-262-13217-6

To Gina

Contents

Series Foreword

This series in learning, development, and conceptual change will include state-of-the-art reference works, seminal book-length monographs, and texts on the development of concepts and mental structures. It will span learning in all domains of knowledge, from syntax to geometry to the social world, and will be concerned with all phases of development, from infancy through adulthood.

The series intends to engage such fundamental questions as

The nature and limits of learning and maturation: the influence of the environment, of initial structures, and of maturational changes in the nervous system on human development; learnability theory; the problem of induction; domain specific constraints on development.

The nature of conceptual change: conceptual organization and conceptual change in child development, in the acquisition of expertise, and in the history of science.

Lila Gleitman
Susan Carey
Elissa Newport
Elizabeth Spelke

Preface

A certain degree of irony is involved in using learnability theory to support a hypothesis concerning the nature of language input: learnability is most widely recognized as a method that has been used to support nativistic claims about language acquisition, whereas much of the work on input has been motivated in part by reactions against such claims. Nevertheless, the formal methods that learnability theory makes available have much to contribute to our quest for understanding of the role that input performs in language acquisition. These methods provide a rigorous framework that may make explicit the contributions that particular properties of input provide to acquisition and, equally if not more important, may reveal the points at which input alone will not suffice. Moreover, learnability theory may permit us to address fundamental questions that may otherwise prove elusive; in particular, I will argue that learnability may allow us to discover which aspects of language input are *necessary* for successful language acquisition.

The hypothesis that I investigate in this monograph is that the linguistic part of children's input—utterances—consists of more than simple strings of words. Rather, I suggest, the speech that children hear contains cues that, in conjunction with the child's emerging knowledge of grammar, allows at least part of the phrase structure of input sentences to be reconstructed. Certainly, the regularity with which languages incorporate multiple devices that may signal phrase structure lends plausibility to this hypothesis. The predominant theme of this work is that input containing cues to phrase structure—*bracketed input*—may allow the child to acquire the complexities of grammar on the basis of very simple sentences, while eliminating the need for certain constraints on acquisition; moreover, because the sentences that children learning language actually hear are very simple, bracketed input may be necessary for language acquisition as we observe it. At the same time, it is important to keep in mind that even given my assumptions about input—and the assumptions adopted in my learnability proof could scarcely be stronger—the constraints on learning required to ensure successful language acquisition are far from trivial.

The Bracketed Input Hypothesis has its roots in work on miniature language learning that I undertook as a beginning graduate student. My advisor, Elissa Newport, was instrumental in pointing me toward this work. In the time since, Elissa has been mentor, collaborator, and friend to me; I find it difficult indeed to exaggerate how much I have benefited from my association with her. My interest in learnability theory was abetted by Susan Goldin-Meadow, Anne Hay, and Annette Zehler, who participated in a seminar I taught and, by forcing me to explain previous work, helped me to clarify my thinking and led me to new insights. An earlier version of the proof presented in this monograph formed the nucleus of my doctoral dissertation. In addition to Elissa Newport, Ann Brown, Doug Medin, and Jerry Morgan served as members of my thesis committee. I appreciate the consultation and conversation for which they made themselves readily available.

The learnability-theoretic research reported here could not have been contemplated, much less completed, without the contributions of previous workers in this area. In particular, I owe a great intellectual debt to Kenneth Wexler. Ken, along with William Cooper and Scott Weinstein, reviewed a previous version of this monograph, and I thank them all for their insightful comments. Several others provided helpful suggestions on aspects of this work: Aravind Joshi pointed out errors I had made in interpreting work on tree automata, Michael Kac and Nancy Hedberg assisted me in formulating some of the linguistic arguments, and Michael Maratsos and William Merriman commented on several aspects of my general argument. Remaining deficiencies of substance or style are entirely due to me.

Research is rarely an individual enterprise, and I have certainly benefited from the collaboration and assistance of several people, including Richard Meier, Jan Goodsitt, Poldi Gerard-Ngo, Heidi Patz, and LuAnne Gunderson. I also thank Lee Jessup, principal, and JoAnn Fitch, Theresa Fitton, Ann Rayburn, and Susan Tennant for allowing me to use the facilities of the Lincoln Trail School in Mahomet, Illinois, in conducting some of the studies reported here. Beyond this, many friends provided me with social and moral support, including Peter and Patti Adler, Jonathon Gray, Bruce Menchetti, Jeanine Clancy-

Menchetti, and Ted Supalla. Elizabeth Stanton, Nancy Spears, and Anne Mark, all of the MIT Press, provided editorial assistance in the preparation of my manuscript, and Elizabeth Greene aided in creating the indices.

Finally, I thank Gina Kuecks-Morgan, my wife, for loving me, for serving as my emotional rudder, for helping me keep my head during times of stress, and for so tolerantly listening to the arguments and examples that I would come up with at the *oddest* moments.

The research reported here and the preparation of this monograph were supported in part by the following grants and agencies: NINCD Training Grant 1 T32 HDO 7205-02 to the Department of Psychology, University of Illinois, NIH Grant PHS NS 16878 to Elissa Newport and Ted Supalla, the Graduate College of the University of Illinois, the Graduate School of the University of Minnesota, and the Center for Research in Human Learning at the University of Minnesota.

From Simple Input
to Complex Grammar

Chapter 1
Introduction

Perhaps the most remarkable observation concerning the child's acquisition of language is its very lack of remarkability: every normal child, bright or dull, succeeds as a matter of course and without explicit instruction in learning a natural language. Of course, in some ways each adult has a different command of language—each of us has a unique set of conversational styles, a unique degree of fluency, and a unique vocabulary. Nevertheless, all speakers of a language must share some core of knowledge, for without shared knowledge it would be impossible for different speakers to carry on any but the most stereotyped interchanges. This common knowledge of language is acquired under widely varying, though invariably limited, conditions of exposure; one of the central goals of any theory of language acquisition must be to account for the fact of language learnability.

Beyond the observation that speakers of a given language have internalized some common knowledge, it may also be observed that no particular language is privileged with regard to acquisition. That is, we know that children acquire whatever language they are exposed to. Thus, a second goal of any theory of language acquisition is to account for the acquisition of any possible human language. Pinker (1979) has provided a further taxonomy of the data for which a successful theory must account; for example, a theory must provide for acquisition within empirically observed limits on the child's language input, the child's cognitive capabilities, and the amount of time it takes for a child to acquire a mature grammar. In addition to accounting for various data concerning acquisition, ultimately we should wish to develop a theory that explains in detail how language acquisition proceeds and succeeds. Such a theory would provide an explicit account of the mental structures and processes that underlie acquisition. As in many other realms of psychological explanation, these constructs must be inferred on the basis of how they interact with observable quantities in a well-specified network of relationships. We can establish what some of the basic components of this network must be: as a rough equation, Language Input $\oplus$ Perceptual Capacities $\oplus$ Learning Mechanism $\oplus$ Maturation $\oplus$ Time = Mature Grammar. At present, though, we are profoundly ignorant both of what the nature of any of these components might be (aside from the knowledge that successful acquisition occurs within fairly strict limits on the amounts of input and time) and of what operations "$\oplus$" might represent. The purpose of this book is to examine one of these components, language input, and to explore the possible contribution of one particular property of input to the process of acquisition of natural language syntax.

Following early observations by Brown and Bellugi (1964) and Ferguson (1964), a substantial literature has been amassed describing various aspects of speech addressed to children learning language. For a recent review, see Hoff-Ginsberg and Shatz (1982). In addition, several researchers have begun to examine whether naturally occurring variability of input is associated with the rate of acquisition (Gleitman, Newport, and Gleitman 1984, Furrow, Nelson, and Benedict 1979, Newport, Gleitman, and Gleitman 1977). Given the methodology of this work, it can only address the issue of what aspects of input are facilitative. This issue is clearly interesting and important, but it is not fundamental. The presence or frequency of facilitative aspects of input may vary across children, all of whom succeed in acquiring a language, but the basic goal of a theory of language acquisition must be to account for learning in the most general case. Thus, the fundamental question concerning input involves the identification of those aspects of input that are necessary.

The determination of which aspects of language input are necessary will impose general limits on the theoretical power of the mental structures and mechanisms underlying acquisition. For any child, that child's learning system, in conjunction with the child's input, must converge on a grammar for the language the child is learning. In general, the fewer aspects of input that are necessary, the more variable input may be across children and, concomitantly, the more powerful the learning system shared by all children must be. In contrast, identification of aspects of language input that may be facilitative may provide insight into the flexibility of this learning system. The notion of power is central to the discovery of boundary conditions on the general form of the language-learning system, whereas the notion of flexibility has implications for the internal details of such a system. Clearly, the former is fundamental. This is why the issue of necessity is of primary importance in the study of language input.

What is entailed in demonstrating the necessity of some aspect of language input? First, certain empirical conditions must be met in order to establish the plausibility of any particular hypothesis. If some type of information in language input is to be judged necessary, that information must be universally and readily available in children's language input, children must be able to represent it appropriately, and it must play some identifiable role in acquisition.[1] It is possible, though, for some type of information to meet these conditions for plausibility while failing to be necessary for acquisition. The crucial question is whether certain aspects of language knowledge cannot be acquired (under otherwise normal conditions of exposure) in the absence of such information. Thus, in addition to considering what happens when some information hypothesized to be necessary is present, it is important to examine (empirically, if possible, but, failing this, within some rigorous formal model of acquisition) what happens when that information is absent. Here I shall briefly identify four possibilities.[2]

First, in the most straightforward sense of "necessity," some particular aspect of information in input is necessary if, in its absence, no languages can be acquired. In this case this information could be said to be *absolutely necessary*. As there are cases of children who have established communicative systems in the absence of any systematic language input (see, for example, Feldman, Goldin-Meadow, and Gleitman 1978; Goldin-Meadow and Mylander 1984), it is unlikely that any type of input information, aside from that which is derived from some general exposure to the human social world, will meet this most stringent criterion.[3]

However, our intuitive understanding of what it means to succeed in acquiring language is not that a child can learn some part of some language but rather that, for any language, a child exposed to a sample of that language can induce a grammar that will completely generate that language. Thus, in the second case it could be that at least some natural languages could be completely learned only given that some type of information is present in input. In this case such information could be said to be *extensionally necessary* (see also Osherson, Stob, and Weinstein 1986). Extensional necessity is concerned only with the acquisition of languages (sets of strings), not with the acquisition of particular grammars underlying those languages, and thus involves what has traditionally been termed *weak generative capacity* (Chomsky 1965). At issue here is whether or not the classes of grammars that can be acquired either in the presence or in the absence of some information in input are equivalent in weak generative capacity (that is, generate identical sets of languages). Unfortunately, this question is in general undecidable because it involves comparisons of infinite sets (see Hopcroft and Ullman 1980). Thus, conclusive arguments regarding extensional necessity are likely to be very difficult to formulate.

Beyond completely acquiring a particular language, successful acquisition entails that the child induce knowledge concerning the structural characteristics of sentences in that language. Thus, in the third case there may be differences in the structural information that is acquired depending on whether some information is present in input. This could come about in one of two ways. It could be that some structural information can be acquired *only* in the presence of some input information. Alternatively, it could be that some structural information would *necessarily* be learned in the presence of such information but not necessarily in its absence. In either event the information in question may be said to be *intensionally necessary*. Intensional necessity is concerned with the acquisition of particular grammars underlying languages and is thus related to what has traditionally been termed *strong generative capacity* (Chomsky 1965), that is, the ability of grammars to generate both sets of strings and structural descriptions for those strings. In certain cases it is possible to distinguish between the strong generative capacities of different classes of grammars; thus, the question of whether some aspect of input is intensionally necessary may be decidable.

Finally, we know that children normally succeed in acquiring language within fairly strict limits on both length of time and type and amount of input. Thus, in the fourth case it could be that an inordinately long time or inordinately complex data would be required to acquire certain languages (or certain grammars) in the absence of certain information in input. In this case such information may be said to be *empirically necessary*. This is the weakest form of necessity, entailing only that the information in question is required to produce successful acquisition within empirically determined limits on the amount and form of input data. In this case such information may not be required *in principle* for acquisition. Nonetheless, empirical necessity is crucial, for it speaks to the conditions under which human language acquisition is feasible.

With these considerations in mind, let us begin to examine how the syntax of natural languages might be acquired. Modern theories of language acquisition have typically assumed that at least part of the basis for the learning of syntax is some sort of distributional analysis. That is, children exploit statistical regularities of equivalence and substitution in the languages to which they are exposed in order to construct internal representations of the categories and patterns that make up the grammars of their languages. To give a simple example, suppose the child hears sentences (1)–(3).

(1) The little boy threw a rock at the dragon.

(2) A doughty warrior threw a rock at the dragon.

(3) He threw a rock at the dragon.

A comparison of (1) and (2) might suffice to indicate that "The little boy" and "A doughty warrior"—though they refer to quite different entities—have grammatically equivalent functions. Further, a comparison of (3) with either of the preceding sentences might suffice to indicate that "He" is both grammatically equivalent to and may be substituted for "The little boy." This fact of substitutability indicates in turn that the words "The little boy" form a grammatical unit.

In truth, the strings of words preceding "threw a rock at the dragon" in (1)–(3) all constitute noun phrases. But this is fortuitous: not all strings occurring in such a position are phrases. For example, consider (4). In (4) the string "Yesterday in a fit of pique someone" is composed of three phrases.

(4) Yesterday in a fit of pique someone threw a rock at the dragon.

Further data are needed to demonstrate that "Yesterday" and "in a fit of pique" are phrases independent of the noun phrase "someone." In general, distributional analyses are not straightforward; rather, it is the complex network of relationships holding across large numbers of sentences that reveals the syntactic structure of a language.[4]

Theories differ considerably in the extent to which they rely upon language input as a guide to acquisition. Chomsky (1965, 1975, 1981), for example, has argued that children come equipped with a biological endowment—a language faculty—that guides their analyses and ensures that they will make generalizations of only a certain sort. At the other end of the spectrum Braine (1971) and, to a lesser extent, Maratsos and Chalkley (1980) have proposed models of acquisition that rely heavily on analysis of the frequency of and correlations among regularities in input while imputing to the child minimal innate capacities. Despite these differences, all these theories implicate distributional analysis as a tool in discovering the grammatical structures of sentences.

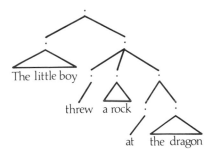

The little boy

threw a rock

at the dragon

Tree 1.1

Most theories of language acquisition have shared the assumption that language input consists of simple strings of words. An alternative view has recently gained currency, however, namely that input effectively consists of *structured* strings (Gleitman and Wanner 1982, Morgan 1983, 1984, 1985, Morgan and Newport 1981, Morgan, Meier, and Newport 1986, Read and Schreiber 1982, Tager-Flusberg 1985). That is, suppose that cues exist in input that allow children, in conjunction with their partial knowledge of grammar, to immediately identify the hierarchical structures of some of the sentences they hear, to "bracket" these sentences, as in (5).

(5) [The little boy] [threw [a rock] [at [the dragon]]].

The results of such bracketing may be seen more clearly in tree diagram 1.1.[5] Intuitively, it appears that bracketing information might aid in replacing the need for distributional analyses: rather than grammatical units being discovered on the basis of comparisons of sets of sentences, such units would be immediately evident. Thus, such information would reduce the amount of data and computation needed for acquisition and, by reducing the need for distributional analysis, might constrain the sorts and extents of false starts the child might make. The hypothesis that phrase structure in the child's language input is cued in such a fashion that the child may readily construct bracketed representations of sentences will be termed the *Bracketed Input Hypothesis*.

The notion that bracketed input might facilitate the acquisition of at least some aspects of grammar seems fairly obvious. However, I am interested in pursuing the claim that bracketed input may be necessary for the acquisition of natural language syntax. My argument will involve both theoretical and empirical examinations of some of the ramifications of the Bracketed Input Hypothesis. In particular, I will be concerned with the consequences of this hypothesis for language learnability. There are powerful arguments that, regardless of how rich the child's language input may be, the inductive hypotheses that the child may consider must be subject to certain constraints. Nevertheless, the precise form of such constraints will depend on the nature of the data upon which induction operates. Hence, the determination of whether bracketing information is a necessary aspect of language input will likely shed some light on the mechanisms of learning underlying the successful acquisition of language.

In the remainder of this chapter I will first sketch how the Bracketed Input Hypothesis meets the empirical conditions for necessity noted above; I will return to these issues and deal with them in greater detail in chapters 4 and 5. Determining whether the Bracketed Input Hypothesis meets any of the four criteria of necessity will require establishing a framework within which the logical status of this hypothesis may be evaluated. In chapter 2 I will review relevant results in the development of learnability theory, and in chapter 3 I will present a learnability-theoretic proof demonstrating that the Bracketed Input Hypothesis allows for the acquisition of complex grammars on the basis of very simple input—input of the sort that can be shown to be available to children learning language. This result argues strongly for the necessity of bracketing information in language input.

Prima Facie Evidence for the Bracketed Input Hypothesis

One of the empirical conditions that must be met if some aspect of information is to be judged necessary for acquisition is that such information must be readily available in children's language input. The ubiquity of phrase-bounded or phrase-related rules in natural languages ensures that this input will contain several potential cues to phrase bracketing. In many ways the phrase is the central organizational unit of natural language grammar. In the syntaxes of languages the orders in which words may occur in sentences are highly constrained; in addition, the occurrence of certain classes of words may depend upon the occurrence of other classes (in English, for example, articles can appear only if there is a following noun). Most typically, these dependencies hold between words that fall within a single phrase; in other cases they are best expressed as obtaining between phrases (for example, subject noun phrases and verb phrases in English must agree in number). Sentences may be organized into families in which pairs of sentences are related by transformational or redundancy rules; in any such pair sentences differ mainly in the organization and ordering of their constituent phrases, and such rules are therefore "(phrase) structure-dependent" (Chomsky 1965).[6] Finally, many languages exhibit morphological processes that operate only within the confines of particular types of phrases: in German, Latin, and Hebrew, for example, the components of a noun phrase must agree (by taking a particular ending) with the head noun of the phrase in gender, number, and, in the former two languages, case.

At an entirely different level of language, phrases are the domains within which certain phonological rules operate (see Scott and Cutler 1984), and the phrasal organization of a sentence plays a role in determining its pattern of prosody (Chomsky and Halle 1968, Cooper and Paccia-Cooper 1980). This all means that there is likely to be a large number of cues—some syntactic, some morphological, some phonological, some prosodic—that converge to indicate phrase boundaries in normal speech.

Children's language input may contain a number of possible additional sources of nondistributional bracketing information. First, presenting children with examples of phrases in isolation would be the most direct way to cue them into what constitutes phrases in their language. In fact, research on speech directed to children learning language indicates that a substantial fraction of mothers' utterances consists of sentence fragments; generally, such fragments consist of individual well-formed phrases (Newport 1977). For example, a mother might say, "Put that block in the truck. The red block. In the truck. Put the red block in the truck." Such a sequence might suffice to indicate that "Put the red block in the truck" consists of three phrases: the first being the entire verb phrase, the second being "the red block," and the third being "in the truck." Individual utterances (for instance, "The red block") can only indicate what constitutes single phrases; how these phrases are combined in larger structures must be deduced from sequences of utterances. In a strict sense, then, sentence fragments are most informative within the context of cross-utterance distributional analysis. However, this may be a very limited sort of distributional analysis, operating on a small number of utterances presented within a short amount of time.

Another possible source of bracketing information, one that also depends on analysis of limited sequences of utterances, might arise from the child's hearing adjacent utterances in which phrases are filled in, left out, or rearranged. For example, a child might say, "Red block," to which the mother might reply, "The red block is on the table." Such a sequence, called an *expansion,* may help the child to identify phrases by adding a phrase (in this case "is on the table") to make a more complete utterance. Newport, Gleitman, and Gleitman (1977) and Hoff-Ginsberg (1981) have shown that the frequency of such expansions in the child's environment is positively correlated with certain measures of language growth. Though other explanations are possible, one reason for this relationship might be that such sequences do operate to reveal syntactic structure to the child.[7]

The alternation of open (content) and closed (function) class words may supply yet another possible source of bracketing information. Closed class words (articles, prepositions, auxiliary verbs, etc.) tend to occur at the peripheries of phrases: in particular languages, in either phrase-initial or phrase-final positions (Greenberg 1963). Thus, if a child hears "Put it in the truck" and can identify "in" and "the" as closed class words, that child may be able to infer that "the truck" and "in the truck" are phrases.[8]

Prosody may provide a final nondistributional source of bracketing information. Cooper and his colleagues (Cooper, Paccia, and Lapointe 1978, Sorensen, Cooper, and Paccia 1978, Cooper and Paccia-Cooper 1980) have identified three acoustic indicators of phrase boundaries in adult-adult speech: pauses, and longer pauses, are more likely to occur between phrases; voice pitch (fundamental frequency) tends to fall and then rise across phrase boundaries; and phrase-final vowels tend to be lengthened. These cues allow structurally ambiguous sentences such as "They fed her dog food" to be typically unambiguous when spoken; here prosody functions to indicate whether or not "her dog" forms a phrase. Several investigators (for instance, Remick 1971, Broen 1972, Snow 1972, Garnica 1977) have noted that speech to children is typically higher pitched, slower, more carefully enunciated, and intonationally "exaggerated." Interestingly, many of the prosodic exaggerations characteristic of speech to children involve the same acoustic variables as do the cues discussed by Cooper et al. In chapter 4 I will present a study investigating whether these cues to bracketing are in fact exaggerated in children's input.

To summarize, bracketing information might be gleaned from language input in a variety of ways in the absence of (or at least with severe restrictions on) distributional analysis. Thus, the Bracketed Input Hypothesis appears to meet the first empirical condition on necessity: it is likely that bracketing information is readily available in input.

The second empirical condition that must be met if some information is to be judged necessary is that children must be capable of appropriately representing such information. Some evidence exists suggesting that children are capable of representing bracketing information—specifically, that they may use prosody in parsing utterances they hear. In a series of experiments Read and Schreiber (1982) demonstrated that 7-year-olds can reliably identify subject noun phrases of sentences except when such phrases are single words (pronouns or generic nouns). The crucial difference between single- and multiple-word subject phrases is that they manifest different intonation patterns: single-word phrases lack phrase-final vowel lengthening and pitch drop. Similarly, Tager-Flusberg (1985) has shown that young children may rely on prosody in parsing certain types of complex sentences. In her study children's comprehension of sentences with subject-embedded relative clauses (for example, "The boy the girl likes ran home") spoken with normal prosody was far superior to their comprehension of similar sentences formed by splicing together words spoken in isolation. Unfortunately, it is impossible to determine on the basis of these results whether 2-year-olds use prosodic cues in guiding their syntactic analyses, or whether the syntactic analyses precede and the correlations between phrase boundaries and prosodic cues are noticed at a later time.

In chapter 4 I will present an experiment demonstrating that young children can use prosodic cues to bracket utterances in an unfamiliar "language" composed of random strings of nonsense syllables. For the present, however, note that children need not be able to construct representations of bracketing for every utterance they hear. In chapter 6 I will take up the issue of how much bracketing information must be represented for any individual sentence.

The third empirical condition that must be met if some type of information is to be judged necessary for acquisition of syntax is that such information must play an identifiable role in language learning. Some indirect evidence exists suggesting that nondistributional bracketing information may actually aid induction of linguistic rules. It is difficult to approach this problem head-on, for it would be impossible to eliminate fragments, repetitions, closed class words, and prosody from a child's language input. Moreover, even if one conducted this monstrous experiment and the child failed to learn language, it is not clear what could be concluded: transformational relations between sentences, closed class words, and prosody are all integral parts of natural languages, and without these characteristics the child's input would not resemble any natural language.

However, as an analogue to the child's acquisition of language, it is possible to investigate the acquisition of miniature languages in the laboratory. In such studies simple languages are constructed that incorporate certain features of natural languages. The characteristics of input can be directly manipulated, so that it is possible to conclude which characteristics are necessary for successful acquisition of the rules of the language. Since the experimental situation is highly artificial, it is not straightforwardly obvious that results from such experiments can be generalized to the child's acquisition of natural language; this problem is compounded by the fact that subjects in these experiments have generally been adults. Thus, it is necessary to exercise caution in interpreting the results of such studies.

In collaboration with Elissa Newport and Richard Meier (Morgan and Newport 1981, Morgan, Meier, and Newport 1986), I have conducted a series of miniature language experiments that are relevant to the issue at hand. In these experiments subjects served in one of three conditions of language input. In one condition subjects saw only simple strings (sentences) from the language, with no cues to phrases aside from those that could be deduced from distributional analysis. In a second condition subjects saw strings with an additional cue (supplied either by prosody, function words, concord morphology, or the spatial organization of a reference world) that served to group words into consistent, nonphrasal groups. In a third condition subjects viewed strings with cues that grouped the words of each sentence into phrases. Subjects in all conditions were exposed to identical sample sets of strings from the language and were given identical tests to assess their acquisition of syntax.

The results of these experiments indicated that only subjects in the last condition—the condition that included an additional, nondistributional source of phrase-bracketing information—succeeded in learning both the phrases and the rules of the language. Subjects in the other two conditions learned some of the simple rules of the language, but they typically failed to learn either the phrases or the more complex rules of the syntax. One of these studies will be presented and discussed in greater detail in chapter 5. In general, though, these results suggest that adults (who are cognitively and linguistically more sophisticated than children) may require nondistributional bracketing information, in addition to bracketing information that may be derived by distributional analysis, in order to succeed in inducing moderately complex syntactic rules. It certainly seems reasonable to question whether children can learn the much more complex rules of natural language syntax solely on the basis of distributional analyses.[9]

Formal evidence concerning the possible facilitative effects of non-distributional phrase-bracketing information on grammatical induction is provided by certain results from the study of automata. An automaton is a computing machine with some well-specified configuration; the field of automata theory is largely concerned with ascertaining what sorts of problems are computable by particular machines. The psychological interest of automata theory is that particular machines may be taken as providing models of human information processing. Miller and Chomsky (1963) describe various types of automata and review early results in automata theory. Anderson (1976) provides an extensive account of, and experimental evidence bearing on, a particular automaton (ACT).

One highly constrained type of automaton is the *finite state automaton*. This machine consists of an infinitely long tape, marked off into segments, and a mechanism (which can be in one of a finite number of states) controlling a tape-reading head. The machine can read the symbol on the segment to which it is currently positioned and, depending on the state it is currently in, it can move one segment to the right and change its state. One of the possible states of a given automaton is its initial state; some subset of the states are specified as final, or "accepting," states. The tape is blank except for a finite string of symbols (one per segment). The machine starts off (in its initial state) positioned at the leftmost symbol; a given string is said to be "accepted" ("accepting" is simply the converse of "generating") if the machine eventually moves to the first tape segment beyond the right end of the string and simultaneously enters an accepting state. Figure 1.1 presents a representative finite state automaton and shows how it computes a simple problem. For further details concerning finite state automata, see Hopcroft and Ullman 1980.

Suppose that the strings of symbols represent sentences of a language. If an automaton can accept all and only the sentences of a particular language, it is said to accept that language. The type of automaton and the class of languages (as defined in the Chomsky hierarchy; see chapter 2 for a brief discussion) it can accept are related: the finite state automata can accept the class of finite state languages; the push-down automata, which incorporate an auxiliary "stack" memory,

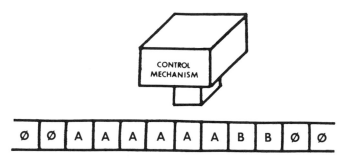

State Transition Matrix

Input	State				
	1	2	3	4	5
A	2	1	5	5	5
B	3	5	4	3	5

State 1 is the initial state; States 1 and 4 are accepting states.
This finite automaton accepts the language (AA)*(BB)*.

Example Derivation of AAAAAABB
1. In state 1, reads A, moves right, enters state 2.
2. In state 2, reads A, moves right, enters state 1.
3. In state 1, reads A, moves right, enters state 2.
4. In state 2, reads A, moves right, enters state 1.
5. In state 1, reads A, moves right, enters state 2.
6. In state 2, reads A, moves right, enters state 1.
7. In state 1, reads B, moves right, enters state 3.
8. In state 3, reads B, moves right, enters state 4.
9. In state 4, reads blank, accepts string.

Figure 1.1
Example of a finite state automaton

can accept the class of context-free languages (a superset of the finite state languages, including many computer languages); and so forth.

However, suppose that, instead of strings, the input to a finite state automaton consists of *trees*. Thatcher (1967, 1973) has shown that, given tree input, the finite state automata can accept the class of context-free languages.[10] This shows that the presence of structural information in input results in a significant increase in computing power. Levy and Joshi (1978) have extended Thatcher's results: they show that if input consists of "skeletal structures" (that is, trees whose nonterminal nodes are unlabeled) and if the number of possible states is known, then the finite state tree automata can accept a significant portion of the class of context-free languages. Moreover, they demonstrate that there is an algorithm by which a finite state tree automaton can construct an acceptive grammar for any such context-free language given input with a bounded limit on complexity. In other words, to put it crudely, given bracketed input, a finite state tree automaton can learn a context-free grammar.[11] The relevance of Levy and Joshi's result to the present enterprise is this: for a given type of computing machine (for example, a human), the inclusion of nondistributional bracketing information in language input can substantially enhance its ability to induce grammars.

In summary, children's language input includes a variety of possible sources of nondistributional bracketing information, and some evidence exists that children are capable of effectively representing such information. Results from laboratory studies of acquisition of miniature languages and from automata theory suggest that such information may be helpful in learning a language. Thus, at first blush the Bracketed Input Hypothesis appears to satisfy all the empirical conditions on necessity.

Does the Bracketed Input Hypothesis meet any of the logical criteria for necessity? In chapter 3 I will argue that it does meet at least the last two criteria I have outlined, those of intensional necessity and empirical necessity. In order to formulate these arguments, however, a rigorous framework must be established within which the consequences for learnability of particular hypotheses concerning the form of language input can be evaluated. I turn now to this task.

A Logical Framework for the Study of Language Acquisition

Generativity is one of the primary hallmarks of human language. In principle, it is possible to coin an infinite number of sentences that conform to the syntactic patterns of a language; indeed, most of the sentences one uses or encounters from day to day are novel. This basic fact strongly suggests that language is rule-governed. Children, though they are exposed only to a finite number of instances of a language, must develop knowledge of general sets of rules that will enable them to cope with new instances. Thus, the acquisition of syntax is an example of inductive learning, learning that progresses from the specific to the general. The child's task of inducing such a general set of rules has been termed the *projection problem* by Peters (1972).

It has long been noted by philosophers (for example, Hume (1919)) that inductive conclusions cannot be rigorously justified—any finite set of data supports an infinite number of generalizations, and additional data may always falsify any particular hypothesis (see also Chomsky 1965). The fact that children's linguistic data necessarily underdetermine the systems of rules that they induce presents serious difficulties with regard to the projection problem, for it is not the case that children induce just any set of rules consistent with their language input; rather, children learn sets of rules that will account for the language to which they have been exposed—including an infinite range of sentences that they have never encountered. As a matter of course, all normal children succeed in discovering a solution to the projection problem for their particular languages; moreover, the rule systems that different children project on the basis of different samples drawn from a language are at least highly similar to one another. If this were not the case, one would be hard pressed to account for the fact that two speakers can agree on whether a particular sentence novel to both of them is a grammatical sentence in their language.

It is fairly trivial to demonstrate that no unbiased inductive mechanism can reliably succeed in solving this sort of projection problem. As a simple analogy to language acquisition, consider a letter series completion problem.[12] The learner's task is to guess a function that will generate the remaining members of the series. Here are the first five letters of a particular series:

A B C E G

The essential question is, How many functions are compatible with the presented data? One possibility is a function that creates triples of letters such that the interval between letters within a triple is equal to the ordinal number of the triple. Thus, the first triple consists of consecutive letters (ABC), the second triple consists of alternate letters (EGI), and so forth. Another possibility is a function that enumerates all the prime numbers and maps them onto corresponding letters (A = 1, B = 2, etc.). In this case the next letter in the series would correspond to the sixth prime number, 11, and would thus be K. Each function corresponds to a unique continuation of the letter series. How many such continuations are there? It is quite simple to show that there are uncountably many continuations and hence uncountably many possible functions.[13] Thus, the probability of guessing a function that generates one particular series is effectively zero.

By enriching the original set of data, it is possible to rule out many previously possible hypotheses. For instance, twenty letters could have been presented instead of five. Or, if we wanted to prejudice the learner toward considering the "triples" solution, some bracketing information could have been included:

(A B C) (E G)...

Or, to return to the problem of acquiring the syntax of a language (considering the presented data to be sentences instead of letters and the complete series to be an enumeration of the grammatical sentences in a particular language), information encoding the meaning and even the derivational history of each sentence could have been included. None of these helps solve the ultimate problem: no matter how elaborate or extensive the presented data are (provided there is a finite amount of data, as must be the case for the child acquiring language), uncountably many distinct generalizations compatible with the data still remain.

At this juncture one might object that many of the infinite set of possible functions are extremely complex, or somehow bizarre, and that some solutions to this problem are therefore more natural than others. Hence, given that we share some notions of what constitutes naturalness, finding a proper solution to this problem is not as difficult as I have made it out to be. Yet this is precisely the point: a completely unbiased mechanism of inductive learning—one that does not embody the prejudices of human psychology—simply cannot have any notion of "naturalness." For such a mechanism, any solution compatible with the data is as good as any other. In other words, the successful solution of an inductive problem like this one can only be guaranteed if the learning mechanism is equipped with a reasonably rich set of constraints on the hypotheses it will consider.[14]

My argument thus far can elicit little disagreement. The next steps are more controversial, however: the extent and nature of constraints on induction must be defined. In general, the relation between necessary aspects of input and the structure of the to-be-learned system will determine the extent of required constraints. Determination of the nature of constraints on induction—in particular, whether they are specific to individual behavioral domains or are general characteristics of information processing—is a deeper issue. Chomsky (1965, 1975, and elsewhere), Peters (1972), and Baker (1979), among others, have argued that because the categories involved in linguistic rules are specific to language ("noun," or "sentential subject," for example), constraints on induction in language acquisition must also be specific to language. Others, including Levelt (1975) and Schlesinger (1982), have argued that constraints on language acquisition must be special cases of

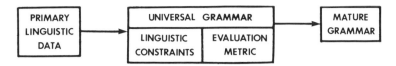

Figure 1.2
The Language Acquisition Device model

more general constraints (see also Piattelli-Palmarini 1980 for further debate on this issue). It appears to me that we do not yet have sufficient data to decide this question. In the interim, if only for heuristic reasons, it is best to consider constraints to be domain-specific. My argument for this is simple: if we assume domain-specificity as a working hypothesis whereas domain-generality is the true state of affairs, this will become apparent as parallelisms and redundancies come to light in accounts of learning across behavioral domains. (If the notion of domain-generality is to have any empirical content, this is how it must be discovered.) On the other hand, if we assume domain-generality as a working hypothesis whereas domain-specificity is the true state of affairs, we may be prevented from formulating adequate theories of learning in any domain. We have much more to lose by wrongly adopting the general view than we do by wrongly adopting the specific view. Therefore, I will consider constraints on language acquisition to be primarily specific to language.

The logic I have argued for here is equivalent to that embodied in the familiar Language Acquisition Device (LAD) model, which is commonly illustrated as in figure 1.2. In the LAD model language acquisition is conceptualized as being an "instantaneous" process. That is, the child has a set of data on the basis of which a set of candidate grammars may be projected, each one compatible with the input. The set of candidate grammars is constrained by the Universal Grammar: that is, a set of innate, language-specific constraints. An optimal grammar is chosen from among the candidate grammars by means of an evaluation metric. Chomsky has argued that the simplifying assumption of instantaneousness incorporated in LAD is unlikely to introduce falsehoods into the account of language learning, but this argument may be incorrect.

First, LAD was not intended to be a psychological model. Thus, arguments that LAD is not psychologically plausible—for example, Pinker's (1982) argument that LAD fails to provide predictions of developmental sequences—although true, are irrelevant to the evaluation of the model. Rather, one must ask whether the LAD model significantly distorts the logic of how syntax is ultimately acquired.

It appears that LAD may misconstrue the logic of language acquisition in two ways. The first problem hinges on the assumption that the child has available a complete corpus from which to infer grammars. If this corpus were invariably free of noise—that is, if it never contained any ungrammatical utterances—this would present no particular difficulties. However, to the extent that children's corpora are noisy, LAD requires that the child's intrinsic constraints be all the stronger. Fodor (1966) made this point quite clearly:

One point about the corpus should, however, be noticed. If it is anything like a randomly selected corpus of adult utterances, it must contain a very substantial number of false starts, slips, grammatical mistakes, and so forth. Most of these the adult speaker is capable of recognizing as distortions of his dialect, hence the attainment of this capacity is part of what the child must master in learning to speak that dialect. Thus the description of the child's task as that of extrapolating from the utterances in his corpus to the sentences of his language makes the task seem simpler than it is. The child's problem is rather to determine which proper subset of the utterances he hears constitute utterances of sentences and to extrapolate that subset. To put it slightly differently, we may think of the linguistic information at which the child arrives as constituting *inter alia* a theory of the regularities in its corpus, a theory about which such regularities are of systematic significance and which are "accidental." The optimal theory need not count every utterance in the corpus as regular because, as a matter of fact, much of what the child hears is almost certain to violate one or another of the grammatical rules that define the dialect from which the corpus is drawn. (pp. 108–109)

Subsequent studies of speech addressed to children learning language have shown that it does not consist of "fragments and deviant expressions of a variety of sorts," as Chomsky (1965:201, fn. 14) characterized it; for example, Newport (1977) reported that of a corpus of 1,500 utterances directed by mothers to their children, only one was truly ungrammatical. Newport did report that a substantial fraction of these utterances were sentence fragments, but, as noted above, these were almost invariably well-formed phrases. The picture that emerges from this research is that the speech children hear contains only a small percentage of noise. However, as Braine (1971) pointed out, even a small percentage of noise can have devastating consequences for an instantaneous hypothesis-testing model: if learners do not have some a priori means of filtering out ungrammatical input, they must settle on grammars that are (incorrectly) consistent with such data.

How might a noninstantaneous acquisition model deal with noisy input? Suppose that a child's grammar is modified to accommodate an ungrammatical input sentence. The grammar will then make incorrect predictions about which sentences are possible in the child's language. However, it is possible to construct real-time hypothesis-testing models in which subsequent exposure to some grammatical sentence will cause the child to reverse this erroneous modification, without adding specific provisions for dealing with noisy data. A detailed description of such a model (the Degree 2 theory of Wexler and Culicover 1980) is given in chapter 2. The essential requirement appears to be that noise is randomly distributed across exemplars of the rules the child must learn. In sum, LAD requires additional constraints to deal with noisy input that do not seem to be required in noninstantaneous models.[15]

The second problem with LAD revolves around the fact that this model is susceptible to an erroneous "hydraulic" interpretation (though this was not intended in the original formulation of the model). The postulation of intrinsic constraints was motivated by the observation that language input could not possibly be rich enough to sufficiently constrain inductive generalizations. The converse of this, seemingly, is that if information available in input is found to be somehow richer, the need for intrinsic contributions from the child is correspondingly reduced. Several writers have succumbed to this fallacy. For example, Levelt (1975) wrote,

'. . . [the child] is confronted with a very limited subset, both in terms of syntax and vocabulary, which is gradually expanded as his competence grows' . . . It should, however, be obvious that from the purely syntactic point of view the urge for strongly nativist assumptions has been diminished by these findings. (pp. 15–16)

Brown (1977) wrote,

. . . it has turned out that parental speech is well formed and finely tuned to the child's psycholinguistic capacity. The corollary would seem to be that there is less need for an elaborate innate component than there first seemed to be. (p. 20)

And Garnica (1977) wrote,

. . . [the finding that speech to children is generally well formed has the direct result] that the importance of the innate mechanisms is reduced. (p. 64)

Leaving aside considerations of whether the hypotheses of uniformly well-formed input and fine-tuning are either empirically supported or theoretically likely to actually be of aid in the acquisition process, arguments such as those cited above are fallacious for two related reasons. First, the informational content of the child's environment merely establishes an upper bound on the richness of the primary linguistic data. Children may not make use of all the information potentially at their disposal—for example, the finding that the sentences addressed to children increase in complexity across time would not establish that they make use of any such ordering.

Second, if children do in fact make use of such information from the environment, this necessarily implies that they have the perceptual and cognitive capacities to do so. Thus, the relative enrichment of primary linguistic data may require somewhat greater information-processing capabilities and may allow somewhat less elaborate constraints on the learner's grammatical hypotheses, but it will not necessarily affect the overall native contributions of the learner. For example, suppose again that it is found that the sentences the child hears increase in complexity across time. Levelt (1974) has shown that such an ordering of input may simplify the learning of certain classes of languages. If children are to make use of this ordering information, however, they must possess the native expectation that their input will be so ordered.

Moreover, it is possible that any additional required information-processing capacities will be specifically linguistic in character. Suppose, for example, that we attribute to children the ability to construct partial structural representations of the utterances they hear on the basis of the prosodic structure of these utterances. As noted previously, Cooper and his colleagues have adduced evidence indicating that phrase boundaries tend to be indicated in speech by lengthening of the final stressed vowel preceding boundaries and by a characteristic fall-rise fundamental frequency contour across such boundaries. Although the perception of lengthening and pitch contours in themselves is not likely to require specifically linguistic capacities (we can perceive these same features in melodies), the use of the correlation of these acoustic features to indicate the extent of phrases (which are linguistic constructs) very well may. The trade-offs involved in enriching input versus constraining grammatical hypotheses are not straightforwardly apparent, but it should be clear that no simple reciprocal relationship holds between contributions from the environment and contributions from the learner.

The LAD model is admirable for its conceptual clarity, but unfortunately it is susceptible to interpretations that distort the logic of acquisition. A slightly more complex model may avoid these difficulties. As dividends, such a model may allow a more psychologically plausible

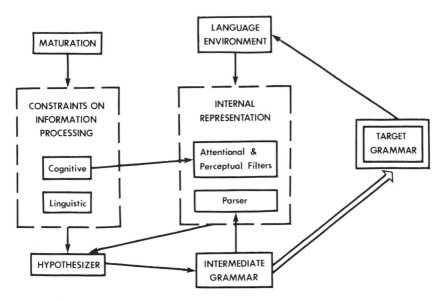

Figure 1.3
Outline of a real-time model of syntax acquisition

characterization of language learning and may even permit predictions concerning the course of development to be deduced. But how should such a model be formulated? Let us begin by considering a moderately detailed real-time acquisition model and then examining how such a model can be simplified in a principled manner.

Figure 1.3 illustrates some of the components likely to be required by an adequate real-time syntax acquisition model. I certainly do not wish to claim that the presented model is either complete or correct as shown (at the least, many details remain to be specified), but merely that, given the present state of knowledge, this model incorporates a set of reasonable assumptions about the general processes that are entailed in the learning of syntax. Below I provide a brief description of the nature of the components of this model and how they interact.

At the broadest level, we know that two things are required for the successful acquisition of language: exposure to some language and constraints on the grammatical hypotheses the learner will entertain.[16] In addition, we know that language acquisition is not "instantaneous"; rather, it is the result of a series of modifications (which may be either incremental or reorganizational in character) to an internal grammar. The model I am proposing implicitly incorporates the general assumption that children's central task is to comprehend the language they encounter; syntax is acquired as a part of this process. Clearly, one's current internal grammar comprises part of the knowledge that is brought to bear on the problem of comprehending speech; I have assumed here that it is only when (but not necessarily always when) comprehension fails that one modifies one's grammar. There are additional possibilities: it is certainly possible that heretofore unnoticed generalizations come to light during acts of successful comprehension and stimulate reorganizations of grammars, and it is also possible that maturational factors alone may prompt reorganizations as well (see Borer and Wexler 1984, Bowerman 1982, Gleitman 1981, and Karmiloff-Smith 1979 for some suggestions along these lines). For the present, however, these additional possibilities are ignored.

The first component of this model is the data available in the learner's environment. Such data may be construed quite broadly: they may include features of the nonlinguistic environment that will enable the learner to identify the referents of utterances, maternal gestures and facial expressions, prosodic components of speech, and so forth. Necessarily, such data will include utterances exemplifying the behavior of the mature grammar that is the target of the learning process.

Whatever the nature of the environment, the child's construction of a grammar operates on an internal linguistic representation of relevant aspects of this environment. Thus, input is subject to filtering by the learner's information-processing capacities. It is unlikely, at least in early stages of acquisition, that children construct a perfectly veridical representation of the utterances they hear: children may be biased to attend preferentially to the beginnings of sentences (Newport, Gleitman, and Gleitman 1977), to the ends of individual words (Slobin 1973), to stressed syllables (Pye 1981), and so forth. It is also likely that non-syntactic aspects of the environment are subject to filtering through the child's attentional and perceptual biases. For example, it has been suggested that, early on, the child represents agent-action-object relations, while excluding other, presumably more complex, relations (Bowerman 1973, Schlesinger 1982). The nature of children's attentional and perceptual filtering of language input is almost certainly subject to change over the course of acquisition as their general cognitive capabilities change. This nonstationarity poses great difficulties for any account of acquisition, for it entails that the data the child operates on will change over time, in ways that are not yet fully understood.

Let us assume that certain features of the environment receive an initial internal representation. These features, linguistic and nonlinguistic, must be related so that they form a coherent utterance-interpretation pair. The function of the parser is to create such representations. Among other things, the parser must assign a structural description to input utterances; thus, clearly, the operation of the parser will be a function of the current state of the learner's internal grammar. In other words, the nature of the learner's complete internal representation will change as the learner's grammar changes. Again, this nonstationarity contributes complexity.

At this point the learner's grammar must be evaluated in light of the current input. Perhaps no coherent utterance-interpretation pair can be constructed given the current state of the grammar. Or perhaps the utterance-interpretation pair is not fully consistent with the current grammar. In either event, provided that adequate processing resources are available, some modification of the learner's grammar is in order. This is the function of the "hypothesizer."

As discussed above, there must be cognitive and/or linguistic constraints on the range of possible modifications that may be hypothesized. Again, it is possible that these constraints change over time, as a function of maturation. This is a third source of internal nonstationarity in this model. At any rate, the outcome of this modification procedure will be a new internal grammar, and the entire procedure must begin anew. Eventually the internal grammar will converge to some degree of equivalence to the target grammar, and after this point no further modification will be required.

As should be clear from the preceding discussion, this model of syntax acquisition is fraught with complexities. Both the nature of the child's representational capacities and the child's internal grammar change with development, and these two processes may interact in quite subtle ways. The nature of grammatical modifications that the child may effect might also vary across time. There are likely to be both cognitive and linguistic contributions to constraints on the child's hypothesizations, but it is certainly not clear at the outset how to distinguish one from the other. Finally, the composition of the language-learning environment and the nature of the linguistic system that is eventually attained are not yet fully understood, although considerable progress has been made in explicating both of these areas.

Even if the model I have presented were entirely accurate, it would not provide a suitable basis for beginning to construct an explanatory

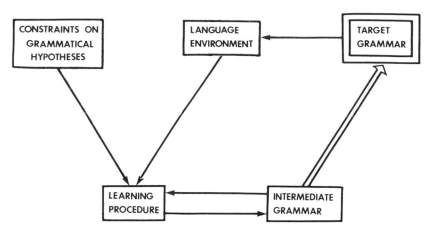

Figure 1.4
Outline of a simplified model of syntax acquisition

theory of syntax acquisition: this model simply has too many degrees of freedom, too many sources of nonstationarity. Rather, given our present lack of knowledge, it is necessary to restrict attention to the core process of constructing a grammar, to consider a less dynamic, less interactive model. Naturally, the sort of explanation constructed on the basis of such a model cannot be complete, but we may hope to be able to specify a set of boundary conditions for acquisition. Such conditions will restrict the possibilities for interactions that must be considered in subsequent investigations of broader models.

Therefore, consider how the real-time model in figure 1.3 might profitably be simplified. In essence, we want to eliminate all the internal sources of nonstationarity. As a working hypothesis, then, consider the model illustrated in figure 1.4 as depicting the central processes of syntax acquisition. The assumptions distinguishing this model from the real-time model presented above are, first, that children operate on a perfectly veridical representation of their input, second, that children's grammars are modified whenever they are inconsistent with input, and, third, that a constant set of cognitive/linguistic constraints governs the possible modifications that might be made. In outline, this is the processing model that has been assumed in attempts to construct formal learnability-theoretic accounts of the acquisition of syntax (see Gold 1967, Hamburger and Wexler 1975, Wexler and Culicover 1980). In this model data from the language environment are compared with the current state of the internal grammar by a learning procedure. If some inconsistency is found, the grammar is modified in accordance with a set of constraints on grammatical hypotheses. Eventually the internal grammar converges on some degree of equivalence to the target grammar. This model is similar to the original LAD model, except that it allows for incremental modifications of the learner's grammar, and it is explicitly related to the real-time acquisition model.

The (obviously false) assumption that children can form veridical representations of their input will eliminate considerable complexity. This is a principled simplification. Suppose it can be shown that, given such perfect representations, a certain set of constraints is required to account for successful acquisition. It is certainly not the case that fewer constraints will be required when the child's imperfect representational capacity is taken into account; on the contrary, the set of constraints will most likely need to be amplified (see Wexler and Culicover 1980 for discussion). However, the set of constraints obtained under this simplifying assumption can be taken as the core of the more elaborate set required in the absence of this assumption.

Similarly, the assumption that the nature of the child's grammatical modifications is constant removes a source of complicating nonstationarity. Pinker (1984) provides extensive discussion of this assumption under the rubric of the "Continuity Hypothesis." I will merely mention that, provided that we make sufficiently powerful assumptions about what sort of modifications the child can perform, the situation described above should again obtain: the set of constraints developed under this working hypothesis can serve as a core when more dynamic aspects are taken into consideration. Note, however, that the situation here is somewhat more complicated, for it is not a priori clear what constitutes "sufficiently powerful assumptions."

Finally, suppose that it is assumed that children always modify their grammars whenever their grammars are inconsistent with their input. By making this assumption, it is possible to avoid the necessity of developing a theory that stipulates the exact circumstances under which changes of internal grammars are initiated. The formulation of such a theory is interesting and important, but at present the analytic tools required for such an enterprise (that is, identifying exactly when a child's grammar is changed) are not available. This particular assumption may create one difficulty: namely, it may in fact be the case that the child has some means for filtering ungrammatical input (such input may be marked by hesitations, immediate self-corrections, and so forth), so that it does not generally serve as data for grammatical modifications. This is not considered here. However, the intrusion of ungrammatical input into the child's hypothesizations need not be disastrous: any incorrect modifications made in accordance with such data can later be undone.

This learnability-theoretic processing model of syntax acquisition avoids the logical difficulties associated with LAD. Ungrammatical input can be handled gracefully, with no need to impute additional capacities to the learner. Taken by itself, this model might be susceptible to "hydraulic" interpretations, but this model has been proposed as an explicit simplification of a real-time model to which such interpretations cannot be applied. Thus, I suggest that this pair of models offers a more adequate alternative to LAD.

The relative simplicity of this learnability-theoretic processing model exacts a rather heavy price: it is extremely restricted in explanatory power with respect to developmental aspects of language acquisition. Learnability theories may provide specifications of the boundary conditions necessary to ensure ultimately successful acquisition of syntax, but because of the particular simplifying assumptions incorporated in these theories, they are typically not well connected to data concerning the developmental course of language acquisition. In chapter 6 I will discuss some of the problems entailed in deriving predictions of acquisition sequences from learnability theories. In general, given the model I have outlined here, only two sources of explanation for developmental patterns are possible: such patterns may be a consequence of the ordering of the data available to the child, or they may result from intrinsic constraints on the orders in which rules may be acquired. However, as I will discuss later, it is doubtful whether either of these factors plays any significant role in language development. For now, note that I do not mean to imply that such learnability-theoretic accounts of language acquisition are immune to empirical disconfirmation, but merely that the range of relevant data is more restricted than one would ideally like. Ultimately, the validity of following the course I have outlined here can only be judged by measuring how successful learnability theory is in solving the conceptual problem of syntax acquisition and how amenable such a theory is to incorporation in more realistic models of acquisition.

Chapter 2
The Development of
Learnability Theory

The central goal of a learnability-theoretic proof is to determine whether a set of assumptions is sufficient to ensure that any language arbitrarily drawn from a particular class of languages can be learned within a finite amount of time. With regard to natural languages, learnability proofs are often constructed by working backward: one begins with the presumption that the class of natural language *is* learnable and proceeds to search for a set of premises that will provide deductive support for this conclusion. The motivation for applying this approach to natural language acquisition stems from the basic observations that any child with normal cognitive endowment who receives sufficient exposure to a language will succeed in learning that language and that no natural language has privileged status with regard to acquisition.

Taken together, these two observations form a logical proposition: For any natural language, if a child has the requisite cognitive abilities, and if that child receives sufficient input, then the child will succeed in acquiring that language. The task of a learnability proof is to provide explicit formulations for each of the following elements of language learning: How is the notion "possible natural language" to be defined? What are the cognitive abilities engaged in learning a language? What constitutes sufficient language input? How is "successful acquisition" to be defined? Once a set of formulations sufficient to account for the learnability of natural languages is discovered, more stringent requirements may be imposed: a fully explanatory theory of language acquisition ought to provide for learnability within empirically defined constraints on time, type and amount of input, and cognitive abilities of children and should ideally provide accurate predictions of possible sequences of acquisition and possible errors made in the course of acquisition (see Pinker 1979).

In this chapter I will review a portion of previous work in learnability theory. The most important learnability result developed to date is the Degree 2 theory of Wexler and Culicover (1980). In chapter 3 I will present a proof that is a modification of Wexler and Culicover's theory. The difference between my proof and Wexler and Culicover's is the inclusion of the Bracketed Input Hypothesis. A comparison of these two proofs will reveal the contributions of phrase-bracketing information to language learnability and will suggest how such information is necessary. Here I will review only work that is directly antecedent to the Degree 2 theory. A broader review of formal approaches to language learning may be found in Pinker 1979; slightly more recent discussions of issues in language learnability appear in Baker and McCarthy 1981 and Pinker 1984.

This review will be organized in three sections. In the first section I will discuss the early (and mostly negative) learnability results that laid the logical foundations for the Degree 2 theory. In the second section I will describe Wexler and Culicover's proof in some detail. In the third section I will propose a set of criteria that may be useful in evaluating attempts to provide a feasible theory of language learnability, and I will discuss how well the Degree 2 theory meets these criteria.

Establishing the Framework of Learnability Theory

The basic methodology of learnability theory derives from a seminal paper by Gold (1967). Gold began by equating successful acquisition with *identifiability in the limit.* In his model acquisition was conceptualized as consisting of a series of discrete trials, in each of which the learner received a unit of information about the input language and hypothesized a grammar for this language. If after some finite number of trials the learner consistently hypothesized the same grammar, and if this grammar correctly generated the input language, the learner was said to have identified the language in the limit.[1] A class of languages was said to be identifiable in the limit if, for any language arbitrarily drawn from the class and for any sequence of information about that language, the learner could identify the language in the limit. Note that this definition of successful acquisition does not require that the learner be aware that it has succeeded in correctly identifying the input language.

Gold's theoretical framework included four major components. The first was the criterion of learning (identifiability). The second was a definition of the form of relevant input. The third was a set of grammatical hypotheses that the learner could consider (or, in other words, the definition of a particular class of languages). The fourth was a learning procedure, which compared the current input datum and the currently hypothesized grammar for consistency and hypothesized a new grammar on those trials in which inconsistency was found.[2] It should be readily apparent how these components map onto the model illustrated in figure 1.4.

Gold investigated the identifiability of the broad classes of languages defined in the Chomsky hierarchy (Miller and Chomsky 1963). Languages are classified in the Chomsky hierarchy according to the type of rules employed in their grammars. *Finite state* languages are at the bottom of the hierarchy; their grammars employ only the most restricted form of rules. Other major classes of languages in the hierarchy are the *context-free,* the *context-sensitive,* and the *recursively enumerable* languages. Progressively more powerful types of rules are allowed for grammars in each successive class of languages.[3] Note that the finite state languages may be generated by context-free grammars, and so forth; thus, each level of the hierarchy is properly included in the next higher level. Generally, grammars capable of generating the natural languages have been considered to be at least as powerful as the context-sensitive grammars (Chomsky 1957), although Gazdar and his colleagues (Gazdar 1982, Gazdar, Pullum, and Sag 1982) have argued that properly augmented context-free grammars may be sufficiently powerful.[4]

Gold considered two basic schemes of input information. In the first scheme input consisted only of positive instances—grammatical strings—of the input language (*text presentation*). In the second scheme input included both positive and appropriately labeled negative instances of the input language (*informant presentation*). Given informant presentation, the class of primitive recursive languages, which is a superset of the context-sensitive languages, can be identified in the limit. However, it is doubtful whether appropriately labeled negative input is available to the child, at least to the extent required by Gold's proof. Parents do not label their own utterances as grammatical or ungrammatical. Possibly, negative information might be supplied by parental corrections of children's grammatical mistakes. But the available empirical evidence indicates that children are generally not corrected for their ungrammatical utterances (Brown and Hanlon 1970) and that, even when such correction is available, children do not make consistent use of it (McNeill 1966).[5] As a result of these empirical findings, most subsequent attention has been focused on language learning from text presentation.

The early findings on identifiability from text presentation were discouraging. Gold proved that if the learner's hypotheses are constrained so that only (and all) those languages at a particular level of the Chomsky hierarchy are candidates for possible languages, then only the class of *finite cardinality* languages—languages comprising finite numbers of sentences—could be identified on the basis of text presentation. The finite cardinality languages form a trivial subset of the finite state languages; clearly, such languages are not candidates for possible natural languages.

Gold's proof that classes of languages in the Chomsky hierarchy that include infinite languages are not identifiable was based on the *Superfinite Theorem:* any class of languages that includes all the finite languages and at least one infinite language on a given vocabulary cannot be identified. ("Vocabulary" may be construed broadly as including, for example, grammatical categories. Natural languages appear to share the same set of grammatical categories—nouns, verbs, and so forth—and at a suitable level of abstraction may be considered as languages on a common vocabulary.) Given the inclusion properties of the Chomsky hierarchy, the Superfinite Theorem guarantees that none of the classes of languages defined in the hierarchy is identifiable. A simple proof of the Superfinite Theorem is given below.

Consider the following class of languages on the vocabulary "a":

$L_0 = a*$ (i.e., a, aa, aaa, ...)
$L_1 = a$
$L_2 = a, aa$
$L_3 = a, aa, aaa$
etc.

This class of languages is not identifiable.

Proof

The learner may be biased in one of two ways. Suppose that the learner is biased to always select the infinite language, L_0, as a hypothesis. Since any possible information sequence from any language in this class is compatible with L_0, no input could ever force the learner to change its hypothesis. Hence, no finite language could be successfully identified. Therefore, suppose that the learner is biased to always select the largest finite language compatible with the information sequence. If the information sequence is drawn from L_0, then the learner will change its hypothesis an infinite number of times (to larger and larger finite languages), but no information sequence would cause the learner to hypothesize L_0. Given either bias, at least one language in the class will not be identifiable by the learner; hence, this class of languages is not identifiable.

This proof can be extended straightforwardly to account for more interesting superfinite classes of languages. In essence, the problem with text presentation is that this type of input provides no way to recover from overgeneral hypotheses. In Gold's words, "The problem with text is that, if you guess too large a language, the text will never tell you that you are wrong" (p. 461).

Clearly, something is amiss here. As a matter of course, children regularly acquire language. But Gold's results show that, given input of a sort that might be supposed to correspond to that available to the child, broad classes of languages are in fact unlearnable. Thus, it appears that either the learnability framework is not a fruitful way to address the problem of language acquisition or the assumptions adopted in Gold's proofs are somehow insufficient. Two clear possibilities for strengthening these assumptions, both noted by Gold, suggest themselves. First, the input available to the child might be richer than was assumed. Second, it is possible that positive results could be obtained using more restricted classes of languages.

Concerning schemes for enriching input, Gold suggested that if an ordering were imposed on input, then learnability of the recursively enumerable languages would obtain. That is, suppose that, for each language, a function is defined that maps between times (trials) and strings: $F(time_1) = string_1$; $F(time_2) = string_2$; and so forth. For the recursively enumerable languages, the set of such functions is enumerable, and each such function is unique. Thus, it is possible to show that after some finite amount of time the learner can identify the function to which it is being exposed, and this is tantamount to identifying the language on which the function is defined.[6]

More generally, Anderson (1976) showed that the class of recursively enumerable languages is *function learnable:* any enumerable set of functions mapping from some domain onto a range of strings, or vice versa, is identifiable. As noted above, one possibility for the domain of such a function is time (conceptualized as discrete units). In a general sense, informant presentation is an example of function learnability, where the function is from strings onto labels of "grammatical" and "ungrammatical." A third possibility, noted by Anderson, is a function mapping from meanings (which may be enumerated by the process of Gödelization) onto strings. Presumably, other types of functions are possible as well. Any conceptualization of input that consists of functionally related domain-range pairs will allow equally powerful learnability results.

For empirical reasons, however, the notion of function learnability appears to be of limited usefulness. First, no reason exists to believe that natural language input includes negative information or is ordered in any useful sense. A mapping from meanings onto strings would appear to provide a more likely basis for acquisition, but here we encounter a second problem: namely, what is required is a functional mapping, and functions are deterministic. That is, a function may map each member of its domain onto at most one member of its range. However, the mapping between meanings and strings is not deterministic in natural languages, since both ambiguity and paraphrase are possible. In fact, Anderson includes a proof showing that the general class of languages including either paraphrase or ambiguity is not function learnable (though this does not rule out the possibility that some subset of this class is learnable). A third problem with function learnability is that it requires use of an enumeration learning procedure. In an enumeration procedure the learner starts out with a "list" of all possible functions. Although there may be infinitely many possible functions, each function occupies a finite place in the enumeration. If the learner encounters a datum that is inconsistent with its current hypothesis, it must test each subsequent function in the list until it finds one that is compatible with all the presented data. Because such a list is so long, such procedures require vast amounts of time and/or memory.[7] In short, it appears that input enrichment alone will not be sufficient to account for the learnability of natural languages.

The second possibility, restricting the classes of languages to be learned, appears to offer a more promising avenue of attack. Gold's negative results were based on the Superfinite Theorem; however, natural languages are infinite, and there is no reason to suppose that children entertain grammars of finite languages as possible candidates. More generally, mathematical investigations initially focused on the classes of languages in the Chomsky hierarchy because of their tractability given available methods. However, the class of natural languages is unlikely to be coextensive with any of these. For example, even if all natural languages could be generated by means of context-free grammars, this does not imply that all context-free languages are potential natural languages. Thus, negative learnability results for supersets of natural languages do not imply that the class of natural languages, properly defined, is unlearnable. Note that this cuts both ways: if it is shown that a broad set of languages is learnable, this does not imply that the natural languages are contained within this set.[8]

Wexler and Hamburger (1973) adopted the tactic of specifying a narrower class of languages. One extensively developed candidate theory for natural languages is provided by the Standard Theory of transformational grammar (Chomsky 1965); hence, Wexler and Hamburger examined the learnability of the class of transformational languages. In this initial work they adopted the assumption that this class of languages shared a universal base. The Universal Base Hypothesis (UBH) (see Chomsky 1965) asserts that all languages share a common context-free base to which transformations are applied to produce surface strings. UBH (as noted by Wexler and Hamburger) is generally considered to be too strong because it specifies that all natural languages have the same underlying order of grammatical categories; in light of the different canonical orderings exhibited by various languages (for example, English subject-verb-object versus German subject-object-verb), this is a dubious contention. However, UBH, coupled with constrained possibilities for transformations, does allow specification of a narrow class of languages. The transformations allowed by Wexler and Hamburger were in fact quite constrained: deletion was prohibited, and transformations were either singulary (applying within one cyclic domain—one clause) or binary (applying to two cyclic domains—one clause embedded within another).[9]

Wexler and Hamburger began by proving a generalized version of the Superfinite Theorem, which I will term the *Infinite Density Theorem*. The Infinite Density Theorem states that any class of languages $\{L_0, L_1, L_2, L_3 \ldots\}$ such that L_0 is the union of all the other languages in the class (that is, contains all strings contained in any other language) and such that any finite subset of L_0 is contained in an infinite number of other languages in the class, is unlearnable. The proof of this theorem is parallel to the proof of the Superfinite Theorem. Because L_0 is the union of all the other languages, if data from any language other than L_0 are presented, the hypothesis of L_0 will never be disconfirmed. On the other hand, because the languages $\{L_1, L_2, L_3 \ldots\}$ are packed with infinite density within L_0, if a finite set of data from L_0 is presented, it will be contained in infinitely many other languages, and thus L_0 need never be hypothesized. Either way at least one language in the class will not be identifiable in the limit. Note that the Superfinite Theorem is a special case of the Infinite Density Theorem, in which $\{L_1, L_2, L_3...\}$ are all finite.

Does a class of transformational languages on a universal base exist that satisfies the conditions of the Infinite Density Theorem? If so, then any superset of this class will be unlearnable. Wexler and Hamburger proceeded to construct such a class as follows: Suppose that the universal base generates an infinite number of two types of strings, A and B. L_0 includes a transformation that converts all type B strings to type B'. For each of the remaining languages L_i, all type B strings with depth of embedding less than or equal to i are converted to type B', and all other type B strings are converted to type A.[10] In this class L_0 is equal to the union of all the other languages, and every finite subset of L_0 is contained in an infinite number of other languages. In general, therefore, transformational languages on a universal base are unlearnable. Again, a positive learnability result for transformational languages might be obtained either by further restricting the class of possible languages (by imposing additional constraints on possible transformations) or by enriching the learner's input.

Learning a transformational grammar entails acquiring a set of transformations that will map between appropriate base structures and surface strings. Wexler and Hamburger's result indicates that text input in conjunction with knowledge of the *general* form of base structures does not provide a sufficient basis for learning a set of transformations that will generate the proper set of surface strings for a particular language. Thus, surface input is not sufficient for a learner to attain *weak equivalence*. Intuitively, providing the learner with information about the *specific* form of base structures underlying surface strings might simplify the task of learning the appropriate mapping. Accordingly, Hamburger and Wexler (1973) abandoned the Universal Base Hypothesis and adopted a stronger assumption about the form of the learner's input, namely, that input consists of (b,s) pairs, where b is a base structure and s is a surface string. As before, the surface strings were the utterances heard by the learner; it was assumed that the appropriate base structure for a sufficient number of such strings could be constructed by the learner on the basis of contextual information in conjunction with knowledge of individual word meanings. Hamburger and Wexler sketched a proof incorporating this assumption (the complete details of the proof are given in Hamburger and Wexler 1975): given (b,s) input, a learner can attain not merely weak equivalence but in fact *moderate equivalence;* that is, with such input a learner can acquire a set of transformations that will map appropriately between all base structures and surface strings.

Because this work represents one of the first significant positive learnability results, and because it laid the foundation for subsequent, more feasible theories of learnability, it is worthwhile to consider some of its details: in particular, the learning criterion, the system of constraints on possible hypotheses, and the learning mechanism.

First, as in Gold's work, if after some point in the sequence of input further input never causes the learner to change its hypotheses, then the learner is said to have succeeded. However, Gold's criterion of identifiability was an absolute criterion, whereas Hamburger and Wexler's criterion (sometimes referred to as *learnability*) was probabilistic. That is, Hamburger and Wexler demonstrated that if a certain set of conditions obtained (to be discussed below), then the learner could be shown to converge upon an appropriate grammar with a probability approaching one.

The constraints on the learner's hypotheses in this work are mainly concerned with defining characteristics of possible grammars. An *Aspects* type transformational grammar (Chomsky 1965), augmented with a number of additional restrictive principles, was assumed to represent the target class of grammars. In this type of grammar a set of context-free rules applies to form a base structure. S(entence) is the essential recursive category; that is, if two (non-S) nodes of the same type appear more than once in the same branch of a tree, an S node must intervene between each two successive appearances. The set of transformations applies cyclically to base structures, applying first to those nodes dominated by the lowest S node in the tree (that is, to the most deeply embedded sentence), then to the nodes dominated by the next lowest S node, and so forth.

Two important types of restrictions were added by Hamburger and Wexler. First, transformations could be at most "height two"; that is, transformations could apply to nodes in the current cyclic domain or in the immediately previous cyclic domain, but they could not move nodes from arbitrary depths of a tree (see Ross 1967 for examples and arguments concerning such unbounded movement). This principle is essentially identical to the principle of Subjacency, proposed independently in Chomsky 1973 for reasons of linguistic description. In subsequent work this principle became known as the *Binary Principle*. Second, Hamburger and Wexler proposed a set of principles that collectively had the effect of restricting transformations from applying to structures created by previous applications of transformations; that is, transformations could apply only to base-generated structures. Two further restrictions are worthy of note: all transformations were obligatory, and the target set of transformations had to be deterministic.

Upon receipt of each (b,s) datum Hamburger and Wexler's learning mechanism applied the (previously hypothesized) transformations currently in the learner's grammar to the base structure to derive a surface string. If the string so derived was identical to the presented string, no changes were made in the learner's transformations. However, if the derived string was not identical to the presented string, or if two transformations could apply simultaneously to an intermediate stage in the derivation, the learner's grammar made a *detectable error*. At this point one of two actions could be taken. Either the learning mechanism could choose at random a transformation that had applied in the faulty derivation to be discarded from the learner's grammar (this action was required in the case of nondeterminism, that is, when two or more transformations could apply simultaneously), or the learning mechanism could add one transformation that could be applied to the fully derived surface structure to produce a new surface string, identical to the presented string.

This learning mechanism distinguishes Hamburger and Wexler's procedure from that of function learnability. Clearly, given (b,s) input, the set of grammars defined by Hamburger and Wexler are function learnable (the property of determinism ensures this). In function learnability, however, grammars are hypothesized and discarded of a piece, and many grammars (functions) that are not even remotely correct must be tested. In contrast, this learning mechanism allows acquisition to proceed rule by rule—certainly a psychologically desirable characteristic.

To return to a description of Hamburger and Wexler's proof, given the restrictions noted above, the sets of candidate transformations for rejection or hypothesization are both finite; thus, in the event of a detectable error the modification selected by the learning mechanism has some nonzero probability of being correct. The core of Hamburger and Wexler's proof hinged on demonstrating that any possible detectable error in the learner's set of transformations would be revealed by some input datum within a finite amount of time. This is possible if there is some limit on the complexity (depth of embedding) of the base structure necessary to reveal any error.

Within each cyclic domain a finite number of possible base-generated structures can serve as input to transformations.[11] However, there may be cross-cyclic interactions of transformations—for example, the application of one transformation may serve to prevent the application of another transformation. Hence, different sequences of single-cycle base structures embedded within each other will in general permit different sequences of transformations to be applied. But, since the number of different single-cycle base-generated structures is limited, there will be a bound on the complexity of base structures in which all possible sequences of single-cycle base structures can occur and hence a bound on the complexity of data necessary to reveal the learner's errors. Thus, for any error, an error-revealing datum will be presented within a finite amount of time. Coupled with the finite probability of making a correct adjustment when an error is revealed, this property, called *Boundedness Degree of Error,* ensures that a learner will converge in a finite amount of time on a correct set of transformations with a probability approaching one.

Thus, Hamburger and Wexler obtained a positive learnability result for an interesting class of languages. However, the bound on the complexity of data necessary to reveal errors in their proof was astronomical—a conservative estimate noted in Wexler and Culicover 1980 was that data with 400,000 levels of embedding would suffice. Thus, the finite amount of time necessary to ensure convergence would be equal to several lifetimes, and the vast complexity of required data would impose enormous processing burdens on the learner. Hamburger and Wexler's proof demonstrates that transformational languages are learnable in principle, but, given empirical constraints on the complexity of children's input, their processing capacities, and the extent of time needed for acquisition, this result is hardly feasible. Clearly, it would be more interesting if a learnability result could be obtained using data with a much lower bound on complexity. In fact, the crowning achievement of Wexler et al.'s research—detailed in Wexler and Culicover 1980—was to prove learnability on the basis of data with no more than two levels of embedding. This result was obtained by imposing an even stricter set of constraints on possible transformations. This culminating proof—the *Degree 2 theory*—is described below.

Toward a Feasible Learnability Result

Consider first the functions that constraints on the form of possible grammars must fulfill. If convergence on the learning criterion is to occur, three properties deriving from constraints on the class of hypothesizable transformations must obtain. First, the number of possible transformations that may be hypothesized must be bounded. This ensures that there is some probability greater than zero that the learning procedure will add a correct transformation to the grammar. Second, the number of transformations that can apply in any derivation must be bounded. This ensures that there is some probability greater than zero that the learning procedure will correctly discard a mistaken transformation from the grammar. Third, the complexity of the datum that will reveal an error in the learner's grammar must be bounded. This ensures that there is some probability approaching unity that errors in the learner's grammar will be revealed within a finite amount of time.

In order to constrain the set of possible transformations, it is necessary to place some upper limit on the possible complexity of a structural description. One reasonable approach is to limit the number of cyclic domains over which a transformation can apply (this is not the only possible approach; see Baker 1977 for an alternative). Therefore, Wexler and Culicover proposed the *Binary Principle*, which states that transformations can apply only to nodes in two adjacent cyclic levels of a tree. In tree 2.1 this means that a transformation operating in the S_0 cycle can only refer to the set of nodes $\{A, B, S_1, C, D, E\}$.[12] This rules out unbounded movement.

By itself, however, the Binary Principle is not sufficient to bound the number of possible transformations. This is because nodes may be raised from an arbitrary depth in previous successive cycles; thus, given a tree with arbitrary depth, an unbounded number of nodes may be in the Binary environment as a result of raising. One solution for this is to adopt constraints on the structures to which transformations may apply. Thus, Wexler and Culicover made a second major assumption constraining the form of possible transformations: the *Freezing Principle*, which states that if a node N immediately dominates a nonbase sequence of nodes, then no node dominated by N can be analyzed by a transformation. To illustrate, suppose that a transformation applying in the S_1 cycle of tree 2.1 raises F and adjoins it to C, as in tree 2.2. Suppose that no base rule expands C as $E + F$ but that this sequence of

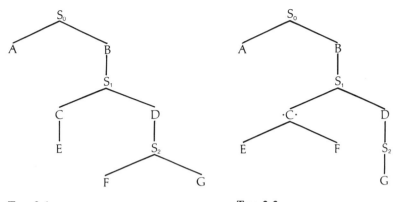

Tree 2.1   **Tree 2.2**

nodes could only result from the operation of some set of transformations. Then C is said to be *frozen* (denoted by $*C*$), and no subsequent
transformation in the derivation can make reference to either E or F. In
other words, transformations can only apply to structures that can be
created by base (phrase structure) rules; given the assumption that all
recursion is through S, only a finite number of nodes can be generated
in any cyclic level by such rules.

In combination, the Binary Principle and the Freezing Principle ensure that the three necessary conditions obtain. By themselves, however, these two principles are not sufficient to ensure learnability from
simple data. Because these two principles ensure that for any transformation there exists a Degree 1 datum (a sentence with one embedding)
to which it may apply, at first it might seem that Degree 1 Error Detectability, and hence Degree 1 Learnability, should follow from these two
constraints. To see why this is not so, consider tree 2.2, in which F was
raised in the S_1 cycle. The terminal string of this tree is $A - E - F - G$.
Suppose, however, that the child's grammar mistakenly adjoins F to
D (as a left sister to S_2). The terminal string of this tree is also
$A - E - F - G$; hence, there is no detectable error.[13] But suppose
further that both components raise C in the S_0 cycle to be a left sister of A. Then according to the target grammar the terminal string
is $E - F - A - G$, whereas according to the child's grammar it is
$E - A - F - G$; this is a detectable error that can only be revealed by a
Degree 2 datum.

As long as the linear ordering of the learner's derived string matches
the ordering of the input surface string, no error is revealed. In other

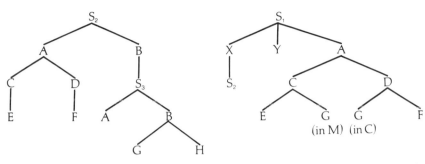

Tree 2.3   Tree 2.4

words, in Wexler and Culicover's theory, because input consists of surface *strings*, order-preserving errors of adjunction such as that described above can only be revealed by the action of subsequent transformations. It could be the case that a permutation transformation operates in the same cycle as the incorrect transformation to reveal the error. If this were always the case, then Degree 1 Learnability would be attainable in this framework; but this cannot be guaranteed. Alternatively, it could be the case both that there is no same-cycle error-revealing transformation and that there is no subsequent-cycle error-revealing transformation; in this case the adjunction error would never be revealed.[14] Again, if this were always the case, then Degree 1 Learnability would be attainable; again, this cannot be guaranteed. Thus, Wexler and Culicover could at best demonstrate Degree 2 Learnability.

It is possible to have complex interactions of transformations producing errors that can only be revealed on Degree 3 or greater data. A large part of Wexler and Culicover's proof is given over to detailing a taxonomy of these interactions and formulating a set of constraints on transformations designed to prevent any such interaction. Here I will give a single example. Suppose that tree 2.3 represents the two lowest levels of an input deep structure. No relevant transformations apply in the S_3 cycle. In the S_2 cycle a transformation raises G: the target grammar adjoins it to C; the child's grammar adjoins it to D. An error has been created. No further transformations apply in S_2, but in the S_1 cycle a structure-preserving transformation raises A, producing tree(s) 2.4. (Irrelevant details are omitted.) Note that since A dominates the error, the terminal strings of the two trees are the same, and no detectable error has occurred. Finally, in the S_0 cycle, C is raised. In the target grammar's derivation C dominates the string $E - G$, but in the child's derivation C dominates only E. Hence, the resulting terminal strings will not be equal. Here a detectable error has been revealed on a Degree 3 datum that could not be revealed on a Degree 2 datum.

In order to rule out the possibility of this sort of derivation and to preserve Degree 2 Error Detectability, Wexler and Culicover assumed the *Raising Principle,* which states, "If a node A is raised, then no node that A dominates may be used to fit a transformation" (p. 143). In this example the Raising Principle would prevent the transformation in S_0 that raises C. Note that the effect of this constraint is not to prevent errors from occurring but to conceal certain errors—namely, those that could only be revealed by data of Degree 3 or greater. The important point here is that complex data should not hold any "surprises" for the learner—if learnability is to follow from simple data alone (Degree 2 or smaller), all errors that could possibly figure in acquisition must be revealed by such data.

The complete Degree 2 proof includes a number of additional constraints (about twenty in all) that function in concert to ensure Degree 2 Error Detectability. Wexler and Culicover 1980 may be consulted for further details, but the examples discussed above should suffice to impart some flavor of this enterprise. Without question, Wexler and Culicover's Degree 2 theory is an interesting and important achievement: it provides a positive learnability result for a class of languages that might reasonably be considered to be nearly equivalent to the class of natural languages, and it provides for learnability from quite simple input. Thus, Wexler and Culicover can lay claim to having developed a feasible learnability result.

Several researchers have criticized aspects of the Degree 2 proof. For example, Pinker (1979, 1981, 1982) and Valian (1981) have leveled criticisms against Wexler and Culicover's learning mechanism; Williams (1981) has suggested that certain of Wexler and Culicover's constraints might be modified; and so forth. Here, however, I will not be particularly concerned with criticizing details of the Degree 2 theory. Rather, I will define a set of general criteria that are desiderata for any learnability theory and discuss how well the Degree 2 theory measures up to these.

Some Criteria for the Evaluation of Learnability Results

I will consider five criteria for the evaluation of learnability results.

1. *Degree of attained equivalence*. The learning criterion employed in learnability theories entails that the learner must converge on a grammar that bears a certain degree of equivalence to the target grammar. This predicted degree of equivalence should be empirically appropriate.

2. *Quantity of input*. The amount of input required by a particular theory must be commensurate with that actually available to the child.

3. *Availability of crucial input*. A theory must ensure that an adequate amount of information deemed crucial for deciding between competing grammars is available in the input to the child. That is, the complexity of such input should be consistent with what the child actually hears. Moreover, if a theory relies on the availability of information in language input beyond that available in simple strings drawn from the target language, it must ensure that both adequate amounts of and feasible sources for such information exist.

4. *Processing demands*. The computational and memorial demands of a theory must be reasonable, given what is known about the limited processing capacities of the child.

5. *Accuracy of linguistic predictions*. Any learnability theory includes a definition of "possible natural language" and thus implies that certain types of constructions will necessarily be ungrammatical in any particular language. Such predictions should be consistent with linguistic data.

These criteria will be discussed in turn.

Degree of Attained Equivalence

Every successful learnability theory requires that the learner eventually converge on a grammar that is consistent with its input. However, this leaves open the extent to which the learner's grammar must be equivalent to the target grammar. Different degrees of equivalence may be defined. Chomsky (1965) defined two types of equivalence: *weak* and *strong*. Two grammars are said to be weakly equivalent if they generate the same set of sentences; they are said to be strongly equivalent if they generate identical sets of meaning–surface structure pairs. Wexler and Culicover (1980) define an intermediate level of equivalence: two grammars are said to be *moderately equivalent* if they generate identical sets of meaning-sentence pairs.

The various learnability theories described above assume different definitions of equivalence. In Gold's model the learner's goal was to attain weak equivalence. Anderson's function-learnability model allows for attainment of moderate equivalence. The Degree 2 theory ensures something more than moderate, but less than strong, equivalence: the learner's grammar will generally generate the same surface structures as will the target grammar. However, in this theory misadjunction errors can only be revealed by the operation of subsequent transformations. Suppose that there is a transformation after which no other transformations can apply (for example, a phrase might be adjoined as a daughter of S, freezing an entire cycle). If the learner makes a misadjunction error in the formulation of such a transformation, its error can never be revealed. Thus, the learner's grammar will assign different structural representations to sentences in which such transformations apply than would be assigned by the target grammar.

Of course, which degree of equivalence children actually attain is an empirical question. It is reasonable to assume that children's grammars are at least moderately equivalent to their parents' grammars—speakers of a given language can understand one another as well as agree on what sentences are possible in their language. But whether children attain strong equivalence or not is a subtler issue. In chapter 5 I will present a study investigating this question. The results of this study suggest that strong equivalence is attainable; on these grounds, theories that allow for strong equivalence are to be preferred. However, further research is needed before this question can be resolved.

Quantity of Input
At present it is not possible to derive meaningful quantitative estimates of the amount of input that particular learnability theories require. Two reasons for this state of affairs exist: first, the amount of input required will be a function of the complexity of the complete grammar the child must acquire, and at present we have no descriptions of complete grammars; second, the amount of required input will also be a function of the percentage of input that enters into the process of grammar construction, and no evidence bearing on this question is available. However, it may be possible to compare the relative amount of input required by different learnability theories. In the absence of any firm data concerning the amount of input children actually make use of, it is

reasonable to assert that, other things being equal, theories that require relatively less input are to be preferred.

Four factors affect the relative amount of input required by a particular theory. The first concerns the generality of the rules the child is hypothesized to be learning. Holding everything else constant, theories that allow for the learning of more general rules may require less input, simply because fewer rules will need to be learned. For example, compare the learnability of transformational grammars (as in Wexler and Culicover 1980) with the learnability of lexical grammars (as in Pinker 1982). In the latter sort of theory the child is taken to be learning the sets of syntactic frames in which individual verbs can occur. Clearly, this sort of theory will require relatively more input. However, this is not a function of the learnability theories per se but is rather a consequence of the type of grammar on which the theories are based. The choice of a correct grammatical theory must be made on independent grounds; thus, with regard to the criterion of quantity of input, learnability theories based on different types of grammars will be incommensurable.

The second factor affecting the required amount of input is the number of types of errors the learner may make in a given theory. In the Degree 2 theory two types of errors are allowable. First, the learner may hypothesize transformations that apply overgenerally (too simple a structural description) or undergenerally (too complex a structural description). Second, the learner may hypothesize transformations in which constituents are adjoined to incorrect positions in the resulting tree (errors in the formulation of the structural changes of transformations). Several abstract examples of such errors were given above. Errors are quite heavily restricted: one could imagine theories in which learners could make ordering errors, theories in which learners could hypothesize irrelevant transformations, and so forth.

Still, it is possible to inquire whether children actually make both types of predicted errors. The literature contains numerous examples of errors of under- and overgeneralization (though perhaps not so many of the latter as might be predicted by Wexler and Culicover's theory). It is less clear whether examples of misadjunction errors exist. Consider the sort of data that might be indicative of such an error.

It has been proposed that English includes a rule, called *Dative Movement*, that relates sentences like "John gave a watch to Mary[dat]" to "John gave Mary[dat] a watch." Suppose that a child misformulates the transformation of Dative Movement so that it produces structures

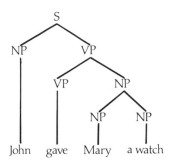

Tree 2.5

like tree 2.5. What happens when this structure is passivized? The result would be the ungrammatical "Mary a watch was given by John." I know of no examples of such errors in the literature. At any rate, a theory that eliminates one or the other of these two types of errors will require less input and, on this criterion, is to be preferred to the Degree 2 theory.

A third factor affecting the required amount of input is the complexity of input needed to reveal errors to the learner. Suppose that a theory is constructed that has the property of Degree 5 Error Detectability. In other words, certain errors will only be revealed by input of complexity of Degree 5 or greater. Compare this to Degree 2 Error Detectability, given which all errors are revealed by input of complexity of Degree 2 or greater. All input satisfying the Degree 5 criterion will also satisfy the Degree 2 criterion, but the converse is not true; hence, input satisfying the Degree 2 criterion will occur with greater frequency. As a result, the total amount of input required will be less in the Degree 2 theory than in the Degree 5 theory.

The fourth factor affecting the required amount of input concerns the likelihood of making a correct modification once an error is revealed. Recall that two types of modifications can be made in the Degree 2 theory: a transformation used in the error-revealing derivation can be discarded, or a new transformation can be hypothesized. The likelihood that an incorrect transformation will be discarded is a function of the number of transformations that must apply in the derivation—in part, a function of the complexity of the error-revealing datum. In the Degree 2 theory it is sometimes the case that subsequent transformations must apply in order to reveal a previous mistaken transformation. Thus, in a theory in which subsequent transformations are never required, the likelihood of making a correct discard will in general be greater. On the other hand, the likelihood of correctly hypothesizing a new transformation depends on the size of the set of hypothesizable transformations. In turn, this is a joint function of the constraints on possible transformations and the types of erroneous transformations that are allowed in this set. Again, in a theory that more severely constrains the types of errors learners may make, the probability of hypothesizing a correct transformation will be greater.

In sum, several factors govern the amount of input that will be required for learnability. One of the more valuable dividends of the Degree 2 result is that the quantity of input required for learnability is reasonably restricted. However, this theory is not optimal in this regard.

Availability of Crucial Input
In every successful theory of learnability, for each pair of possible languages, there must exist some datum (or data) that is sufficient to distinguish between those languages. At a minimum, a learner who succeeds in learning a language L must receive in input data distinguishing L from every other language in the class of possible languages. This is the diagnostic, or crucial, input.

Some theories of learnability may not include any explicit definition of this crucial input. For example, in Anderson's function-learnability proofs (or in Pinker's (1982) learnability proof for lexical-interpretive grammars) no explicit bound on the complexity of required input is stipulated; it is simply shown that some such data exist. However, it may be the case, as in Hamburger and Wexler's (1975) proof, that the required input is of such overwhelming complexity that it causes the entire theory to be infeasible. Clearly, the Degree 2 theory avoids this difficulty. We have all encountered sentences at least as complex as "This is the cat that ate the rat that stole the cheese." Moreover, the property of Degree 2 Error Detectability does not imply that all errors will require Degree 2 input to be revealed; in fact, it may be that most errors in the Degree 2 theory can be revealed by Degree 0 or Degree 1 input. How complex are the data actually available to children learning language?

Newport (1977) reports that the utterances addressed to a group of children between 12 and 27 months in age had an MLU (Mean Length of Utterance in morphemes) of 4.24; compare this to her report of an MLU of 11.94 for adult-adult speech. Concomitant with their extreme

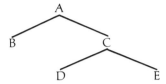

Tree 2.6

shortness, these utterances had a minimum of embedding and conjunction; Newport reports that, in speech addressed to children, the mean number of S nodes per utterance was 1.08. This means that the occurrence of Degree 1 input is relatively rare; presumably, the occurrence of Degree 2 input is significantly rarer. Hence, we may question whether sufficient Degree 2 data are present in children's input.

In addition, if the learner is to approach or attain anything more than weak equivalence, it must have available some source of structural information. Without such information the learner could never correct errors that result in sentence structures different from those assigned by the target grammar. Thus, for learnability theories that do include a source of structural information in input, one must ask whether this proposed source is plausible.

In the Degree 2 theory structural information is supplied by the base structure that the learner constructs on the basis of nonlinguistic aspects of its input (in conjunction with knowledge of word meanings). Wexler and Culicover note that this is a very strong assumption and are at some pains to provide justification. They propose that the hierarchical relations between grammatical categories in deep structures are subject to intrinsic constraints and that deep structures in various languages differ only in that categories may be ordered differently. This hypothesis is called the *Invariance Principle*. To see what is entailed by this hypothesis, consider tree 2.6.

The Invariance Principle states that all languages must observe the same hierarchical relations, but the ordering of terminal elements can vary from language to language. But note how possible orderings are constrained. Suppose that tree 2.6 is a "mobile" rather than a standard tree. Thus, certain orders are possible (*BDE, BED, DEB, EDB*), but others are not (*DBE, EBD*), because they would result from impermissible transformations of tree 2.6. In order to learn which of the possible orderings are observed by the languages they are learning, children merely need to be given early exposure to sentences that present canonical ordering.

Wexler and Culicover's hypothesis has three difficulties. First, the Invariance Principle predicts that four orderings of subject-verb-object should be possible (SVO, SOV, OVS, VOS), but two, which are in fact attested, should be impossible (VSO, OSV). The problem here is that the Invariance Principle suggests that subject and verb should form a single constituent in the last two types of languages, but, so far as I am aware, no evidence supports this suggestion.

Second, it does not seem to be the case that children are presented with only canonically ordered sentences in early stages of acquisition. Newport, Gleitman, and Gleitman (1977) report that the sentences addressed to children include examples of declaratives, imperatives, *wh*-questions, and yes-no questions. In fact, in their data the proportion of declaratives—which are canonically ordered—actually increases with the age of the child. Since the deep structure orderings of languages are revealed by canonical sentences, discovering these orderings cannot be a simple task.

Third, because the grammatical system they employ is deterministic, Wexler and Culicover must assume that the child can construct different deep structures for sentences that are paraphrases of one another, such as (1) and (2).

(1) I found a dollar on my way home.

(2) On my way home, I found a dollar.

If indeed cues exist in the nonlinguistic environment that would invariably allow the child to construct distinct deep structures for these sentences, they must be exceedingly subtle. One solution to this problem would be to allow optional transformations, thus eliminating the need for distinct deep structures. Without determinism, however, Wexler and Culicover's proof cannot go through.

In sum, any learnability theory that strives for a result stronger than weak equivalence must provide for a source of structural information. Theories may differ as to what they consider this source to be; at present it is not clear what source is most plausible. In the absence of evidence, theories that require a single source of structural information should be preferred over theories that implicate multiple sources of such information. At the same time theories that involve highly abstract representations of structural information are less preferable than theories that involve more concrete representations.

Processing Demands

Any theory of data-driven language acquisition makes certain assumptions about the processing capacities of the learner: it must have the perceptual abilities needed to extract relevant features of linguistic and nonlinguistic input, the computational abilities needed both to compare these features to those entailed by its present hypotheses and to modify its hypotheses on the basis of these comparisons, and the memorial capacity to hold in memory whatever information is needed for these computations. It is clear that the processing resources of the child during the crucial years of two to five are quite limited, though the precise nature of these limitations is not entirely clear at present (see Brown, Bransford, Ferrara, and Campione 1983, Huttenlocher and Burke 1976, and Mandler 1983 for discussion). Therefore, any solution to the projection problem that makes excessive processing demands on the learner loses value as a potential explanation; in general, other things being equal, theories making minimal demands on processing capacities are to be preferred.

As an example of a theory that fails to meet the criterion of reasonable processing demands, consider Gold's original model. In this model the learning procedure was an enumeration procedure. In such a procedure the grammars of each language in the class to be learned are listed, or enumerated. The learner progresses through the list serially, testing each grammar against all of its input, until it finds a grammar that is consistent with this input. One of the implausible aspects of enumeration procedures is that in general the learner must hypothesize, test, and reject entire grammars, not individual rules. In Gold's work the learner was assumed to have perfect memory for input, another implausible assumption. Even with perfect memory, learning via enumeration procedures takes astronomical amounts of time, simply because so many grammars must be tested; if more plausible restrictions on memory are assumed, the time for learning increases in proportion. Enumeration procedures do not provide a reasonable model of the processing capacities of the human child.

In contrast, the learning procedure incorporated in the Degree 2 theory seems much more plausible. Changes to internal grammars are effected rule by rule. The learner needs no memory for previous input: it simply compares its current grammar with the latest datum. It is not clear how much time is needed for this learning procedure to attain convergence; as noted above, this amount of time is a function of the required amount of input.

Pinker (1981) has criticized one aspect of Wexler and Culicover's learning mechanism as being implausible. He argues that in selecting a new hypothesis for inclusion, the learner must first enumerate all possible hypotheses: this is an intolerable computational burden. However, it is not at all clear that any such enumeration is required. The set of possible hypotheses is jointly determined by the set of constraints on possible hypotheses, the learner's current grammar, and the current input datum. All the learner must do is select some hypothesis that falls in this set. Intuitively, we never enumerate all possible hypotheses before selecting one as the solution for a problem; for example, in the letter series completion example discussed in chapter 1 it would be impossible to enumerate all possible hypotheses, regardless of constraints on time (since there are uncountably many hypotheses). Nevertheless, it is possible (in a fairly short period of time) to come up with a possible solution. We do not need to count all the balls in the urn before selecting one, and neither does Wexler and Culicover's learning procedure.

However, certain assumptions in the Degree 2 theory do seem to require unreasonable levels of processing resources. One example is the Assumption against String Preservation, which states roughly that no two phrase markers in any derivation may have the same orderings of terminal elements. This assumption entails that the learner be able to hold all phrase markers in a derivation in memory and to compare them pairwise. The derivation of a Degree 2 sentence may include a large number of intermediate phrase markers and consequently may require a tremendous number of comparisons. Thus, unreasonable memorial and computational demands may be made on the learner.

Otherwise, the Degree 2 theory seems to entail reasonable assumptions on processing capacity. The learning procedure in this theory is quite reasonable, and the property of Degree 2 Error Detectability ensures that the learner's resources need not be taxed by overly complex input.

Accuracy of Linguistic Predictions
In any theory of learnability the form of the learner's input and the constraints on its possible hypotheses jointly define a universal set of possible grammatical rules. Every possible subset of this set defines a possible language. In certain theories not all such languages are allowable. For example, if grammars are required to be deterministic, as in the Degree 2 theory, then languages generated by nondeterministic sets of rules must be disallowed. The composition of the set of all languages

allowed by a particular theory constitutes a hypothesis about the nature of possible natural languages—namely, they must be coextensive with this set.

In other words, constraints that are adopted for purposes of learnability may also have linguistic implications. If the Binary, Freezing, and Raising Principles are operating to constrain the child's acquisition of language, we might also expect that they operate in defining grammaticality distributions: sentences whose derivations violate one or another of these constraints ought to be ungrammatical. Conversely, linguistic evidence can serve as an independent source of confirmation or disconfirmation for particular constraints incorporated in learnability theories.[15]

This important point was first noted by Wexler and his colleagues (see especially Wexler, Culicover, and Hamburger 1975 and Culicover and Wexler 1977), and they have adduced impressive amounts of linguistic evidence supporting their assumptions. However, Wexler and Culicover (1980) also note counterexamples to certain of their assumptions, including the Freezing Principle and the Raising Principle. Other counterexamples have been noted elsewhere (Fodor 1984, Rochemont 1982, Williams 1981). A complete evaluation of the grammaticality predictions of the Degree 2 theory would entail detailed examination of a large number of linguistic arguments; this unfortunately goes beyond the scope of this work.

However, on the view that the nature of language is determined in part by the demands of learning and that theories of learnability can provide an explanatory basis for syntactic constraints, the failure of linguistic predictions made by a particular theory must count heavily against that theory. It may be possible to appeal to theories of markedness in attempting to explain why exceptions appear to constraints required for learnability, but these arguments are plausible only if they provide explicit accounts of how a marked, exceptional rule may be acquired. No such argument has been advanced in defense of the Degree 2 theory; thus, the accuracy of some of the assumptions of this theory is open to question.

Summary
The Degree 2 theory performs reasonably well on the criteria I have proposed: the amount of required input is relatively restricted, crucial input is not overly complex, processing demands are generally reasonable, and, at worst, the predicted degree of attained equivalence is not

far wrong. As I have noted, the source of structural information implicated in this theory is not totally plausible, though it is not clear what the alternative might be. Finally, Wexler and his colleagues have adduced much linguistic evidence supporting their learnability assumptions, but certain central assumptions have clear counterexamples, and thus their validity is in doubt. In discussing each of these criteria, I have alluded to ways in which the results of the Degree 2 theory might be improved upon. Many of these improvements are realized in the Degree 1 Learnability proof presented in the next chapter.

Chapter 3

A Degree 1 Learnability Proof

At the outset I suggested that bracketing information in language input might simplify the learning of syntax by eliminating many of the child's false starts and thereby reducing the need for distributional analyses. In this chapter I will explore the contributions of the Bracketed Input Hypothesis to a learnability-theoretic model of language acquisition. The result of this enterprise will be a proof demonstrating the learnability of transformational grammars from input that need never be more complex than Degree 1—that is, sentences with a single level of embedding. This result embodies numerous advantages over previous learnability results.

First, let us consider informally how bracketed input might contribute to learnability. In Wexler and Culicover's proof complexities arose from the distinction made there between "errors" and "detectable errors." In their proof, if the learner hypothesized a transformation that created an order-preserving adjunction error (all nodes in correct linear order, but some node attached incorrectly), this could only be revealed by interactions with subsequent transformations. Suppose that the learner hypothesized a raising transformation that created such an error. In order to allow for the possibility that the only error-revealing subsequent transformation might be another raising, Wexler and Culicover had to assume an additional level of embedding in crucial input. Therefore, they could at best show Degree 2 Error Detectability.

Given bracketed input, however, the distinction between "errors" and "detectable errors" can be erased: if the learner were to hypothesize a transformation resulting in a misadjunction error, the *structure* of the learner's derived string s' would not match that of the input string s.[1] To make this a bit more concrete, consider a simple example.

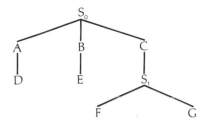

Tree 3.1

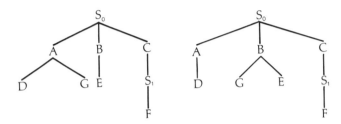

Tree 3.2   **Tree 3.3**

Tree 3.1 represents a possible input deep structure. Suppose that the target grammar includes a transformation that raises G and adjoins it to A, to the right of D; the learner hypothesizes a transformation that raises G and adjoins it to B, to the left of E. The resulting trees are 3.2 and 3.3, respectively. In both cases the resulting surface string is $D - G - E - F$. Hence, in Wexler and Culicover's theory no detectable error has been created. Given bracketed input, however, the input string s would be represented by the learner roughly as $[D - G][E][F]$. Since the learning procedure requires that the learner hypothesize transformations that produce strings that match its input, it could never hypothesize the transformation that produced tree 3.3, with its derived bracketed string $[D][G - E][F]$. In general, transformational interactions are no longer necessary to reveal errors; in particular, the extra level of embedding needed to allow raising transformations to reveal errors can be dispensed with. Thus, retaining Wexler and Culicover's other assumptions, Degree 1 Error Detectability—and, hence, Degree 1 Learnability—follows directly.

In addition, the assumption of bracketed input should allow certain otherwise necessary constraints to be relaxed. For example, assumptions that Wexler and Culicover were forced to make in order to ensure that errors are not concealed across multiple cycles are no longer needed. These include the Raising Principle discussed in chapter 2 (a modification of this constraint will be incorporated in my proof, but for other purposes) and the Assumption against String Preservation, which entails that the learner store in memory and compare all stages of particular derivations. The point here is not merely to be able to complete a proof with a minimal set of assumptions, but rather to include a set of assumptions that are psychologically plausible and natural.

This proof will differ from Wexler and Culicover's in two ways. As I have noted, it will incorporate the Bracketed Input Hypothesis. That is, I will assume that the learner's input consists of (b,bs) pairs, where *b* continues to represent a base or deep structure, but where *bs* is a *bracketed* string (or a skeletal structural description) rather than a simple string. I will also employ a slightly different method of proof. Wexler and Culicover's method of proof involved showing that an algorithm exists by which a Degree 2 error-revealing phrase marker could be constructed from a higher-degree error-revealing phrase marker. But this focus is incorrect: it is irrelevant whether a given error is detectable in any particular phrase marker or within any particular family of phrase markers; rather, what is crucial is whether a given error is detectable or not. Accordingly, I will attempt to show a weaker result, namely, that if an error occurs in a phrase marker of arbitrary degree, then there exists a Degree 1 phrase marker (which may or may not be systematically related to the higher-degree phrase marker) on which the same error occurs. This is all that must be shown; the existence of any algorithm like the one incorporated in Wexler and Culicover's proof is immaterial for learnability.

Certain problems that arise under Wexler and Culicover's method of proof by construction can be avoided using the method of proof by existence. I will give two examples illustrating this. In the first example the structure-preserving raising of a frozen node blocks a subsequent transformation, which would move a node *E* in a non-structure-preserving manner.[2] In the subsequent cycle there is a raising transformation that raises *E* only in the event that it is not dominated by a frozen node. Thus, this appears to be an example in which an error is possible on a Degree 2 phrase marker but not on a Degree 1 phrase marker.

The Degree 2 base structure is shown in tree 3.4. The Degree 1 base structure (which is equivalent to the phrase marker that would result

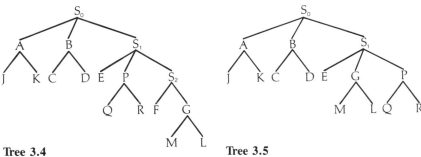

Tree 3.4   Tree 3.5

from application of Wexler and Culicover's construction algorithm) is shown in tree 3.5.

The transformations that operate are as follows:

T_1: $F - M - L - X \Rightarrow F - L + M - X$
T_2: $E - P - X - G \Rightarrow E + G - P - X$
T_3: $E - M - L - X \Rightarrow M - L + E - X$
T_4: $A - B - E \Rightarrow A + E - B$
T_4': $A - C - E \Rightarrow A + E - C$

In this case rule T_4 is in the target grammar, whereas rule T_4', which is undergeneral, is in the learner's grammar.

T_1 applies in the S_2 cycle of the Degree 2 phrase marker 3.4, causing G to be frozen. In the S_1 cycle T_2 operates to raise G (to a point where G could have been base-generated). The structural description of T_3 is not met, so it cannot apply. Finally, in the S_0 cycle, T_4 can apply, but T_4' cannot. Thus, an error is revealed. These operations are illustrated schematically in tree 3.6.

Now see what happens in the Degree 1 phrase marker 3.5. In the S_1 cycle T_1 cannot apply because F is not present. Likewise, the structural description of T_2 is not met. However, T_3 can apply, with the consequence that E is frozen under G, as in tree 3.7. Since G cannot be analyzed, neither T_4 nor T_4' can apply. Hence, no error can occur on this Degree 1 phrase marker.

Under the method of proof by construction, it was necessary to make an additional assumption, the Principle of Transparency of Untransformable Base Structures (TUBS), that would rule out examples like this one. In essence, TUBS would require that G have an alternative

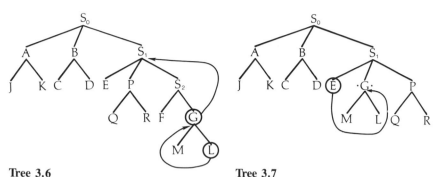

Tree 3.6   **Tree 3.7**

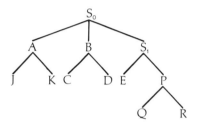

Tree 3.8

expansion, say $G \Rightarrow T + U$, which would block the application of T_3 and thus permit application of T_4 (T_4' would not apply). Unlike most of the other constraints in the Degree 2 theory, TUBS is a constraint on the grammar as a whole rather than on any particular rule, and, as Williams (1981) has pointed out, it is quite unnatural.[3] Under the method of proof by existence, however, TUBS is not necessary: there does exist a Degree 1 base structure to which T_4, but not T_4', can apply. This structure is given as tree 3.8.

From inspection of the Degree 2 base structure given in tree 3.4, it should be apparent that $S \Rightarrow E + (G) + P$ is a base rule; hence, phrase marker 3.8 is a possible base structure. Now T_1, T_2, T_3, and T_4' do not apply, but T_4 does. This is a Degree 1 base structure that can illustrate the error in question.

However (one might object), suppose that a different transformation applies in the S_1 cycle of phrase marker 3.8 that blocks subsequent application of T_4. In this case TUBS might still be needed. It is instructive to see why this ploy will not work.

Suppose that an additional transformation is added to both components:

T_0: $E - Q - R \Rightarrow Q - R + E$

Here T_0 permutes E so that P is frozen. Once again, T_4 cannot analyze E and therefore cannot apply. But consider what happens in the S_1 cycle of the Degree 2 phrase marker 3.4. The structural description of T_0 is met here, but so is the structural description of T_2. However, if we require grammars to be strictly deterministic (that is, if only one transformation can fit at a time), then neither the target grammar nor the learner's grammar can include both T_0 and T_2, so the situation described cannot arise (unless there is some required ordering of these transformations; this is discussed in the next example). In sum, given the method of proof by existence, no justification exists for the inclusion of TUBS.

As a second example, consider a case in which an intracyclic transformation permits the raising of a node that is subsequently raised again, this time perhaps erroneously. However, when this node appears in the lower cycle of a Degree 1 phrase marker, it is frozen and cannot be raised (erroneously or otherwise). The base rules of the grammar are given below:[4]

$$S \Rightarrow \left(\begin{Bmatrix} A \\ H \end{Bmatrix} \right) \begin{Bmatrix} B \\ F \end{Bmatrix} (S)$$

$B \Rightarrow D\,E$
$F \Rightarrow (C)\,(H)\,G$

The relevant transformations are as follows:

T_1: $A - D - E - X \Rightarrow D - A + E - X$
T_2: $B - X - H \Rightarrow H + B - X$
T_3: $H - D - E \Rightarrow D - H + E$
T_4: $X - G - Y - H \Rightarrow X - H + G - Y$
T_4': $G - X - H \Rightarrow H + G - X$

T_4 is in the target grammar; T_4', which is an undergeneral rule, is in the learner's grammar.

In the Degree 2 phrase marker 3.9 no transformations apply in the S_2 cycle. T_1 applies in the S_1 cycle, freezing B. T_2 applies to raise H. T_3 cannot apply because its context is not met (as a result of freezing), so H remains an eligible (analyzable) node. Finally, in the S_0 cycle, T_4, but not T_4', can apply.

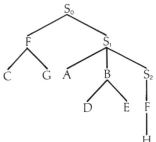

Tree 3.9

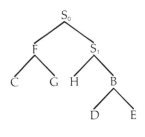

Tree 3.10

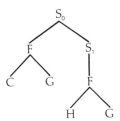

Tree 3.11

Tree 3.10 is the Degree 1 phrase marker that would result from 3.9 by the method of construction. In 3.10 neither T_1 nor T_2 can apply. Transformation T_3 does apply, however, freezing B. Now H is no longer eligible for raising, and no possible error can be revealed by this phrase marker.

One way to rule out cases like this would be to adopt a constraint on the ordering of transformations: extracyclic transformations must apply before intracyclic transformations.[5] Now, in the S_1 cycle of tree 3.9, H cannot be raised, since the context required for its raising is produced by an intracyclic transformation. Thus, T_4 cannot later apply to raise H in the S_0 cycle.

Under the method of proof by existence, an alternative solution is possible. In fact, given these base rules, there is a Degree 1 phrase marker to which T_4 (but not T_4') can apply. This is shown in tree 3.11. Here no transformations apply in the S_1 cycle; since H is an eligible node, it can be raised in the S_0 cycle.

By dispensing with Wexler and Culicover's ordering constraint, certain other problems can be avoided. Suppose that a grammar has the following base rules:

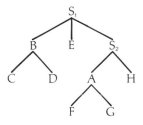

Tree 3.12

    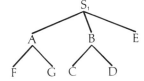

Tree 3.13   **Tree 3.14**

S ⇒ (A) B E (S)
S ⇒ A (H)
A ⇒ F G
B ⇒ C D

Suppose further that it has the following transformations:

T_1: F – G – H ⇒ F + H – G
T_2: B – X – A ⇒ A + B – X
T_3: C – D – E ⇒ C + E – D
T_4: F – X – E ⇒ F + E – X

Given the ordering constraint, there exists a Degree 2 phrase marker in which an error can occur, but there does not exist any Degree 1 phrase marker on which a comparable error can occur. The two lower cycles of the Degree 2 phrase marker are shown in tree 3.12. T_1 applies in the S_2 cycle, freezing A. Then T_2 applies in the S_1 cycle, raising A. T_3 cannot apply, because there is material to the left of C;[6] T_4 cannot apply because A has been frozen and F is unanalyzable. Thus, E can be raised (perhaps erroneously) in the S_0 cycle (not shown).

However, E cannot be raised in any possible Degree 1 phrase marker. E appears in the S_1 cycle in two Degree 1 phrase markers. These are shown as trees 3.13 and 3.14. In tree 3.13 T_3 applies, freezing B. Since E is dominated by a frozen node, it cannot be affected by following transformations. In tree 3.14 T_4 applies, freezing E and A. Again, E cannot be raised.

Now see what happens in tree 3.12 when the ordering constraint is abolished. T_1 again applies in the S_2 cycle. In the S_1 cycle both T_2 and T_3 fit. Two possible courses of action might be taken. We might require grammars to be strictly deterministic, in which case T_2 and T_3 cannot coexist in the same grammar. If we eliminate T_2, then T_3 will apply in tree 3.12, causing E to become unanalyzable. If we eliminate T_3, then E remains analyzable in tree 3.13. Alternatively, we could adopt an ordering convention: if an intracyclic and an extracyclic transformation simultaneously fit a tree, the intracyclic transformation applies first. In this case T_3 would apply *before* T_2 in tree 3.12, making E ineligible. Given either possibility, E will be equally eligible or ineligible in Degree 1 and Degree 2 phrase markers.

These examples should suffice to illustrate the potential advantage of proof by existence over proof by construction. Note, however, that adoption of this method will not by itself suffice to guarantee Degree 1 Learnability. The examples given in chapter 2 illustrating Wexler and Culicover's assumptions (see, in particular, the example motivating the Raising Principle) are still valid: with only linear surface information available in input, Degree 2 Learnability appears to be the limiting result. Thus, the key question remains: given surface bracketing information in input, is it the case that, for any error that is revealed by a Degree 2 or greater phrase marker, there exists a Degree 1 phrase marker that also reveals that error? I will address this question in my proof, to which I now turn. I will formally demonstrate that, given a particular set of assumed constraints on the hypotheses that the learner can consider, this question can be answered in the affirmative.

The remainder of this chapter will consist of three sections. In the first I will define and give examples of the assumptions incorporated in my proof. The second section will contain the proofs of six theorems, culminating in the proof of Degree 1 Learnability. The final section will contain a brief evaluation of this proof in light of the criteria advanced in chapter 2. Since the essential difference between the Degree 1 proof and Wexler and Culicover's Degree 2 theory is the inclusion of the Bracketed Input Hypothesis in the former, a comparison of these two results will reveal the ways in which bracketed input may be necessary.[7]

Assumptions

I will begin by listing and defining the assumptions incorporated in the Degree 1 proof, along with explanations of the terminology and notations that will be used. The proof rests on eight assumptions.[8] Three of these, Determinism, Precedence of Intracyclic Transformations, and Single Application of Transformations, have to do with the general functioning of grammars. Of the remaining five, one is a constraint on the base component, and the other four are constraints on the form or function of individual transformational rules. After defining all eight assumptions, I will give examples showing why each of the last five is required for the proof.[9]

First, I will assume that, in general, possible grammars are of the type defined in Chomsky 1965. That is, a context-free base generates base structures; lexical insertion applies at this level, subject to constraints on subcategorization. The transformational component applies to lexicalized base structures to produce surface structures. This component is cyclic: transformations apply first to the most deeply embedded clause, then to the next most deeply embedded clause, and so forth.[10] In the examples given below I will ignore lexical items—the terminal nodes of the trees that follow are lexical categories, dominating particular items, but the identity of these is irrelevant, and they will therefore be omitted.

Second, I will employ the same learning procedure and learning criterion used by Wexler and Culicover. Crucially, I am assuming that input is in the form of (b,bs) pairs, where *b* is a base structure and *bs* is a bracketed string. That is, I am assuming not only that the learner has access to information concerning the linear order of words in input sentences, but also that the learner can construct a representation of how these words are grouped together to form hierarchical phrases.

Definitions and terminology required for the proof are as follows:

Definition: eligible node. If a transformation can analyze a node, that node is said to be eligible. Conversely, if a node is unanalyzable, it is said to be ineligible.

Definition: cycle. The nodes in a given cycle are defined to be all nodes dominated by a given *S* node, but not dominated by any embedded *S*; any embedded *S* itself is also not in the given cycle.

Terminology: The *binary context* of a phrase marker includes all nodes that are eligible, given the Binary Principle (see below). For a given phrase marker P, this will be denoted by BC(P). The binary context consists of an *upper context* and a *lower context*. The upper context, denoted by UC(P), includes all eligible nodes in the current cycle; the lower context, denoted by LC(P), includes all eligible nodes in the immediately preceding cycle.

Definition: intracyclic and *extracyclic*. A transformation will be said to apply intracyclically if all the nodes in its structural description are in UC(P). If some node in the transformation is in LC(P), it will be said to apply extracyclically. ("Extracyclic" is equivalent to Wexler and Culicover's term "S-essential.") The application, rather than the form, of a transformation determines its classification, since a given transformation may apply either intracyclically or extracyclically in different phrase markers.

Definition: context. Nodes in the structural description of a transformation that are not permuted, deleted, or copied by that transformation form the context of the transformation.

The eight assumptions required for the proof are as follows:

1. *Principle of Determinism*. A transformational component is said to be deterministic if at each stage of every derivation one and only one transformation can apply (perhaps excepting the case noted below covered by the Principle of Precedence of Intracyclic Transformations (PIT)) and if that transformation can fit the phrase marker in only one way. The Principle of Determinism states,

The target grammar is deterministic. In the limit, the learner's grammar is also deterministic, though it may not always be so in the course of acquisition. If at a given stage in a derivation more than one transformation can apply, or a given transformation can be fit in more than one way (subject to the PIT exception), then that derivation is filtered, and an error is revealed.

If a derivation is filtered due to a violation of Determinism, this means that it is aborted at the point of nondeterminism and no surface string is produced. Thus, errors due to violations of Determinism will always result in the discarding of a previously hypothesized transformation.

2. *Principle of Precedence of Intracyclic Transformations (PIT)*. This principle states,

If an intracyclic transformation and an extracyclic transformation simultaneously are fit by a phrase marker, the intracyclic transformation applies first.

PIT is the opposite of Wexler and Culicover's Ordering of S-Essential Transformations (OSET), which required that extracyclic transformations apply before any intracyclic transformations.

3. *Principle of Single Application of Transformations (SAT)*. This principle states,

In a given cycle a transformation may apply at most one time.

I have included this assumption to ensure that the child's grammar is effective; that is, no derivations involve infinite loops. There may be instances where a transformation creates an environment in which a second transformation applies, undoing the results of the first transformation, which could otherwise then apply again, and so forth. If a derivation does involve an infinite loop, the least egregious result is that no surface structure can ever be derived. But it is unclear what to do in such cases; the transformations involved in the loop may or may not be erroneous. The simplest solution is to prohibit such loops, via SAT.

4. *Principle of S-Optionality*. This principle states,

Whenever S appears on the right-hand side of a base rule, it is always optional. Furthermore, no rule A $\Rightarrow$ (S) *is possible.*

This principle was also included in Wexler and Culicover's proof. The second part of the Principle of S-Optionality follows from the fact that grammatical categories in the base are divided into lexical and nonlexical types. Lexical categories (such as noun, verb, and adjective) can dominate only lexical material. Nonlexical categories (such as NP, VP, and AP) can be expanded as strings of nonlexical and/or lexical categories. Given this distinction, it follows that there can be no base rule of the form $A \Rightarrow (S)$, since if A is a lexical category it cannot dominate S, and if A is a nonlexical category it must always have a nonnull expansion. More generally, we can conclude that there can be no base rule of the form $A \Rightarrow (X)$, where X represents any grammatical category.

5. *Binary Principle*. The Binary Principle defines eligibility as follows:

In a given cycle a transformation may analyze only those nodes in the current cycle and in the immediately preceding cycle.

This definition is equivalent to that given in Wexler and Culicover 1980; an illustrative example is given here in chapter 2.

6. *Principle of Transparency of Lower Context* (TLC). This principle states,

No node in any LC(P) may be used to fit the context of a transformation. Moreover, any node in LC(P) that is not explicitly referenced in the structural description of a transformation is transparent and need not be fit by a variable.

TLC implies that all nodes in LC(P) (including the embedded S itself) are transparent to intracyclic transformations and that no intracyclic transformation can explicitly reference any such node. With regard to extracyclic transformations, TLC implies that the only nodes in LC(P) that can be referenced are nodes that are permuted (that is, raised), deleted, or copied. Among other things, this implies that lowering transformations are not possible and that movement transformations cannot be governed by material in a higher cycle. TLC is a slightly stronger version of Wexler and Culicover's Principle of No Bottom Context.[11]

7. *Principle of Intracyclic Ineligibility of Raised Nodes* (IRN). This principle states,

If a node A *is raised, no node that* A *dominates may be used to fit any intracyclic transformation.*

IRN is similar to Wexler and Culicover's Raising Principle, except that IRN permits implicitly raised nodes to be raised or extracyclically deleted in subsequent cycles.

8. *Principle of Uniqueness of Extracyclic Transformations* (UET). UET is identical to Wexler and Culicover's Principle of Uniqueness of S-Essential Transformations. This principle states,

In a given cycle at most one extracyclic transformation may apply, raising, deleting, or copying a single node in LC(P). If additional extracyclic transformations are fit by a phrase marker, they are ignored.

In combination with TLC and IRN, UET implies that in a given cycle at most one node in LC(P) can ever be referenced in the set of transformations applying in that cycle.

This completes the list of assumptions included in the Degree 1 proof. Below I will give examples for the Binary Principle, Transparency of Lower Context, Intracyclic Ineligibility of Raised Nodes, Uniqueness of Extracyclic Transformations, and S-Optionality, showing how each of these rules out some possibility in which an error is revealed by a Degree 2 or greater phrase marker, but not by any Degree 1 phrase marker. Since I have begun by assuming this entire set, these examples will demonstrate that each of these assumptions is relatively necessary, given the others. I will also discuss some linguistic evidence bearing on TLC, IRN, and UET. Wexler and Culicover have previously provided linguistic evidence for most of the other assumptions.

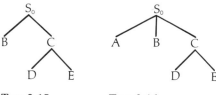

Tree 3.15   Tree 3.16

Before turning to these examples, however, consider briefly the types of errors permitted in the Degree 1 proof. Errors can occur because an incorrect transformation is hypothesized, a correct transformation has been discarded, or a required transformation has not yet been hypothesized. What sort of incorrect transformations can be hypothesized? Recall how the learning procedure works: if the surface structure derived by the learner's transformational component does not match the input surface structure, the learner must hypothesize a transformation that applies to the derived surface structure and produces the input surface structure. Since, by hypothesis, the bracketing of the derived surface structure must match the bracketing of the input surface structure, nodes that are moved by the hypothesized transformation must be correctly attached. In other words, misadjunction errors are not allowed. This leaves two possible types of errors: the hypothesized transformation can apply overgenerally (usually as a result of too little stipulated context) or undergenerally (usually as a result of too much stipulated context).[12] Errors that arise because of incorrect discarding or lack of hypothesization can simply be considered as cases of maximal undergeneralization. Below I give some examples of possible types of errors.

First, consider one possible type of an overgeneral permutation error. Trees 3.15 and 3.16 are two Degree 0 base phrase markers. Suppose that the target grammar includes the rule $B - D - E \Rightarrow B - E + D$, whereas the learner's grammar includes the rule $X - D - E \Rightarrow X - E + D$. Both of these rules will apply to tree 3.15, permuting D and E. In fact, this base structure could have been the datum that led to the hypothesization of the learner's incorrect rule. The learner's rule will also apply to tree 3.16, but the target grammar rule will not (again, I am assuming that there are no implicit end variables). In this case the learner's rule is overgeneral because an explicit context element in the target grammar rule has been replaced by a variable. One important point is illustrated by this example: not all applications of overgeneral

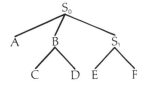

Tree 3.17   **Tree 3.18**

(or undergeneral, for that matter) transformations are incorrect. Thus, it will not be sufficient to show that there is a low-degree phrase marker to which an incorrect transformation applies (or fails to apply); rather, it is necessary to show that there is a low-degree phrase marker to which an incorrect transformation applies (or fails to apply) *erroneously*.

A second possible type of overgeneral error exists. Trees 3.17 and 3.18 are two Degree 1 base phrase markers. The target grammar includes the following rules:

T_1: $A - C - X \Rightarrow C + A - X$
T_2: $F - B \Rightarrow B$
T_3: $C - D - E \Rightarrow C - D$

The learner's grammar includes the following rules:

T_1: $A - C - X \Rightarrow C + A - X$
T_2: $F - B \Rightarrow B$
T_3': $B - E \Rightarrow B$

In tree 3.17 no relevant transformations apply in the S_1 cycle. In the S_0 cycle T_1 applies in both grammars to adjoin A to B as a sister of D. The target grammar rule T_3 cannot now apply, because B dominates the sequence $C - A - D$, so E is not deleted. However, the learner's grammar rule T_3' can apply, so E is overgenerally deleted. In tree 3.18 again no relevant transformations apply in the S_1 cycle. In the S_0 cycle T_2 applies in both grammars to delete F. Now both T_3 and T_3' can apply to delete E, since both B and $C - D$ are present. In this example the learner's rule T_3' is overgeneral because a sequence in the target rule context has been replaced by a node dominating that sequence. Previous transformations may destroy the dominated sequence while leaving the dominating node analyzable.

It is also possible to construct examples of undergeneral transformations. I will not go through this is any detail, but suppose that in the first example the rule $X - D - E \Rightarrow X - E + D$ is in the target grammar, whereas the rule $B - D - E \Rightarrow B - E + D$ is in the learner's grammar. Or, in the second example, suppose that the rule $B - E \Rightarrow B$ is in the target grammar, whereas the rule $C - D - E \Rightarrow C - D$ is in the learner's grammar. In either case an undergeneral error will result.

With this taxonomy of errors in mind, I now turn to examples of the assumptions of my proof. For each assumption, I will give one or two examples demonstrating why it is required for Degree 1 Error Detectability. That is, I will relax each assumption in turn while holding all of the others constant. In each case it will be possible to show that there are then errors that are revealed only by Degree 2 or greater phrase markers. Note that the given examples are not the only instances in which each assumption is required. Thus, alternative formulations may rule out the particular examples illustrating a given assumption, but these will not necessarily obviate the need for the assumption.

Binary Principle
Given the Binary Principle, transformations applying in a given cycle can refer only to nodes in the current cycle and in the immediately preceding cycle; they cannot "look" further down the tree, and unbounded movement is therefore ruled out. The question I wish to pursue now is this: if the Binary Principle is relaxed while retaining the other assumptions I have made, are there errors that can be revealed only by Degree 2 or greater data? If we can answer this question in the affirmative, this demonstrates that the Binary Principle is *relatively necessary* for the proof of Degree 1 Error Detectability.

At first glance it would seem that the Binary Principle might not be necessary, given the other constraints (particularly TLC). In order to show the necessity of the Binary Principle, the following sort of example would have to be constructed. In the S_0 cycle of a Degree 2 phrase marker some node E is erroneously raised from the S_2 cycle. This entails that E is not an eligible node in the S_1 cycle of this phrase marker. This sort of phrase marker can be constructed. Suppose that the next-to-last transformation in the S_1 cycle of this phrase marker is a non-structure-preserving extracyclic raising that triggers the subsequent intracyclic deletion of E. Since this E is no longer present, it will not be eligible for raising in the S_0 cycle. Thus, only the E in the S_2 cycle is eligible, and an error can be created on a Degree 2 phrase marker. In addition to this, however, it must be shown that E cannot be erroneously raised in any Degree 1 phrase marker. In such a phrase marker E would be base-generated in the S_1 cycle, but it would be rendered ineligible (deleted) by some intracyclic transformation applying in this cycle. Suppose that this is indeed the case for every possible Degree 1 phrase marker in which E appears in the S_1 cycle. This leads to a paradox: if E is always deleted by the operation of transformations in the cycle in which it was generated, this node could never be raised. This means that E could not be raised from S_2 in the S_0 cycle of the Degree 2 phrase marker. In short, if the requisite Degree 2 phrase marker can be constructed, this entails that the required Degree 1 phrase marker cannot be, and vice versa.

However, the correctness of this argument hinges on how the Principle of Uniqueness of Extracyclic Transformations is interpreted when the Binary Principle is relaxed. In this situation (as Wexler and Culicover noted) UET may be interpreted in one of two ways. First, it could be interpreted as meaning that in any given cycle only one extracyclic transformation may apply. Alternatively, it could be interpreted as meaning that in any given cycle only one extracyclic transformation may apply to each of the previous, but currently eligible, cycles. Given the Binary Principle, there is only one such cycle, so these interpretations are equivalent. In the absence of this principle, however, these interpretations have different implications: the first interpretation entails that at most one extracyclic transformation can apply in any given cycle (though it can now operate on nodes from any previous cycle); the second interpretation entails that in a given cycle one extracyclic transformation may apply to some node in each of the previous cycles. Given the first interpretation, the argument sketched above goes through: the Binary Principle is not necessary. However, I can think of no compelling reason why this interpretation must be adopted.

Given the interpretation of UET in which one extracyclic transformation can apply to each previous cycle, it is possible to construct an example demonstrating the relative necessity of the Binary Principle. The crux of this example is that the interaction of the multiple extracyclic transformations applying in the S_0 cycle of a Degree 2 phrase marker may cause an error to be revealed that cannot appear in any Degree 1 phrase marker. Following Wexler and Culicover, I will adopt a constraint on the ordering of extracyclic transformations: they must apply to successively "shallower" preceding cycles. That is, in the S_0 cycle of a Degree 2 phrase marker extracyclic transformations apply first to the S_2 cycle and then to the S_1 cycle. In the example given below, which is adapted from Wexler and Culicover, the erroneous raising of a node from the S_1 cycle is conditional upon the previous raising of a node from the S_2 cycle. When the latter node is base-generated in a Degree 1 phrase marker, the nodes it dominates are eli-

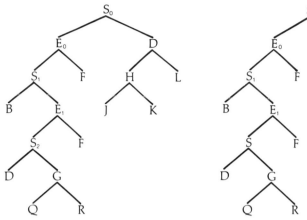

Tree 3.19

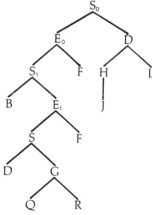

Tree 3.20

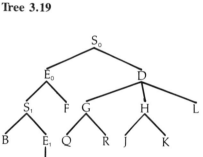

Tree 3.21

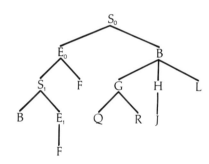

Tree 3.22

gible, and they trigger a transformation that conceals the error. The Degree 2 and Degree 1 phrase markers used in this example are shown as trees 3.19 through 3.22.

The following transformations are in the target grammar:

T_1: X – G – H – L ⇒ X – G + H – L
T_2: X – B – Y – G – Z – K – L ⇒ X – Y – G – Z – K – B + L
T_3: E – X – B – Y ⇒ X – B – Y
T_4: Q – X – B – Y ⇒ Q – X – Y
T_5: E – Q – X – J – L ⇒ Q – X – J – L

The following transformations are in the learner's grammar:

T_1: X – G – H – L $\Rightarrow$ X – G + H – L
T_2': X – B – Y – G – H – L $\Rightarrow$ X – Y – G – H – B + L
T_3: E – X – B – Y $\Rightarrow$ X – B – Y
T_4: Q – X – B – Y $\Rightarrow$ Q – X – Y

For the target grammar, in tree 3.19 no transformations apply in either the S_2 or the S_1 cycle. In the S_0 cycle T_1 applies, raising G and adjoining it as a left sister of H. Then T_2 applies (note that G is required for this transformation), raising B and adjoining it as a left sister of L. Since B is now to the right of E_0, T_3 can apply, deleting E_0 and all nodes it dominates (including S_1).[13] T_4 cannot apply, because Q, which was implicitly raised with G, is ineligible by IRN. Similarly, for the learner's grammar, T_1, T_2', and T_3 apply, with the same effects as before.

Now see what happens in the Degree 2 phrase marker, tree 3.20. For the target grammar, T_1 again applies, raising G. But now, since there is no K, T_2 cannot apply. Because B has not been raised, T_3 cannot apply; since Q is ineligible, T_5 cannot apply, so E_0 is not deleted. For the learner's grammar, T_1 applies, raising G, T_2' applies erroneously, raising B, and T_3 applies, deleting E_0. Thus, the learner's overgeneral error is revealed by this phrase marker.

However, in the Degree 1 phrase markers 3.21 and 3.22 no error is revealed. In 3.21, for the target grammar, T_2 applies, raising B. Again, B is to the right of E_0, and E_0 is deleted. But now, since G has been base-generated in the S_0 cycle of this phrase marker, Q is eligible, and T_4 can apply, deleting B. No evidence remains that B was ever raised; both its original position and its derived position have been deleted. Similarly, for the learner's grammar, T_2' applies, raising B, T_3 applies, deleting E_0, and T_4 applies, deleting B. The phrase markers derived by the target and learner's grammars are identical.

Finally, in 3.22, for the target grammar, only T_5 applies, deleting E_0 (and B, which it dominates). For the learner's grammar, T_2' applies, erroneously raising B. Then T_3 applies, deleting E_0, and T_4 applies, deleting B. Although B has been erroneously raised by the learner's grammar in 3.22, no evidence of this remains. Again, the phrase markers derived by the two grammars are identical (even though the transformations applying in the two derivations differ). In short, the overgenerality of the learner's rule T_2' cannot be revealed by any Degree 1 phrase marker.

If the Binary Principle is reinstated, G cannot be raised from the S_2 cycle in either of the Degree 2 phrase markers 3.19 and 3.20. Hence, B

cannot be raised (erroneously or correctly) in either of these phrase markers, and no error is revealed on any phrase marker whatsoever. Given the Binary Principle, the learner's two errors (overgenerality of T_2' and lack of T_5) cancel each other out. Although the target and learner's grammars are different, they will generate the same set of phrase markers. The Binary Principle *is* relatively necessary.

Transparency of Lower Context
TLC ensures that nodes in lower context cannot supply context for transformations. Since only nodes in upper context can supply such context, the number of possible transformations is sharply reduced.[14] This aids in learnability by increasing the likelihood of hypothesizing a correct transformation. It is fairly simple to construct an example showing that TLC is relatively necessary.

In this example the following rules are in the target grammar:

T_1: $C - D - C - X \Rightarrow D - C - X$
T_2: $D - C - X \Rightarrow C + D - X$
T_3: $C - D - E - C - X \Rightarrow C - D - C + E - X$
T_4: $C - D - F - X - C - E \Rightarrow C - D - C + F - X - E$

The following rules are in the learner's grammar:

T_1: $C - D - C - X \Rightarrow D - C - X$
T_2: $D - C - X \Rightarrow C + D - X$
T_3: $C - D - E - C - X \Rightarrow C - D - C + E - X$
T_4': $A - F - X - C - E \Rightarrow A - C + F - X - E$

The Degree 2 phrase marker on which an error is revealed is tree 3.23. In this phrase marker, for the target grammar, no transformations apply in the S_2 cycle. In the S_1 cycle T_1 applies, deleting C_{1a}.[15] Then T_2 applies, moving C_{1b} so that it is adjoined to A as a left sister of D. That is, C_{1b} now occupies the position originally held by C_{1a}. T_3 applies, raising C_2 from the S_2 cycle. The effect of these three transformations is to return the S_1 cycle to its original state. However, because of the Principle of Single Application of Transformations, T_1 (and hence T_2) cannot apply again. In the S_0 cycle no transformations apply. In particular, T_4 cannot apply, because no C is present in this cycle to supply the needed context.

The derivation proceeds identically through the S_1 cycle for the learner's grammar. T_1 applies, deleting C_{1a}, T_2 applies, permuting C_{1b} so that it is the left sister of D, and T_3 applies, raising C_2 and returning this cycle to its original state. In the S_0 cycle T_4' applies, erroneously

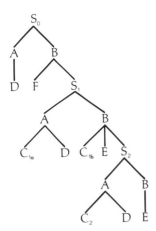

Tree 3.23

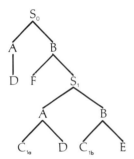

Tree 3.24

raising C_2. Assuming that no further transformations apply, an error has been revealed by a Degree 2 phrase marker.

This erroneous raising cannot occur in any Degree 1 phrase marker. C can only be raised from the S_1 cycle when it is immediately to the left of E, but T_1 and T_2 conspire to ensure that this cannot happen unless C is raised into this position. As illustration, consider the Degree 1 phrase marker 3.24. In the S_1 cycle T_1 applies, deleting C_{1a}. Then T_2 permutes C_{1b} so that it is no longer adjacent to E. T_4 cannot apply, because its structural description is not met. But T_4' cannot apply either, because the S_1 cycle no longer contains the required substring $C - E$.

Note that if TLC is reinstated, there is no longer an error on either the Degree 2 or the Degree 1 phrase marker. In particular, the learner's transformation T_4' cannot apply in the S_0 cycle of tree 3.23 because the

Tree 3.25

node E in the S_1 cycle cannot be used to fit its context. Thus, this example demonstrates the relative necessity of TLC.

As I noted earlier, TLC is a slightly stronger version of Wexler and Culicover's Principle of No Bottom Context (NBC). According to NBC, nodes in lower context cannot supply context for transformations, but they must be represented by variables if they intervene between context in the upper context and the node in lower context that is operated upon. For example, suppose that there is a transformation $X - D - E \Rightarrow X - E + D$. Given NBC, this transformation cannot apply to the partial phrase marker 3.25, because C intervenes between D and E. In contrast, given TLC, in which nodes in lower context are transparent, this transformation can apply to phrase marker 3.25.

Given NBC, transformations can apply to nodes at the boundaries of embedded sentences that cannot apply to nodes internal to such clauses. Does linguistic evidence support this distinction? To the extent that it does, this constitutes an argument that NBC should be employed in place of TLC, which makes no such distinction.

In English certain putative transformations operate on embedded subjects but not on other embedded NPs. These include Equi-NP Deletion, Raising to Object, and Raising to Subject. These transformations relate the (a) and (b) sentences in (1), (2), and (3), respectively.

(1) a. I persuaded John [John] to leave.
    b. I persuaded John to leave.
(2) a. I expected that John would leave.
    b. I expected John to leave.
(3) a. It seems that John has left.
    b. John seems to have left.

Given NBC, this preferential treatment of subjects is easily explicable: the crucial segments of the structural descriptions of the transformations can be written as V – (NP) – NP – X. Nonsubject embedded

NPs can never directly follow the matrix verb, so these transformations can apply only to embedded subjects.

In contrast, given TLC, subjects of embedded clauses cannot be uniquely identified by structural descriptions of transformations. Thus, in a sentence like "It seems that John has left Mary," in which there are two embedded NPs ("John" and "Mary"), unless the embedded subject can somehow be labeled, it seems that a problem with Determinism ought to arise.[16] In fact, this does not occur: only "John" can undergo Raising to Subject.

NBC predicts that phrases occurring at the ends of embedded sentences also ought to receive preferential treatment. It might seem that *Tough* Movement, which relates (4a) and (4b), corroborates this prediction. However, the object of an embedded clause can undergo *Tough* Movement when it is followed by additional material as well, as illustrated in (5).

(4) a. It is tough to please John.
    b. John is tough to please.

(5) a. It is tough to please John completely.
    b. *It is tough to please completely John.
    c. John is tough to please completely.

In fact, to my knowledge, no linguistic evidence supports this prediction that transformations apply preferentially to clause-final embedded phrases.

Even worse, NBC predicts that for languages with VSO order in embedded clauses, the embedded verb and object should be transformed preferentially with respect to the embedded subject. Again, I know of no evidence supporting this prediction; I suspect that the situation is rather the opposite of that predicted by NBC. If this turns out to be true, this implies that there must be some way of marking the embedded subject that does not depend on its position at the boundary of the embedded sentence. But if such marking exists, no evidence remains in support of the distinction between phrases that are peripheral and phrases that are nonperipheral in embedded sentences. In short, no compelling linguistic evidence argues for the replacement of TLC by NBC. Thus, I retain the stronger constraint.

Intracyclic Ineligibility of Raised Nodes
According to IRN, nodes that are implicitly raised cannot subsequently supply context for intracyclic transformations.[17] In general, it is not

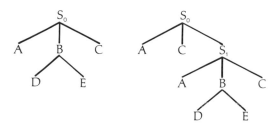

Tree 3.26   **Tree 3.27**

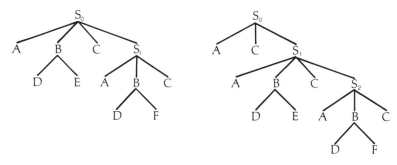

Tree 3.28   **Tree 3.29**

possible to guarantee that nodes raised in the S_0 cycles of Degree 1 and Degree 2 phrase markers dominate the same material. Thus, without IRN it is possible that some transformation, dependent on these implicitly raised nodes, operates to reveal an error in Degree 2, but not Degree 1, phrase markers. This possibility is illustrated in the following example.

Suppose that the target grammar includes the following rules:

T_1: $A - D - X \Rightarrow D - X$
T_2: $A - C - B \Rightarrow A + B - C$
T_3: $D - E - F \Rightarrow F + D - E$

The learner's grammar includes the following rules:

T_1': $A - B - X \Rightarrow B - X$
T_2: $A - C - B \Rightarrow A + B - C$
T_3: $D - E - F \Rightarrow F + D - E$

In the Degree 0 phrase marker 3.26 both T_1 and the overgeneral T_1' apply, deleting A. No error is revealed on this phrase marker. Similarly, in the Degree 1 phrase marker 3.27 no error is revealed. For the target grammar, T_1 applies in the S_1 cycle, deleting A. In the S_0 cycle T_2 applies, raising B. Then T_1 applies, deleting A. For the learner's grammar, T_1' applies in the S_1 cycle, deleting A. In the S_0 cycle T_2 raises B and T_1' deletes A. Finally, in the other possible Degree 1 phrase marker relevant to this example, again no error is revealed. This is shown in tree 3.28. Here, for the target grammar, T_1 applies in the S_1 cycle, deleting A. In the S_0 cycle T_1 again applies, deleting A. Then T_3 applies, raising F. For the learner's grammar, T_1' applies in the S_1 cycle, deleting A. T_1' applies again in the S_0 cycle, again deleting A, and T_3 applies, raising F. The Degree 0 and Degree 1 phrase markers derived by these grammars are identical.

However, an error is revealed in the Degree 2 phrase marker 3.29. For the target grammar, T_1 applies in the S_2 cycle, deleting A. T_1 also applies in the S_1 cycle, again deleting A. Now T_3 applies, raising F and adjoining it to the left of D. In the S_0 cycle T_2 applies, raising B. But since F intervenes between A and D, T_1 cannot apply. The derivation for the learner's grammar proceeds similarly. In the S_2 cycle T_1' applies. In the S_1 cycle T_1' and T_3 apply. In the S_0 cycle T_2 applies, raising B, which dominates a nonbase sequence of nodes. Since B supplies the context for T_1', it can apply again in the S_0 cycle, deleting A. Thus, the learner's overgeneral error is revealed by this Degree 2 phrase marker, but not by any phrase marker of lower degree.

If IRN is reinstated, the learner's error is revealed by phrase marker 3.27. In the S_1 cycle T_1 (in the target grammar) and T_1' both apply to delete A. In the S_0 cycle, in both grammars, T_2 operates to raise B. Now T_1 cannot operate, since, by IRN, D is unanalyzable, but T_1' can apply, since B remains analyzable. This example illustrates the relative necessity of IRN.

IRN is a weakened version of Wexler and Culicover's Raising Principle. The Raising Principle stipulates that implicitly raised nodes cannot be analyzed by subsequent transformations, intracyclic or extracyclic. IRN allows implicitly raised nodes to be extracyclically raised or deleted, but they cannot be analyzed by subsequent intracyclic transformations. Wexler and Culicover adduce several linguistic examples in support of the Raising Principle; however, since all of these examples involve *Wh*-Movement (an extracyclic rule) out of a raised constituent, none of them provides support for IRN.

The groups of sentences shown in (6), (7), and (8) are similar to the examples provided by Wexler and Culicover.

(6) a. A review of a new book came out last week.
   b. A review came out last week of a new book.
   c. What did a review come out last week of?

(7) a. The reports which you had me collect are sitting on the table.
   b. The reports are sitting on the table which you had me collect.
   c. Which are the reports sitting on the table you had me collect?

(8) a. I expressed my belief that the United States should give away a million tons of wheat each week to Mary.
   b. I expressed my belief to Mary that the United States should give away a million tons of wheat each week.
   c. Exactly how many tons of wheat did you express your belief to Mary that the United States should give away each week?

Sentence (6b) results from (6a) by application of the rule of Extraposition of PP. Since this rule extracts material from an NP, it is considered to be a raising. In (6c) the object of the extraposed PP has been *Wh*-Moved. Wexler and Culicover claim that sentences such as this are ungrammatical, though I personally find (6c) to be acceptable in the intended reading. Sentences (7a) and (7b) are related by the rule of Extraposition of Relative Clause, again a raising. *Wh*-Moving a constituent of the extraposed relative creates the clearly ungrammatical (7c). In this case, however, depending on the derived structure of (7b), it is possible that the ungrammaticality of (7c) results from a violation of the Binary Principle. Finally, (8a) and (8b) are related by the rule of Extraposition of Sentential Complement. *Wh*-Movement of a constituent from the extraposed complement produces (8c), which Wexler and Culicover claim to be ungrammatical. Again, I find this sentence to be acceptable. Note that IRN does not predict that any of the (c) sentences are ungrammatical; if they are, some alternative explanation is required.

IRN and the Raising Principle agree in predicting that no constituent of any extraposed phrase can be analyzed by an intracyclic rule. The sentences in (9) provide an example of this.

(9) a. A boy from Mrs. Smith's class ran away (to the city).
   b. A boy ran away (to the city) from Mrs. Smith's class.
   c. Mrs. Smith's class was run away (to the city) by the boy from.
   d. Mrs. Smith's class was run away (to the city) from by the boy.

Extraposition of PP relates sentences (9a) and (9b). (9b) is ambiguous, for "from Mrs. Smith's class" can be taken as a modifier of either "a boy" or "ran away." (9c) results from application of Passive (an intra-cyclic rule) to the structure underlying the first reading of (9b); this sentence is clearly ungrammatical, as predicted. (9d) results from application of Passive to the structure underlying the second reading of (9b); at least in the version without "to the city," this sentence is acceptable.

Williams (1981) and Rochemont (1982) have noted certain counter-examples to the linguistic predictions made by the Raising Principle. In (10b) a relative clause is extraposed from a *Wh*-Moved NP by Extraposition from NP. Again, *Wh*-Movement is a raising, so this appears to be a violation of the Raising Principle. In (11b) a PP has been extraposed from an NP that has previously undergone Raising to Subject. Again, this Extraposition of PP seems to violate the Raising Principle.

(10) a. Which man that was running away did you see?

b. Which man did you see that was running away?

(11) a. A book by John seems to have appeared.

b. A book seems to have appeared by John.

The Raising Principle would not be violated if these extraposition transformations applied before the raising transformations. However, Ross (1967) has supplied evidence arguing that these extrapositions are last-cyclic and therefore must apply after the raisings, which are cyclic. Williams and Rochemont both offer an identical alternative solution: let the Raising Principle apply only to cyclic transformations. However, it is not clear how the learner is to distinguish between cyclic and last-cyclic, or "stylistic," rules. Nor is it clear whether the learnability result will go through under this revised version of the Raising Principle.

The examples in (10) and (11) do not violate IRN, because the extrapositions are themselves raisings. No violation of IRN occurs because IRN does not cause any material to become ineligible for extracyclic transformations. These examples do, however, violate UET, since they require two extracyclic transformations to apply in the same cycle. Each of these rules involves an extraction from a different cyclic domain (in the case of (11) Raising to Subject involves extraction from an S, whereas Extraposition of PP involves extraction from an NP), but only one constituent is extracted from each domain. If UET is modified to allow for such possibilities (this possibility was raised in the discussion of the Binary Principle), it would no longer be violated by the above examples. I do not believe that this would raise any difficulties for the Degree 1 proof, although I have not explicitly investigated this; the original version of UET is assumed in the proof.

In summary, IRN makes a weaker, but apparently more accurate, set of linguistic predictions than does the Raising Principle: certain clear counterexamples to the Raising Principle are not violations of IRN. If in fact (6c), (7c), and (8c) are ungrammatical, eventually some explanation for this must be found, but there is no reason to expect to find learnability-theoretic bases for all linguistic constraints.

Uniqueness of Extracyclic Transformations
I will show that if a node is erroneously raised in a Degree 2 or greater phrase marker, then it can also be erroneously raised in a Degree 1 phrase marker. However, with multiple raisings it is possible that other nodes are previously raised in the Degree 2 phrase marker that cannot be raised in the Degree 1 phrase marker.[18] Supposing that these previous raisings are structure-preserving, it will be possible to base-generate the raised nodes in the upper context of the Degree 1 phrase marker. The problem is that implicitly raised nodes, by IRN, will not be eligible in the Degree 2 phrase marker; but, since they are base-generated in the Degree 1 phrase marker, they will be eligible. Thus, a subsequent raising transformation may apply erroneously in the Degree 2, but not the Degree 1, phrase marker. This will be ruled out by the Principle of Uniqueness of Extracyclic Transformations.

Consider first the two lower levels of the Degree 2 phrase marker 3.30. Later, in the S_0 cycle, E will be erroneously raised. The following transformations are in the target grammar:

T_1: $A - D - E - X \Rightarrow A - D - X$
T_2: $A - X - F \Rightarrow A + F - X$
T_3: $L - A \Rightarrow L + A$
T_4: $L - G - X - E \Rightarrow L + E - G - X$

The learner's grammar includes rules T_1, T_2, and T_3, but, instead of T_4, it includes a rule T_4':

T_4': $L - A - E \Rightarrow L + E - A$

No transformations apply in the S_2 cycle of phrase marker 3.30. In the S_1 cycle T_2 applies, raising F (and, implicitly, E). By IRN, D and E are ineligible for intracyclic transformations, so T_1 cannot apply. Now see what happens in the S_1 cycle of the Degree 1 phrase marker 3.31: T_1 applies, deleting E. In this phrase marker, since E is no longer present,

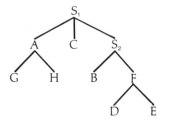

Tree 3.30

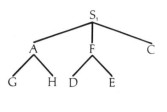

Tree 3.31

Tree 3.32

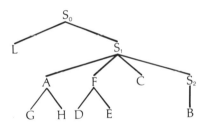

Tree 3.33

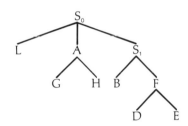

Tree 3.34

it cannot be raised in the S_0 cycle, erroneously or otherwise. However, a Degree 1 phrase marker exists in which E can be raised: the S_1 cycle of this phrase marker is shown as tree 3.32.

Now consider what happens in the S_0 cycles of the Degree 2 and Degree 1 phrase markers. These are given, partially derived through the S_1 cycle, as trees 3.33 and 3.34. In the Degree 2 phrase marker T_3 applies, raising A. Note that, by IRN, the nodes dominated by A are not eligible. Thus, T_4 cannot apply, since it refers to G. However, T_4' can apply, and it does so erroneously. In the S_0 cycle of the Degree 1 phrase marker T_1, T_2, and T_3 cannot apply. However, since G is an eligible node in this phrase marker, either T_4 or T_4' can apply—but the application of T_4' will not be erroneous. Thus, there is an error on a Degree 2 phrase marker that cannot be revealed by any Degree 1 phrase marker.

This possibility may be ruled out by invoking UET. Now, if T_3 applies extracyclically to raise A in the Degree 2 phrase marker, T'_4 cannot apply, so no error will occur. If T_3 does not apply, two possibilities obtain: either the phrase marker is as shown in 3.33, so that the structural descriptions of T_4 and T'_4 are not met, or A is base-generated in the S_0 cycle of the Degree 2 phrase marker, in which case either T_4 or T'_4 can apply. In any event no error will occur on the Degree 2 phrase marker.

Some linguistic counterevidence to UET may exist. Williams (1981) offers the following comments on this constraint:

This constraint says that at most one thing can be extracted from an S. It is a theorem of nearly every model of grammar that two things (and, in the best models, at most two things) can be extracted from an S. When both NP raising and wh-movement apply, we get the most commonplace violations of [UET]:

(16) the man *who Bill* seems t to like t[19]

Here both of the italicized NPs have been removed from the embedded S. (pp. 76–77)

I believe that Williams is incorrect. UET states that in each cycle at most one extracyclic transformation can apply, but, under either of the interpretations noted in the discussion of the Binary Principle, it doe not necessarily imply that "at most one thing can be extracted from an S."

The derived structure of Williams's (16) is shown in tree 3.35. If we assume that there are separate S and S' cycles, no violation of UET occurs here.[20] In the S_0 cycle only one NP, "Bill," has been raised. Likewise, in the S'_0 cycle only one NP has been *Wh*-Moved. The Binary Principle may be violated here, but UET is not.

The Binary Principle could be saved in one of two ways. First, we could interpret it as saying that transformations can "look through" at most one S'. In this case the *Wh*-Movement from S_1 into S'_0, because it crosses only one S', would not violate the Binary Principle. This interpretation of the Binary Principle would imply that three things can be extracted from the embedded S_1, one each in the S'_1, S_0, and S'_0 cycles.

Alternatively, we could interpret the Binary Principle as saying that transformations can look through at most one S, and we could also suppose that *Wh*-Movement is strictly cyclic. That is, "who" is *Wh*-Moved into COMP in the S'_1 cycle and then raised from COMP to COMP in the S'_0 cycle. This interpretation of the Binary Principle im-

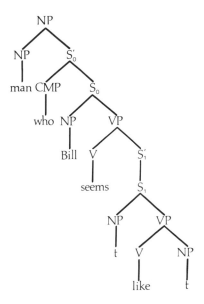

Tree 3.35

plies that at most two things can be extracted from the embedded S_1, one each in the S_1' and S_0 cycles.

Independent linguistic arguments exist in accord with each of these interpretations. Rizzi (1978) has noted that Italian has more restricted possibilities for *Wh*-Movement than English and, on this basis, has suggested that these two languages differ in that S is the bounding node for Italian, whereas S' is the bounding node for English. This is consistent with the first interpretation. On the other hand, Chomsky (1973) has argued that *Wh*-Movement is strictly cyclic; this is consistent with the second interpretation.

Regardless of which interpretation turns out to be correct, examples such as Williams's (16) do not provide evidence against UET. On the contrary, UET explains why only a limited number of constituents can be extracted from embedded sentences.

Principle of S-Optionality
S-Optionality states that whenever S appears on the right-hand side of a base rule, it is an optional category. Suppose, on the contrary, that there is some rule $A \Rightarrow B\ S$. In this case it is simple to show that an error may be revealed on a Degree 2 or more complex phrase marker that cannot be revealed by any phrase marker of lower degree.

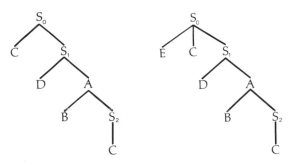

Tree 3.36   **Tree 3.37**

In this example the target grammar includes the transformation $C - B \Rightarrow C + B$, whereas the learner's grammar includes the transformation $X - C - B \Rightarrow X - C + B$. In the phrase marker 3.36 both the target rule and the learner's rule apply, raising B. In the phrase marker 3.37, however, only the learner's rule applies, erroneously. Since B only occurs as a sister of S, there is no Degree 1 phrase marker in which it can be raised. The Principle of S-Optionality is required to rule out possibilities such as this.

I have given examples showing how each of the assumptions I adopted constraining transformational and phrase structure rules serves to eliminate certain possibilities of errors being revealed only by Degree 2 or greater data. Since I began by assuming the entire set of constraints, these examples suffice to show that each constraint is relatively necessary, given the others. I am now ready to proceed with my proof.

Theorems

In this section I will prove six theorems, culminating in the proof of Degree 1 Learnability. The first two theorems will establish that identical sets of transformations apply to base Degree 2 (or more complex) phrase markers and to base Degree 1 (or simpler) phrase markers. The third theorem will demonstrate that if a transformation applies erroneously to a Degree 2 or more complex phrase marker, then there exists some Degree 1 phrase marker to which the same transformation applies erroneously. The fourth theorem will show that if an error is concealed in a Degree 1 phrase marker, then either it is concealed in every Degree 2 or more complex phrase marker as well, or there exists an alternative Degree 1 phrase marker in which the error is not concealed. Theorems 3 and 4 permit the proof of the fifth theorem, Degree 1 Error Detectability. Finally, given Theorem 5, this system meets the criteria set forth in Hamburger and Wexler 1975, thereby permitting the proof of the sixth theorem, Degree 1 Learnability.

Theorem 1: Equivalence of Untransformed Degree 2 and Degree 1 Phrase Markers

If a transformation T applies to a base Degree 2 (or more complex) phrase marker, then there exists a base Degree 1 or 0 phrase marker to which T applies.

Proof
First, suppose that T applies extracyclically in the S_0 cycle of some base Degree 2 phrase marker P. By the Binary Principle, we know that T can only refer to nodes in the S_0 and S_1 cycles of P. Suppose that T applies to some node E in LC(P), which dominates the node S_2. By S-Optionality, we know that this S_2 node can be dropped without disturbing the remainder of LC(P). When we drop this node, we have a Degree 1 phrase marker P' to which T applies. Similarly, if some other node dominates S_2, we can drop S_2 without changing the status of E. In other words, if an extracyclic transformation T applies to some Degree 2 (or more complex) phrase marker with a binary context B, T will also apply to any Degree 1 phrase marker with the same binary context.

Second, suppose that T applies intracyclically in the S_0 cycle of some base Degree 2 phrase marker P. Given TLC, we know that no nodes in LC(P) are analyzed by T. By S-Optionality, we know that S_2 and all nodes it dominates can be dropped without affecting the eligible structure of UC(P). When we drop this node, we have a Degree 1 phrase marker to which T applies. In other words, if an intracyclic transformation T applies to some Degree 2 (or more complex) phrase marker with an upper context U, T will also apply to any Degree 1 (or 0) phrase marker with the same upper context. This completes the proof of Theorem 1.

Theorem 2: Equivalence of Untransformed Degree 1 and Degree 2 Phrase Markers

If a transformation T applies to a base Degree 1 or 0 phrase marker, then there exists a base Degree 2 (or more complex) phrase marker to which T applies.

Proof

Suppose that T applies in the S_0 cycle of a base Degree 1 or 0 phrase marker. By the definition of "cycle," we know that the application of T cannot be affected by any material in higher cycles. Therefore, we can embed this Degree 1 or 0 phrase marker in a phrase marker of arbitrary degree, and T will still apply. Conversely, suppose that some node in the Degree 0 phrase marker or in the lower context of the Degree 1 phrase marker can dominate an S. We can embed a phrase marker of arbitrary degree at this point. If T applies intracyclically, by TLC and PIT, we know that it must still apply to the higher-degree phrase marker constructed by this embedding. If T applies extracyclically, by the Binary Principle, we again know that it must apply to this higher-degree phrase marker. This completes the proof of Theorem 2.

In conjunction, Theorem 1 (which, by the way, is identical to Wexler and Culicover's Theorem 1) and Theorem 2 show that identical sets of transformations apply to base Degree 2 (or more complex) and base Degree 1 (or simpler) phrase markers. More generally, these two theorems show that if the binary contexts of two phrase markers are identical, then the same transformation must apply to both, regardless of their respective degrees. If only one transformation applied in each derivation, or if only one transformation applied in each cycle, this might complete the proof. However, as I hope I have made clear by the examples above, transformations can interact to produce consequences that would not follow from the application of any single transformation. Thus, versions of Theorems 1 and 2 must be shown to hold for partially derived phrase markers as well.

As should be apparent from the examples given above illustrating their relative necessity, the constraints that have been assumed on the grammatical system seriously curtail the possibilities for transformational interactions. In order to prove Degree 1 Learnability, it is necessary to demonstrate that two properties hold, given these limitations on interactions. First, it must be demonstrated that if an error-producing transformation applies to a phrase marker of Degree 2 or greater, then there exists a Degree 1 phrase marker to which the same transformation applies. Second, it must be demonstrated that if an error-concealing transformation applies to a Degree 1 phrase marker, then either this transformation also applies to phrase markers of Degree 2 or greater, or there exists another Degree 1 phrase marker (on which the same error occurs) to which the transformation cannot apply. This ensures that if an error is always concealed in Degree 1 phrase markers, it will always be concealed in higher-degree phrase markers. In tandem, these two properties—which I will call Degree 1 Error Revealing and No Degree 1 Error Concealing, respectively—allow demonstration of the crucial learnability property—Degree 1 Error Detectability. Certain results that will be obtained on the way to proving Degree 1 Error Revealing will be useful in the proof of No Degree 1 Error Concealing, so I will take up the former first.

Theorem 3: Degree 1 Error Revealing

Let P be a phrase marker of Degree 2 or greater, partially derived through the S_1 cycle. Let T be a transformation that applies erroneously to some node E in P. Then there exists some Degree 1 phrase marker P′, partially derived through the S_1 cycle, to which T erroneously applies.

Comment
Again, it is not sufficient merely to show that T applies to P′, since T may apply nonerroneously. That is, if T is overgeneral, T will apply to the entire range of phrase markers to which the correct analogue would apply. It is only when T applies to some phrase marker outside of this range that an error is revealed. With respect to undergeneral transformations, these will be revealed by phrase markers outside the range of the undergeneral transformation, but inside the range of the correct transformation. Theorem 4 (No Degree 1 Error Concealing) will suffice to ensure that undergeneralization errors will be revealed on Degree 1 input; thus, Theorem 3 will only address overgeneralization errors.

Proof
Four cases must be considered. These result from the crossing of two factors: T may apply either intracyclically or extracyclically, and other transformations may or may not apply before T. I will take up each of these below.

Case 1
T applies intracyclically, and no transformations apply before T.

T must apply to UC(P), which is base-generated. Obviously, however, there is a Degree 1 base phrase marker P' such that UC(P) = UC(P'). By Theorem 1, if T applies to P, T must also apply to P'. This completes the proof of Case 1.

Case 2
T applies extracyclically, and no transformations apply before T.

UC(P) is base-generated, and UC(P') = UC(P) can also be base-generated. What must be shown is that if E is in LC(P), then there exists a Degree 1 phrase marker P' such that E is in LC(P'). Thus, extracyclic transformations that apply erroneously to E in P will also apply erroneously to E in P'.

It must be demonstrated that if a transformation can apply in the S_0 cycle of P' either to delete or permute E so that it is no longer eligible, or to delete or permute some other node so that E is no longer eligible, then there exists some alternative Degree 1 phrase marker P'' such that UC(P'') = UC(P) and no such transformation applies in the S_0 cycle of P''. At first glance the proof of this seems to be rather simple: suppose that, in every possible base Degree 0 phrase marker in which E occurs, some transformation applies to render E ineligible. If this were the case, however, E would have been rendered ineligible in the first cycle in which it appeared in P. Hence, E could not be raised (erroneously or otherwise) in the S_0 cycle of P. Note that, if some transformation applies to every base structure in which E appears, by Determinism, no raising transformation that might serve to block the transformation could apply earlier. However, we have assumed that E is raised in the S_0 cycle of P. Therefore, at least one Degree 1 base phrase marker must exist in which no transformation applies to render E ineligible.

If only one transformation could apply in each cycle, this would complete the proof of Case 2. However, it is possible that interactions of transformations result in E becoming ineligible in each Degree 0 phrase marker in which it appears. But now it is not immediately possible to guarantee that there will never be some raising in a higher-degree phrase marker that would block one of these interactions. In fact, the proof of Case 2 turns out to be somewhat more complex. In short, the following proposition must be shown to be true:

Lemma 1
Let P_0 be a fully derived phrase marker of Degree 1 or greater,
such that E is in $UC(P_0)$. There exists some fully derived Degree 0
phrase marker P_0' such that E is in $UC(P_0')$.

In other words, what I want to do now is to disregard the S_0 cycle in
both P and P'. If I can demonstrate that E is eligible in both $UC(P_0)$ and
$UC(P_0')$, then it will follow that any overgeneralization error of the type
in Case 2 will be revealed by a Degree 1 phrase marker. The only requirement on the configuration of the base phrase marker P_0' is that it
include the node E. Lemma 1 will be proved if I can show that for each
such E, some Degree 0 phrase marker exists in which it is not rendered
ineligible.

First, consider what sorts of transformations might result in the ineligibility of E. There are two possibilities: either a transformation deletes
E, or a transformation deletes some node dominating E. For conve-
nience, in the remainder of the proof of Lemma 1 I will use "T_0" to
refer to one of these sorts of transformations. We know that no T_0 could
have applied in P_0, since E remains eligible. Is there a P_0' in which no T_0
can apply?

Suppose that E is originally in $UC(P_0)$. No T_0 can apply in P_0 because
once E has been deleted, no subsequent transformation can reinsert E.
Let P_0' equal $UC(P_0)$. Note that at each stage of a derivation at most
one, and only one, transformation can be fit. Therefore, all transformations that apply in P_0 up to the first extracyclic transformation must also
apply to P_0'; conversely, all (intracyclic) transformations that apply in
P_0' must also apply in P_0 before any extracyclic transformation. Therefore, if some T_0 applies in P_0', it must also apply in P_0. However, by
assumption, no such T_0 can apply to P_0, and thus no T_0 can apply to P_0'.

Alternatively, E could have been raised into $UC(P_0)$. Now, let all
transformations apply in P_0 up to and including the raising of E. Let P_0'
equal this partially derived P_0, replacing any nodes dominating nonbase
structures with base-generated structures. All subsequent transformations that apply to P_0 must also apply to P_0'. We know that none of these
is a T_0; therefore, no T_0 can apply to P_0'.

Unfortunately, this argument is erroneous. Since nonbase structures
in P_0 were replaced by base-generated structures in P_0' and nodes raised
(and therefore ineligible) in P_0 are now eligible, it is possible that additional transformations may apply to P_0' that would be blocked by the
nonbase material in P_0. One of these transformations may be a T_0.

At this point it might be possible to invoke something equivalent to Wexler and Culicover's TUBS, which would ensure that no additional transformations can apply in P_0'. However, given the method of proof by existence, there is an alternative way to proceed. It is possible to "rewind" the derivation of P_0 to the cycle in which E first appeared. Let P_0' be equal to this cycle. Now the argument given above applies: all intracyclic transformations that apply to P_0' must also apply to this cycle of P_0, but, by assumption, none of these can be a T_0. This completes the proof of Lemma 1.

Lemma 1 demonstrates that not every combination of transformations applying to Degree 0 base phrase markers results in the ineligibility of E. Therefore, there must exist some Degree 1 phrase marker, P', partially derived through the S_1 cycle, such that E is in $LC(P')$. Since I have assumed that $UC(P) = UC(P')$ and no transformations apply before the incorrect transformation, this implies that the transformation must apply erroneously to E in P'. This completes the proof of Case 2.

Case 3
T applies extracyclically, and transformations apply before T.

Given UET, this means that only intracyclic transformations apply before T. Let $UC(P) = UC(P')$. Given TLC, if an intracyclic transformation applies in $UC(P)$, it must also apply in $UC(P')$. Therefore, after all intracyclic transformations apply, $UC'(P) = UC'(P')$. In Case 2 I showed that any E eligible in $LC(P)$ must be eligible in $LC(P')$. Thus, T can apply erroneously in P'. This completes the proof of Case 3.

Case 4
T applies intracyclically, and transformations apply before T.

Let $UC(P') = UC(P)$. First, suppose that only intracyclic transformations apply before T. Obviously, the same set of transformations must apply to both P and P'. Therefore, at the point at which T applies $UC(P')$ is exactly equal to $UC(P)$; if T applies erroneously to P, it must also apply erroneously to P'.

Now suppose that an extracyclic transformation applies before T. Lemma 1 ensures that any raising that applies in P can also apply in some P'. It may be the case that the nodes dominated by the raised node are different in the two phrase markers. Given IRN, however, the eligible structures of the two phrase markers will not be different. Therefore, if T applies erroneously to P, it must likewise apply to P' This completes the proof of Case 4.

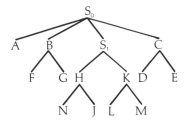

Tree 3.38

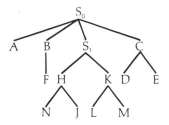

Tree 3.39

I have now shown that whether T applies extracyclically or intra-cyclically, and whether other transformations do or do not apply before T, some Degree 1 phrase marker exists to which T applies erroneously. This completes the proof of Theorem 3.

Theorem 3 shows that if a transformation applies erroneously to a phrase marker of Degree 2 or greater, then there exists some Degree 1 phrase marker to which this transformation also applies erroneously. By itself, however, Theorem 3 is not sufficient to guarantee that any error so produced will be revealed on a Degree 1 phrase marker. It is possible that some subsequent transformation undoes or erases the error. So long as this error-concealing transformation applies equally to phrase markers of Degree 1 and Degree 2 or greater, this creates no problem. However, if an error-concealing transformation applies to all phrase markers of Degree 1, but only to some phrase markers of Degree 2 or greater, in which a particular error occurs, this error will only be revealed by input of degree greater than 1. Thus, I must show that the property of No Degree 1 Error Concealing holds. This will be accomplished in the proof of Theorem 4. Before turning to this proof, though, I will give some examples illustrating how errors can be concealed.

I will give three examples, all involving the pair of phrase markers 3.38 and 3.39. In the first example an error is concealed when a moved phrase is returned to its original position. In the second example an erroneous raising occurs; the raised node is subsequently deleted by a transformation that can apply either intracyclically or extracyclically, thus concealing the error. In the third example a node is erroneously moved; a subsequent transformation moves this node again, whether it is in its original or moved position, thereby concealing the error.

For the first example, the target grammar includes the following rules:

T_1: $A - F - C \Rightarrow F - A + C$

T_2: $B - A - C \Rightarrow A + B - C$

The learner's grammar includes the following rules:

T_1': $A - B - C \Rightarrow B - A + C$

T_2: $B - A - C \Rightarrow A + B - C$

In the target grammar, for phrase marker 3.38, no transformations apply in the S_1 cycle. Because of the presence of G, T_1 cannot apply in the S_0 cycle, and the structural description of T_2 is not met, either. For phrase marker 3.39, again no transformations apply in the S_1 cycle. In the S_0 cycle T_1 applies, permuting A. The structural description of T_2 is now met, and it moves A back to its original position. In the learner's grammar T_1' (an overgeneral transformation) and T_2 both apply to phrase marker 3.39, as was the case for the target grammar rules. However, these rules can also apply to phrase marker 3.38. T_1' produces an error, applying here overgenerally, but T_2 conceals the error by returning A to its original position. By the way, this example illustrates why the Principle of Single Application of Transformations is required. T_1, T_1', and T_2 are all structure-preserving, and without this restriction they could apply iteratively. That is, T_1 produces the context for T_2, which produces the context for T_1, and so forth; without SAT, an infinite loop would result.

In the second example the target grammar includes the following transformations:

T_3: $X - B - H - C \Rightarrow X - B + H - C$

T_4: $X - B - H - C \Rightarrow X - B - C$

The learner's grammar includes transformations T_3' and T_4:

T_3': $X - F - H - C \Rightarrow X - F - H + C$

T_4: $X - B - H - C \Rightarrow X - B - C$

In the target grammar T_3 applies in the S_0 cycle of both 3.38 and 3.39, raising H. Then T_4 applies intracyclically in both phrase markers, deleting H. In the learner's grammar T_3' (an undergeneral transformation) and T_4 both apply to 3.39, raising and intracyclically deleting H, respectively. In 3.38, however, T_3' cannot apply, so H is erroneously not raised. But now T_4 applies extracyclically to delete H, thus erasing any evidence that T_3' is erroneous.

In the third example the target grammar includes the following rules:

T_5: $A - F - C \Rightarrow F - A + C$
T_6: $X - H - Y - C \Rightarrow X - Y - C + H$
T_7: $X - A - Y - C - H \Rightarrow X - Y - C - H + A$

The learner's grammar includes the following rules:

T_5': $A - B - C \Rightarrow B - A + C$
T_6: $X - H - Y - C \Rightarrow X - Y - C + H$
T_7: $X - A - Y - C - H \Rightarrow X - Y - C - H + A$

In the target grammar T_5 applies to 3.39 but not to 3.38. In both phrase markers T_6 applies, raising H, then T_7 applies, moving A to the right of H. In the learner's grammar T_5' (an overgeneral rule) applies correctly to 3.39, but it also applies erroneously to 3.38. Again, T_6 applies in both phrase markers, raising H, and T_7 applies in both phrase markers, permuting A. Thus, in both grammars, for both phrase markers, A ends up at the end of the string. Although the learner's rule T_5' produces an error in 3.38, it is concealed by the application of T_7.

Other possibilities for error-concealing transformations exist, but these examples should suffice to illustrate how such transformations work in general. Note that both overgeneral (the first and third examples) and undergeneral (the second example) errors can be concealed. With this in mind, I turn to the proof of Theorem 4.

Theorem 4: No Degree 1 Error Concealing

Let P be a phrase marker of Degree 2 or greater to which some transformation T_E applies (or fails to apply) erroneously. Let P' be a Degree 1 phrase marker such that $UC(P) = UC(P')$, to which T_E also applies (or fails to apply) erroneously. If an error-concealing transformation T_C applies to P', then either T_C applies to each P or there exists some Degree 1 phrase marker P'' to which T_E applies (or fails to apply) erroneously, but to which T_C does not apply.

Proof
Here we need only consider error-concealing transformations that apply intracyclically, in the S_0 cycle of P'. I will show first that Theorem 4 holds for each of the cases considered in Theorem 3, by which we know that, for each P in which a transformation applies erroneously, there exists some P' as defined above.

Case 1
T_E applies intracyclically, and no transformations apply before T_E.

First, suppose that no extracyclic transformations apply between T_E and T_C. By assumption, $UC(P) = UC(P')$. By TLC, we know that no material in the S_1 cycle of these phrase markers can permit or prevent the application of transformations in the S_0 cycle. Thus, the same set of transformations must apply to both phrase markers, and, after each transformation applies, $UC'(P) = UC'(P')$. Therefore, if T_C applies to P', it must also apply to P.

Now suppose that some extracyclic transformation applies between T_E and T_C. Since it was not stipulated that $LC(P) = LC(P')$, there are two possibilities: either the same extracyclic transformation applies in both P and P', raising the same node E, or different transformations apply in P and P', raising some node E in the former and some node F in the latter. Suppose that the same extracyclic transformation applies in both phrase markers. By Lemma 1, we know that this is possible. By assumption, $UC(P) = UC(P')$. Therefore, the same transformations apply to both phrase markers up to and including the extracyclic transformation. By IRN, we know that after this transformation applies, $UC'(P) = UC'(P')$. Therefore, if T_C applies to P', it also applies to P.

Therefore, suppose that different extracyclic transformations apply to P and P'. After these transformations apply, $UC'(P)$ is no longer equal to $UC'(P')$. Thus, if T_C applies in P', it may not apply in P. However, by Lemma 1, we know that some Degree 1 phrase marker P'' exists such that the same extracyclic transformation applies in both P and P'', raising E. After this transformation applies, $UC'(P) = UC'(P'')$. Therefore, if some T_C applies in P'', it will also apply in P; conversely, if no T_C applies in P, no T_C applies in P''. This completes the proof of Case 1.

Case 2
T_E applies extracyclically, and no transformations apply before T_E.

By assumption, $UC(P) = UC(P')$. By IRN, after T_E applies, $UC'(P) = UC'(P')$. Therefore, if some TC applies to P', it must also apply to P. This completes the proof of Case 2.

Case 3
T_E applies extracyclically, and transformations apply before T_E.

By assumption, $UC(P) = UC(P')$. Given UET, only intracyclic transformations can apply before T_E. By Lemma 1, we know that if T_E applies in P, it can also apply in P'. Given IRN, we know that after T_E

applies, $UC'(P) = UC'(P')$. Therefore, if T_C applies in P', it must also apply in P. This completes the proof of Case 3.

Case 4
T_E applies intracyclically, and other transformations apply before T_C.

As in Case 1, two possibilities obtain: either no extracyclic transformation applies between T_E and T_C, or some extracyclic transformation applies between T_E and T_C. In Case 1 I have already shown that, given the first possibility, if T_C applies in P', it also applies in P. Similarly, I have already shown that, given the second possibility, either T_C applies in both P and P', or else there exists some alternative Degree 1 phrase marker P'' to which T_E, but not T_C, applies. This completes the proof of Case 4.

I have shown that Theorem 4 holds in each of the four possible circumstances in which some T_E applies. Now suppose that T_E is an undergeneral transformation that fails to apply in P. By assumption, $UC(P) = UC(P')$, and, by Lemma 1, we know that if a node is raised in P, the same node can be raised in P'. By IRN, nothing dominated by this node is eligible in either P or P'. Therefore, the same sets of transformations apply in both P and P'; if T_E does not apply in P, it will not apply in P', either.

We can construct three cases in which T_C applies to P', depending on whether no transformations, only intracyclic transformations, or intracyclic and extracyclic transformations apply before T_C.

Case 5
No transformations apply before T_C.

By assumption, $UC(P) = UC(P')$. Therefore, if T_C applies to P', it must also apply to P. This completes the proof of Case 5.

Case 6
Intracyclic transformations apply before T_C.

By assumption, $UC(P) = UC(P')$. Given TLC, we know that the same set of intracyclic transformations applies to both phrase markers, after which $UC'(P) = UC'(P')$. Therefore, if T_C applies to P', again it must also apply to P. This completes the proof of Case 6.

Case 7
Transformations apply before T_C, including an extracyclic transformation.

Given TLC and UC(P) = UC(P'), we know that the same set of transformations applies to the two phrase markers up to the extracyclic
transformation. It is possible that the same raising transformation applies to both phrase markers, in which case UC'(P) will always be equal
to UC'(P'). Thus, T_C must apply to both P' and P. Alternatively,
different extracyclic transformations may apply to P and P', raising E
and F, respectively. Now UC'(P) is no longer equal to UC'(P'), and T_C
will not necessarily apply to P. However, by Lemma 1, we know that
there exists an alternative Degree 1 phrase marker P" in which E is
raised. The same set of transformations applies to both P and P": if T_C
does not apply to P, it will also not apply to P". This completes the
proof of Case 7.

Cases 1 through 4 show that errors resulting from overgeneral applications of transformations are not uniquely concealed in Degree 1
phrase markers. Cases 5 through 7 show that this holds for errors resulting from undergeneral applications of transformations as well. This
completes the proof of Theorem 4.

Having proven that the properties of Degree 1 Error Revealing and
No Degree 1 Error Concealing both hold, I can now proceed to the
proof of Degree 1 Error Detectability.

Theorem 5: Degree 1 Error Detectability

Let P be a phrase marker of Degree 2 or greater. Let P' be a
Degree 1 phrase marker. If an error is revealed in some P, there
exists some P' in which the same error is revealed.

Proof
By Theorem 3, we know that if a transformation applies erroneously to
some phrase marker P, then some phrase marker P' exists to which the
same transformation applies erroneously. In the proof of Theorem 4
I noted that we also know that if some transformation erroneously fails
to apply to P, then there exists some P' on which the same undergeneral error occurs. By Theorem 4, we know that if some error-
concealing transformation applies in P', then either it applies to each P
in which the same error is revealed, or there exists some alternative
Degree 1 phrase marker P" in which the same error is revealed but in
which the error-concealing transformation does not apply. From this it
follows that if there is some phrase marker of Degree 2 or greater in
which an error is revealed but not subsequently concealed, then there

exists some Degree 1 phrase marker in which the same error is revealed and also not subsequently concealed. This completes the proof of Theorem 5.

Given Theorem 5, I am now ready to prove Degree 1 Learnability.

Theorem 6: Degree 1 Learnability

Let G be the target grammar, and let L(t) be the learner's grammar at time t. Let input be of Degree 1. Then, for all $e > 0$, there is some time t such that the probability that L(t) = G is at least $1 - e$.

Proof
Note that Theorem 6 differs from Wexler and Culicover's learnability theorem (their Theorem 9) in that it states that the learner's grammar will become strongly equivalent to the target grammar in the limit. Wexler and Culicover's theorem stated that the learner's grammar will become moderately equivalent to the target grammar in the limit. Nevertheless, the proof of Theorem 6 is parallel to the proof of Wexler and Culicover's learnability theorem; that is, it is identical to the learnability proof given by Hamburger and Wexler (1975, Theorem 6) except that the Bounded Error Detectability result used there (their Theorem 3) is replaced by the Degree 1 Error Detectability result provided by Theorem 5. Therefore, the proof will not be repeated here. For details, see Hamburger and Wexler 1975 and Wexler and Culicover 1980 (see especially note 55, pp. 565–566). QED.

Evaluating the Feasibility of the Degree 1 Proof

In this section I will briefly discuss how the Degree 1 proof fares on the five criteria I proposed in chapter 2: quantity of input, degree of attained equivalence, availability of crucial input, processing demands, and accuracy of linguistic predictions.

Quantity of Input
Three factors predominantly affect the relative quantity of input required by learnability models. These are the number of types of errors permitted to the learner, the complexity of input required to reveal errors, and the likelihood that an error, once revealed, will be corrected. On all three of these factors the Degree 1 model performs better than the Degree 2 model. First, errors of over- and undergeneralization

are permitted in both models. However, misadjunction errors (errors in which the learner's grammar derives correct linear structures but incorrect hierarchical structures), which are permitted in the Degree 2 model, are not allowed in the Degree 1 model, by virtue of the fact that the learner must hypothesize transformations that produce bracketed strings identical to those available in input. Second, in my proof Degree 1 input, rather than Degree 2 input, will suffice to reveal all possible errors. Third, in the Degree 2 model subsequent transformations, or even subsequent cycles of transformations, were required to reveal certain types of errors. In the Degree 1 model this is never the case: all errors can be revealed simply by the application of an erroneous rule to some phrase marker other than that on which the rule was originally hypothesized. Therefore, in general, error-revealing derivations will be shorter in the Degree 1 model than in the Degree 2 model; this means that the likelihood of correctly rejecting an erroneous transformation will be greater in the former. Also, in the Degree 1 model hypothesized transformations must produce strings with the same bracketing, as well as the same ordering, as input strings. This means that the set of hypothesizable transformations will be smaller in the Degree 1 model than in the Degree 2 model; consequently, the likelihood of hypothesizing a correct transformation will be greater in the former.

One additional factor favors the Degree 2 model: in this model certain errors the learner may make will never be detected. In contrast, in the Degree 1 model input is such that all errors may be revealed (this is the difference between moderate and strong equivalence).[21] Thus, the Degree 1 model, but not the Degree 2 model, will require input to reveal and correct all errors. However, it seems that the first three factors should easily outweigh the last. Therefore, we can safely conclude that relatively less input will be required by the Degree 1 model than by the Degree 2 model.

Degree of Attained Equivalence
The learnability theorem of the Degree 1 proof entails that the learner attain a grammar strongly equivalent to the target grammar, whereas the learnability theorem of the Degree 2 proof entails only moderate equivalence. It is not a priori clear which version of equivalence is empirically correct. In chapter 5 I will present a study suggesting that speakers do in fact acquire grammars that are strongly equivalent to the grammars generating their input. Given the results of this study, it

seems that the Degree 1 model is superior to the Degree 2 model with respect to this criterion.

Availability of Crucial Input

Crucial input is simpler in the Degree 1 model than in the Degree 2 model. In the Degree 1 model most errors will be revealed by Degree 0 input; only erroneous extracyclic transformations will require Degree 1 input to be revealed. Studies of speech addressed to children show that such speech contains little embedding (Newport 1977); certainly, the incidence of Degree 2 input must be quite rare. Thus, it is safe to conclude that sufficient Degree 1 input is available to the child, whereas sufficient Degree 2 input might not be. I will take up this issue in greater detail in the discussion of the empirical necessity of bracketed input.

In the Degree 2 model there is one source of structural information: the base structure representation that the learner constructs. In addition to this, in the Degree 1 model I have assumed that the learner's construction of bracketed strings supplies a second source of structural information. In chapter 1 I discussed some potential sources of information that would permit such bracketing to be constructed; in chapter 4 I will present two studies that provide preliminary evidence that such information may be sufficiently available in input and that children can construct representations of bracketing. In chapter 6 I will discuss some ways in which assumptions concerning structural information in input might be constrained. For the moment, however, the plausibility of sources of structural information may be greater in the Degree 2 model, simply by virtue of the fact that that model makes fewer assumptions.

Processing Demands

The input required to provoke grammatical modifications is simpler in the Degree 1 model than in the Degree 2 model. It seems quite likely that more complex input will tend to strain the child's processing resources; later I will discuss some evidence indicating that the child's rate of comprehension of Degree 2 input is extremely low. In addition, Wexler and Culicover's proof included certain assumptions (for example, the Assumption against String Preservation) that required that the learner hold in working memory and compare all stages of every derivation. This appears to entail unreasonable processing demands. No such assumptions are included in the Degree 1 proof. Also, Wexler and Culicover's Raising Principle requires that certain nodes be marked as unanalyzable throughout derivations. This would seem to demand extra memory capacity. In contrast, the Principle of Intracyclic Ineligibility of Raised Nodes incorporated in the Degree 1 proof requires only that certain nodes be marked as unanalyzable in single cycles, thus reducing memory load. Overall, it appears that the processing demands entailed by the Degree 1 model are more reasonable than those entailed by the Degree 2 model.

However, this ignores processing demands required for the representation of input. The assumption that the learner creates a bracketed string representation has been added to the input assumptions of the Degree 2 model. Creating such a representation—parsing input strings—must involve some processing resources. In chapter 6 I will discuss some ways in which the required extent of bracketing might be limited; here note that since the required degree of input complexity is low, the resources required for constructing representations of such input will likely be limited. At this point, however, it appears that the Degree 1 model may require greater processing resources than the Degree 2 model for the representation of input, whereas the opposite is clearly true for grammatical modifications.

Accuracy of Linguistic Predictions
The Degree 1 proof goes through with many fewer assumed constraints on grammatical hypotheses than was the case for the Degree 2 theory. As a result, the linguistic predictions made by the Degree 1 proof are weaker and therefore less likely to be incorrect. Beyond this, certain of the assumptions incorporated in my proof, including Determinism, S-Optionality, Binary Principle, Transparency of Lower Context, and Uniqueness of Extracyclic Transformations, are equivalent to assumptions of the Degree 2 theory. Linguistic evidence adduced by Wexler and Culicover for and against these principles weighs equally with regard to both proofs.

Two of the eight assumptions of the Degree 1 proof, Intracyclic Ineligibility of Raised Nodes and Precedence of Intracyclic Transformations, are clearly different from assumptions incorporated in Wexler and Culicover's theory.[22] Earlier I discussed certain counterexamples to Wexler and Culicover's Raising Principle and showed how IRN circumvents these. Overall, the linguistic predictions of IRN are more accurate than those of the Raising Principle. Wexler and Culicover do not present any evidence in support of their OSET assumption, which is the converse of PIT. I believe that the relevant evidence here would involve demonstrating that certain otherwise possible transformations may be blocked by the presence of a raised constituent. Though I know of no such examples, it is possible that some do exist, so that at present no linguistic basis exists for preferring either OSET or PIT.

Since my central focus here is not on the learnability-theoretic basis of constraints on grammars, a complete evaluation of the linguistic predictions following from the assumptions of the Degree 1 proof would take us beyond the scope of the present work. This brief discussion should suffice to indicate, however, that the linguistic predictions of the Degree 1 proof are very likely more accurate than those of Wexler and Culicover's Degree 2 proof.

In summary, on four of the five criteria I have proposed—quantity of input, availability of crucial input, processing demands, and accuracy of linguistic predictions—the Degree 1 model appears to fare better than the Degree 2 model. For the remaining criterion, degree of attained equivalence, the evaluation of these two models depends on empirical evidence that is not yet available (but see chapter 5). To my knowledge, these are the only two models that can reasonably lay claim to providing feasible accounts of language acquisition at this time. Therefore, I submit that the Degree 1 model developed in this chapter constitutes the most feasible learnability model for language acquisition currently available. Perhaps needless to say, the truth of this assertion depends upon the validity of the Bracketed Input Hypothesis.

Is Bracketed Input Necessary?

The Degree 1 proof clearly shows how bracketed input may operate in facilitating the acquisition of syntax. At the outset I asserted that bracketed input may in fact be necessary for successful acquisition. Since the essential difference between the Degree 1 and Degree 2 proofs is the assumption of bracketed input in the former, a comparison of these two results may reveal which of the criteria of necessity I proposed in chapter 1 are fulfilled by this assumption.

These two proofs also differ in method. However, the inclusion of the Bracketed Input Hypothesis in Wexler and Culicover's system would immediately produce Degree 1 Learnability of grammars that are strongly equivalent to grammars generating learners' input. Thus, the difference in method of proof is irrelevant to the determination of the empirical and intensional necessity of bracketed input. At worst, the effect of the use of the method of existence in the Degree 1 proof may be to render unnecessary certain constraints on grammatical hypotheses that would be required if the method of construction had been used; however, I have not investigated this possibility. If this effect does in fact obtain, then this has implications for the weak generative power of the grammatical theory allowed by the Degree 1 proof. This would limit the conclusions that could be drawn concerning the extensional necessity of bracketed input.

Extensional Necessity

Some aspect of input information may be judged *extensionally necessary* if there are certain languages that can be acquired only in the presence of such information. With respect to the extensional necessity of bracketing information and the comparison of the Degree 1 and Degree 2 proofs, two issues must be addressed. First, do the grammatical theories permitted by these two proofs generate the same sets of languages (that is, are they weakly equivalent)? If they do not, then do the languages generable under the constraints of the Degree 1 proof more closely conform to the natural languages? I believe that there are certain languages that can be generated under the Degree 1 system but not the Degree 2 system; I do not know whether these languages are part of the class of natural languages.

Wexler (1981) briefly addressed the issue of whether the Degree 2 constraints permit the generation of any non-context-free languages. He showed there that these constraints do allow the language $A^n B^n C^n$, which is known to be a context-sensitive language, to be generated. What range of context-sensitive languages can be generated by the Degree 2 system is unclear, but I will argue here that the language $A^i B^j C^i D^j$, which is also a context-sensitive language, can be generated only by the Degree 1 system.

Let the context-free base component consist of the following two rules:

S $\Rightarrow$ A (S) (B) E
E $\Rightarrow$ (C) D

Let the transformational component consist of the following six rules:

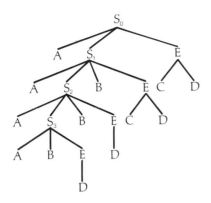

Tree 3.40

T_1: A – C – D $\Rightarrow$ A – C
T_2: A – D $\Rightarrow$ A
T_3: A – B – D $\Rightarrow$ B – D
T_4: A $\Rightarrow$ $\emptyset$
T_5: X – E – Y – D $\Rightarrow$ X – Y – E + D
T_6: X – E – Y – C $\Rightarrow$ X – Y – C + E

This grammar generates the language $A^i B^j C^i D^j$.[23] Here I will provide an example of how the string *AABBBCCDDD* may be derived. The base structure is shown in tree 3.40. In the S_3 cycle T_3 applies, deleting *A*. In the S_2 cycle T_3 again applies, deleting *A;* then T_5 applies, raising *E* from the S_3 cycle and adjoining it as a sister to *D*. Up to this point the string dominated by S_2 is *BBDD*. In the S_1 cycle only T_5 applies; after this S_1 dominates the string *ABBBCDDD*. Finally, in the S_0 cycle, T_1 applies, deleting *D*, and then T_6 applies, raising *E* and adjoining it as a sister of *C*. S_0 dominates the string *AABBBCCDDD*.

However, this grammar is impossible in the Degree 2 theory. Neither T_4 nor T_6 would be a possible rule in this system, because they both require the analysis of nonbase sequences of nodes, and this is ruled out in that system by the Freezing Principle. This problem might be avoided by using a slightly different pair of base rules:[24]

S $\Rightarrow$ (A) (S) (B) (E)
E $\Rightarrow$ (C) (D)

Now the derivation could proceed as in the Degree 1 system through the S_3 cycle. But now another problem arises. Recall that in the Degree 2 theory extracyclic transformations apply before intracyclic transformations. This means that in the S_2 cycle T_5 must apply before T_3. The application of T_3 is blocked by the previous application of T_5 (since this rule produces a frozen structure); eventually this grammar under the Degree 2 system would derive the string *AAABBBCCDDDD,* which is not in the desired language. Perhaps the $A^iB^jC^iD^j$ language could be generated under the Degree 2 system using a different base grammar and set of transformations, but none of the combinations I have tried succeeds: in general, the Freezing Principle seems to block required transformations.

I do not know what range of languages can be generated by the Degree 1 system but not the Degree 2 system, but it appears that the grammatical theories allowed by these systems are not weakly equivalent. This may well be academic, though, unless there are natural languages generable under the former, but not the latter, system. Certainly, constructions of $A^iB^jC^iD^j$ sort do not appear to occur in natural languages; an example might be something like "*Paul and Tom, and Mary, Sue, and Kate laughed and cried, respectively, and sang, danced, and played the flute, respectively, respectively." Beyond this, it seems that the relevant differences between these two systems concern the constraints on grammatical hypotheses incorporated in each, and these may result in part from the differing methods of proof employed, rather than from the different assumptions concerning input information. In sum, it is unclear whether bracketing information is extensionally necessary, though this possibility has not been ruled out.

Intensional Necessity
An aspect of input information may be judged *intensionally necessary* if certain aspects of grammatical structure cannot be acquired in the absence of such information. Given phrase-bracketing information in input, children's grammars should be strongly equivalent to the grammars generating their input. That is, children's grammars will generate the same set of sentences as the input grammars, and the phrase structure of every sentence generated by children's grammars will match the phrase structure generated by the input grammars. More generally, assuming that a number of learners are exposed to a language generated by the same underlying grammar, the acquired grammars of all of the learners should be strongly equivalent.

However, this is not the case in the absence of bracketing information. The problem centers around the fact that, without such information, learners may make misadjunction errors—producing correct linear orders of sentences but incorrect hierarchical phrase structures of these sentences. A mistaken rule that produces a misadjunction error can only be revealed as such if another rule operates on its output. In other words, if there is input providing positive distributional evidence for particular structures, if there are syntactic tests, then misadjunction errors can be corrected; otherwise, they will go undetected.

Suppose that a rule T moves a phrase to one of two possible points of adjunction. Suppose further that no other rule operates on the output of this rule. Thus, there is no syntactic test for determining which point of adjunction T should utilize. Then, in the absence of bracketing information, half of the learners should induce one output phrase structure, and half should induce the other. On the other hand, given bracketing information, all learners should induce the same output phrase structure. The critical empirical question with respect to intensional necessity is whether or not learners induce uniform output phrase structure analyses for rules such as T.

Rules of this sort do exist in English, and in some cases it is possible using indirect means to assess what sort of output phrase structures have been induced by children. In chapter 5 I will present a study examining one such rule. To foreshadow the results discussed there, this study indicates that different speakers of English show significantly greater agreement on the structures of the constructions in question than would be expected by chance. Thus, children do appear to induce grammars that are strongly equivalent to their input grammars. It is bracketing information that enables the acquisition of strongly equivalent grammars; hence, bracketing information appears to be intensionally necessary.

Empirical Necessity

Some aspect of input information may be judged *empirically necessary* if acquisition can succeed in the absence of such information only given inordinate amounts of time or complexity of data. Bracketed input allows for Degree 1 Learnability, and one dividend of this result is that the overall amount of data required for a learner to converge on a grammar is severely reduced, relative to the amount that would be required in the absence of bracketing information. Fewer data mean less time. However, we cannot yet make quantitative assessments of the amount of data required by a particular learnability result. Degree 1 Learnability (with bracketed input) requires less time than does Degree 2 Learnability (without bracketed input), but it may turn out that the time requirements of Degree 2 Learnability are reasonable.

Table 3.1
Frequency of embedded sentences in children's input

	Degree 0	Degree 1	Degree 2	Children's sequiturs to Degree 2 input
Stage I				
Adam	218	14	1	0
Eve	243	16	0	0
Sarah	396	19	0	0
Total	857	49 (5.4%)	1 (0.1%)	0
Stage II				
Adam	276	26	3	2
Eve	294	20	0	0
Sarah	229	16	2	1
Total	799	62 (7.2%)	5 (0.6%)	3
Stage III				
Adam	—	—	—	—
Eve	276	31	2	0
Sarah	252	18	0	0
Total	528	49 (8.5%)	2 (0.3%)	0
Stage IV				
Adam	181	31	1	0
Eve	345	34	4	0
Sarah	326	32	0	0
Total	852	97 (10.2%)	5 (0.5%)	0
Stage V				
Adam	258	48	2	1
Eve	307	21	1	0
Sarah	200	22	1	0
Total	765	91 (10.6%)	4 (0.5%)	1
Total	3801	348 (8.4%)	17 (0.4%)	4

The remaining question, then, is whether the complexity of data that would be required in the absence of bracketing information in input is commensurate with that actually available to children. Newport's (1977) estimate of 1.08 S nodes per utterance in young children's input suggests that embedding is fairly rare in the input to language learning, but this does not rule out the possibility that children are exposed to Degree 2 sentences. In order to address this question, I have tabulated the occurrence of Degree 0, 1, and 2 sentences in input in several transcripts from Roger Brown's subjects Adam, Eve, and Sarah.[25] The results of this tabulation are shown in table 3.1.

As can be seen in this table, the incidence of Degree 2 sentences in children's input is extremely low: only about 4 per thousand sentences.

Although there is a trend toward increasing proportions of embedded sentences in input, this trend is concentrated in Degree 1 sentences, which increase from 54 per thousand to 106 per thousand as children progress from Stage I to Stage V. In contrast, no change in the incidence of Degree 2 sentences related to the child's progress in acquisition is evident. Degree 2 input is very rare throughout the stages of acquisition studied by Brown.

The simple availability of Degree 2 input does not ensure that it will be employed in acquisition. Rather, it is likely that some degree of comprehension by the child constitutes a minimal standard for judging what input can play a role in acquisition. Of course, the fact that a child understands a particular sentence does not guarantee that that sentence will be used in guiding acquisition. However, given both the complexity and the rarity of Degree 2 input, one might expect that such sentences will pose particular difficulties for children.

In performing the tabulation, I also examined children's responses to Degree 2 input sentences. In several cases responses clearly indicated a failure of comprehension: "What?", "Huh?", and "Eh?" are some examples. In other cases the child's failure to make any response, mimicking of the final part of the Degree 2 sentence, or repetition of the child utterance immediately preceding the Degree 2 sentence suggest failure of comprehension. In only four cases (less than 1 per thousand input sentences) did the child's response to a Degree 2 input sentence constitute a sequitur. The four interchanges in which a sequitur response occurred are given in table 3.2. Even in these cases it is less than obvious that the child did in fact comprehend the Degree 2 input sentence.

The likelihood that Degree 2 input is required for acquisition is further reduced by consideration of the fact that as the required complexity of input increases, the probability of occurrence of any sentence revealing a given error decreases. The number of possible base structures increases geometrically with the number of levels of sentence embeddings: supposing that 100 Degree 0 base structures are possible in English (I suspect this is an underestimate), then 10,000 Degree 1 base structures and 1,000,000 Degree 2 base structures are possible. Suppose that some erroneous rule T_E can only be detected in input sentences sharing one particular base structure. If Degree 2 input is required to reveal that T_E is erroneous, only 1 in 1,000,000 Degree 2 sentences will suffice.

Table 3.2
Children's sequiturs to Degree 2 input

Adam, Stage II:
Parent: Careful. What are you blowing?
Child: Blowing tree down.
Parent: I don't think you're quite strong enough to blow a tree down.
Child: Blow Ursla [observer] down.

Adam, Stage II:
[Construction crane goes down the street and disappears.]
Child: Where go?
Parent: It's gone to do a job. Don't you suppose that someone's just waiting
  for it to come?
Child: Waiting derrick?

Sarah, Stage II:
[Child emerges from bathroom with panties down and says she has to go.]
Parent: Didn't you go? I thought you said you just went.
Child: I want . . . I want went.

Adam, Stage V:
[Child and observer are playing with a grinder.]
Child: Hey, you wanna make it a little smaller again?
Observer: Yes, or else you could ask your mother if there is anything else
  she wants ground up.
Child: Yeah.

In short, assuming perfect parsing abilities on the child's part, assuming that every parsed input sentence can be used to correct errors,
assuming that error-revealing input sentences occur only after the child
has made the relevant error, and assuming that very few errors will
require Degree 2 input for their correction, languages could be Degree 2 learnable (rather than Degree 1 learnable) only if Degree 2 sentences occurred with great frequency in input. Clearly, the first three of
these assumptions are wrong, and Degree 2 input does not occur with
the required frequency. Simply put, the claim that anything more complex than Degree 1 input is required for acquisition is without empirical
basis.[26]

It is bracketing information that enables acquisition to succeed on
the basis of Degree 1 input. All of the available evidence points to the
conclusion that in fact language acquisition does proceed on the basis
of such input and cannot require input of any greater complexity. Thus,
bracketing information is empirically necessary.

In summary, the answer to the question of whether bracketed input
is necessary depends upon which criterion of necessity is considered.
Phrase-bracketing information may not be required in principle for

learnability of the class of natural languages. However, such information may be required for the induction of the structure of certain types of syntactic constructions in natural languages. Finally, bracketing information is definitely necessary for language acquisition to proceed in the face of strict limits on data, for children to learn complex grammars from simple input.

Chapter 4

On the Availability and Representation of Bracketing Information

The learnability proof given in chapter 3 indicates that bracketing information may be necessary for the acquisition of syntax. The results obtained there are quite powerful, but it remains to be determined whether the key assumption of the proof—the Bracketed Input Hypothesis—is justified. In order to demonstrate that bracketing information can be used in acquisition, it must be shown that a sufficient amount of such information is encoded in children's language input and that children have the information-processing capacities to appropriately represent such information. Demonstrating these points bears only on the plausibility of bracketing information being used in acquisition; in order to determine whether such information is in fact used in learning, it will be necessary to examine the course and outcome of acquisition. In chapter 5 I will return to this issue; here I present studies concerning the availability and representation of bracketing information.

First, though, I wish to emphasize the exploratory nature of the research presented in this chapter and the next. No systematic investigation of any of the predictions concerning the Bracketed Input Hypothesis has yet been conducted. My purpose here is to discuss some of the issues that arise in attempting to determine whether particular aspects of language input are necessary and to demonstrate some of the methods that might be brought to bear on these issues. All of the empirical conditions identified above must be met; therefore, the Bracketed Input Hypothesis (or any other comparable hypothesis concerning necessary input, for that matter) is easily falsifiable. In fact, the results of all of the studies described below are consistent with this hypothesis. Given the diversity of the predictions examined, this convergence provides at least initial confirmation of the validity of the Bracketed Input Hypothesis.

Prosodic Encoding of Structural Information in Children's Input

In chapter 1 I discussed a variety of means by which bracketing information might be encoded in language input. First, since the phrase is the basic unit of organization in natural language syntax, patterns of equivalence and substitution (distributional evidence) will tend to converge on a phrase structure analysis of sentences. Such patterns may be made particularly salient to the child through the discourse devices of partial-plus repetition and expansions (see Newport, Gleitman, and Gleitman 1977, Hoff-Ginsberg 1981): parents may revise a sentence in consecutive utterances so that aspects of its phrase structure are made clear (for example, "Give *the ball* to me. Give *it* to me."). Second, the phrase is the smallest unit above the word that receives a coherent semantic interpretation. Thus, there may be general semantic cues to the bracketing of sentences. In addition, this means that a meaningful utterance may consist of a single phrase; in fact, single-phrase utterances are quite common in speech to children (Newport 1977). Third, individual languages typically include some morphological or syntactic means of marking phrase bracketing. In certain languages all words in a phrase must agree in case, number, gender, definiteness, and so forth; such agreement is often marked by the affixation of a particular morpheme to each word. In many languages word form classes fall into two categories: content words (for example, nouns, verbs, adjectives) and function words (for example, determiners, prepositions, auxiliary verbs). Function words generally occur at the periphery of phrases and thus may supply cues to bracketing.

The use of any of the above cues, however, entails that the child must have performed some preliminary syntactic, morphological, or lexical analysis. For example, until function words have been identified as such, they can supply little information relevant to bracketing. This restriction may not apply to a final type of bracketing cue—that supplied by prosody. It has been widely noted (Cooper and Paccia-Cooper 1980, Crystal 1969, Lehiste 1970) that several prosodic dimensions may supply cues to phrase boundaries. In English these include the lengthening of the final stressed vowel of a phrase, the occurrence of pauses between phrases, and the fall and rise of fundamental frequency across phrase boundaries. In fact, in cases where other cues to bracketing do not unambiguously specify the structure of a sentence, prosody may do so; for example, the sentence "They are eating apples" is typically unambiguous when spoken.

I do not mean to imply that the use of prosodic cues in assigning phrase bracketing to sentences is entirely straightforward. First, it is unlikely that all languages employ the same sets of prosodic cues to mark phrase boundaries. In certain languages, for example, vowel length is phonemic; I would suspect that those languages do not use vowel lengthening as a cue to the ends of phrases. Tone languages, like Chinese, use pitch patterns to make lexical distinctions and probably do not use such patterns to mark boundaries between phrases. The possibility exists, however, that all languages draw upon a universal, limited set of prosodic cues to phrase boundaries and employ all those that are not preempted for other purposes. But even if this is so, children will have to perform some prosodic analyses of the languages they are exposed to in order to ascertain which cues are viable.

Moreover, prosodic cues to phrase structure may be conditioned by other factors as well. The length of a particular vowel, for example, may depend upon intrinsic factors (for example, whether the vowel is tense or lax), the character of the consonants by which it is surrounded, whether the syllable in which it occurs is stressed or not, whether that syllable receives emphatic stress in a particular utterance, the number of preceding and succeeding syllables in an utterance, the characteristics of the individual speaker, the affective context of an utterance, and so forth. Such multiple determination of prosody has made the quantitative measurement of prosodic cues to phrase structure quite difficult. In the most intensive research on such cues, conducted by Cooper and his colleagues (summarized in Cooper and Paccia-Cooper 1980 and Cooper and Sorensen 1981), these extraneous factors were controlled for by giving lists of specially constructed sentences to subjects and having them practice reading these sentences aloud until they could reliably produce them without introducing unwanted stress. This work is obviously open to criticisms of its artificial method.

Finally, prosodic cues may not always supply entirely accurate bracketings of sentences. In particular, the hierarchical arrangements of phrases may be poorly cued by prosody. Rather, prosody seems typically to supply cues to the boundaries of individual phrases without supplying information about the relations among these phrases; hence, the bracketing supplied by prosodic cues may be "flatter" than that required for a complete structural analysis. See Selkirk 1980 for a description of some of the restructuring effects of intonation. In other cases the bracketing supplied by prosody may be misleading. The example typically cited is "This is the cat that chased the rat that stole the cheese . . ." (see Chomsky and Halle 1968). Here prosodic breaks occur before each instance of "that"; the resulting units, though they could be phrases in other sentences, are not constituents of this sentence. It is unclear, however, how prevalent such prosodic restructurings are in children's input.

Despite these difficulties, the possibility that prosody supplies cues to phrase bracketing in language input is most intriguing. Since the use of such cues need not depend on prior syntactic or semantic analyses, it is possible that prosody supplies the child with an entree into syntactic systems. I do not mean to be advocating the sort of "prosodic bootstrapping" discussed and dismissed by Pinker (1984): clearly, prosody alone provides an insufficient basis for identifying either the categories of individual phrases or the hierarchical relations among phrases. More simply, I mean to suggest that prosody may provide the basis for delineating the domains within which other further (syntactic, morphological, and semantic) analyses operate optimally.

The common observation of prosodic differences between adult-adult and adult-child speech (see Broen 1972, Garnica 1977, Remick 1971, Snow 1972) lends further interest to the examination of these cues. In general, speech to children has been observed to be carefully enunciated, more likely to include pauses, slower, and intonationally exaggerated relative to speech to adults. Several of these characteristics correspond to the prosodic cues to phrase bracketing that have been identified. Therefore, it is possible that these cues are made more salient in speech to children than in normal adult-adult speech. In the present study several aspects of prosody relevant to phrase bracketing were examined in mothers' reading speech to their young children.

Method

Subjects Thirty-four mother-child dyads participated in the study. In half of these dyads the child was approximately 2 years old (mean age = 2;0, range = 1;10 to 2;2); in the other half the child was approximately 4 years old (mean age = 4;1, range = 3;10 to 4;5). All subjects were from the Minneapolis–St. Paul metropolitan area and were predominantly white and middle-class.

Materials Seven matched pairs of experimental sentences were constructed, each containing a monosyllabic target word whose vowel was flanked by stop consonants. Target words were so chosen to facilitate

Table 4.1
Experimental sentences used in the prosody study

1. "You are really BAD, Ball," said Pete.
   "You're a really BAD ball," said Pete.
2. He chased it off the BED with a broom.
   I chased it off the BED in my room.
3. "I'll BET," it said, nodding.
   "I'll BET it said nothing."
4. It was too BIG—two feet around!
   It was too BIG to see around.
5. Pete said, "STOP!" jumping up and down.
   Pete said, "STOP bouncing up and down!"
6. "The ball was STUCK till you yelled."
   The ball was STUCK in the hall.
7. He climbed to the TOP, and he stared.
   He climbed to the TOP of the stairs.

Note: Target words are given in capitals. In each pair of sentences the target word occurs in phrase-final position in the first sentence and in phrase-nonfinal position in the second. Sentences are punctuated as they appeared in the story subjects read.

the accurate measurement of vowel durations. In one sentence in each pair the target word occurred in phrase-final position (either at the end of an S, a VP, or an NP), whereas in the other the target word occurred in a phrase-nonfinal position. Aside from this structural difference, the sentences of each pair were designed to be as similar to one another as possible. In all pairs the two sentences had identical total numbers of syllables and identical numbers of syllables preceding the target word. In six of the seven pairs the lexical material preceding the target word was shared by both sentences. Lexical material following the target word differed across sentences in most of the pairs, but this material was chosen to be as phonologically similar across sentences as possible. The set of experimental sentences is given in table 4.1.

A 450-word children's story was written incorporating the fourteen experimental sentences. These sentences occurred in keeping with the flow of the story and were punctuated according to standard conventions of written English. The story was printed on eight pages, with each sentence of the story appearing on a separate line. Facing each page of text was a picture illustrating some aspect of the story.

Procedure Reading sessions were conducted in an ordinary laboratory room containing a table and chairs and a small selection of toys. Mothers were informed that the purpose of the study was to monitor their children's reactions to stories read by familiar and unfamiliar adults. They were then asked to practice reading the story twice, once to themselves and once aloud to the adult experimenter, before reading the story to their children. The importance of reading the story verbatim, even if this was not how the mother usually read to her child, was stressed.

Reading sessions were tape-recorded using a remote microphone. After each mother had finished reading the story to her child, she was informed of the true nature of the study, and her consent to analyze the tape-recorded data was obtained. Although many of the mothers acknowledged suspecting that it was their reading that was under observation, none of them reported either suspecting that their prosody was being observed or noting the presence of pairs of similar sentences scattered through the story.

The adult-directed and child-directed versions of the experimental sentences for each mother were low pass filtered at 3,300 Hz and digitized at a rate of 10,000 samples per second with a resolution of eight bits, using a Tecmar Lab Tender A-D converter, an IBM PC computer, and software developed by the author.[1] The resulting digitized waveforms were stored on disk and displayed for measurement on a 640-by-400 pixel graphics screen using a Tecmar Graphics Master video controller. Two cursors could be positioned to section off a portion of a waveform; the duration of the marked section of the waveform was automatically calculated and displayed on screen. In order to facilitate accuracy of measurements, portions of waveforms could be magnified up to 50 times, and marked sections of waveforms could be played out through a D-A converter.

In measuring target-word vowel durations, the initial point was taken to be the onset of the stop consonant burst preceding the vowel, and the final point was taken to be either the ending of the periodic portion of the waveform corresponding to the vowel or, in cases where the following word began with a stop consonant and no pause between words was perceptible, the onset of the consonantal burst following the vowel.

Figures 4.1–4.4 illustrate how the measurements were made for a token of the word "top." In figure 4.1 the waveform corresponding to an utterance of "He climbed to the top, and he stared" is displayed; here the cursors have been positioned roughly around "top." In figure

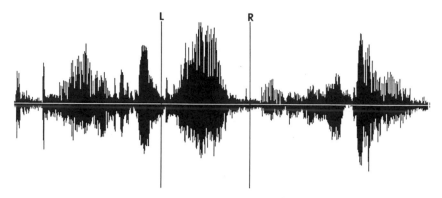

Figure 4.1
Rough segmentation of /tap/. L-R duration 470.0 msec.

Figure 4.2
Rough segmentation of initial burst of /t/. L-R duration 50.0 msec.

4.2 the marked section of the waveform has been magnified, and the cursors have been positioned around a small portion of the waveform corresponding to the consonantal burst. In figure 4.3 this burst has been magnified, and the left-hand cursor has been aligned exactly with the onset of the burst. The offset of the vowel could be similarly magnified, allowing the precise positioning of the right-hand cursor. In figure 4.4 the entire waveform is again displayed, with the two cursors now exactly positioned at the beginning and end of "top." Nominal accuracy of the duration measurements was 0.1 msec, although ambient noise occurring during the recording sessions often made this level of accuracy impossible to achieve.[2]

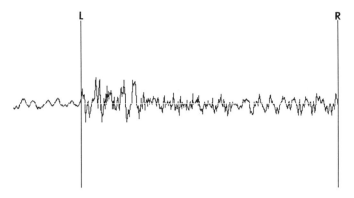

Figure 4.3
Marking of onset of /t/. L-R duration 39.7 msec.

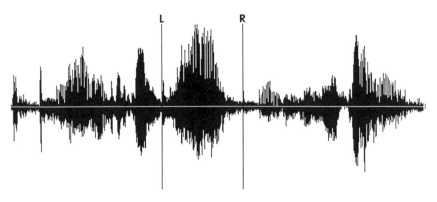

Figure 4.4
Exact segmentation of /tap/. L-R duration 423.5 msec.

If a perceptible pause occurred following the target word, its duration was measured as well. Pauses were defined as those portions of the waveform falling between the offset of the target-word vowel (or the offset of the target-word final consonant release, if it could be readily identified) and the onset of the initial consonant of the following word. In practice, only pauses with durations in excess of 100 msec were coded. For further details of the procedure, see Morgan 1986.

Results and Discussion
The hypotheses of interest with respect to the target-word duration data were (1) whether target-word durations were greater in child-

directed speech than in adult-directed speech, (2) whether target-word durations were greater when targets occurred in phrase-final position than when they occurred in phrase-nonfinal position, and (3) whether phrase-final target-word lengthening was exaggerated in child-directed speech relative to such lengthening in adult-directed speech. Accordingly, two (child vs. adult addressee) by two (final vs. nonfinal position) analyses of variance were conducted on these data for each target word across all 34 dyads. For further analyses of these data broken down by child age, see Morgan 1986. In general, a substantial amount of variability in average target-word length across speakers was evident. Since this variability was not germane to the hypotheses under examination, it was removed by transforming durations to corresponding z-scores. These z-scores were calculated for each speaker on a word-by-word basis.

First, there were consistent main effects of addressee: for all seven words, target-word durations were significantly longer in child-directed speech than in adult-directed speech. Thus, as expected, the slower speech rate evident in child-directed speech is due in part to the lengthening of at least stressed vowels in content words. Since durations of reduced vowels in content words and of vowels in function words were not measured, it is unclear whether there is a completely general effect of vowel lengthening in child-directed speech or whether this effect is confined to particular types of vowels. A few function-word vowel durations were measured in child-directed and adult-directed speech, and these measurements suggested that there may be no difference in the length of such vowels depending on addressee. In addition, function-word vowel durations were consistently smaller than content-word vowel durations. If this finding holds up given more systematic sets of measurements, this suggests that vowel duration may provide a reliable acoustic cue to the form class membership of individual words.

Second, there were consistent main effects of position: for all seven words, target-word vowel durations were significantly longer when the words occurred in phrase-final position than when they occurred in phrase-nonfinal positions. These results are consistent with the findings reported in Cooper and Paccia-Cooper 1980, though all of the structural positions investigated there were not examined in this study. Phrase-final vowel lengthening was quite robust: 84% of the adult-directed phrase-final target words were longer than their nonfinal counterparts (72% were at least 10% longer), and 82% of the child-directed phrase-final target words were longer than their counterparts (74% were at least 10% longer).

The speech examined in this experiment was recorded under more natural conditions than those in effect in the studies reported by Cooper and Paccia-Cooper. Because the subjects in this experiment did not practice reading the key sentences with "normal" sentence stress, it is possible that the presence of emphatic stress may have been confounded with structural position for some of the words. However, the lengthening effect is consistent across all of the target-word pairs, including those in which the phrase-final target never received emphatic stress; those phrase-final target words that were emphasized were not stressed by all subjects; and certain phrase-nonfinal target words occasionally received stress. Thus, it seems likely that the lengthening phenomena observed here are due to the structural positions of the target words and not to the extraneous factor of stress.

Third, in several cases phrase-final target-word lengthening was exaggerated in child-directed speech: for three of the target words, there were significant addressee-by-position interactions, such that the relative lengthening of phrase-final targets was greater in child-directed speech than in adult-directed speech. Thus, lengthening of phrase-final vowels appears to occur reliably in speech to children, and in at least certain instances the lengthening of such vowels is exaggerated. However, such exaggeration is not completely general.

In fact, one of the target words exhibited relatively greater lengthening in adult-directed speech: a significant interaction occurred for the word "stuck." Analyses of the simple main effects of each of these four significant interactions revealed that the durations of child-directed phrase-final targets were significantly longer than the corresponding adult-directed targets in the first three cases but not in the case of "stuck." On the other hand, for "stuck," the duration of the child-directed phrase-nonfinal target was significantly longer than the corresponding adult-directed target. The phrase-nonfinal "stuck" sentence occurred at a crucial point in the story, and the majority of mothers stressed this word when reading to their children (many of the mothers drew out the initial /s/ to a great extent, though this was not included in the measurement of this target). It seems likely that the large difference in the duration of the phrase-nonfinal "stuck" in child-directed vs. adult-directed speech may be due to the effects of emphasis. However, the lack of difference for the phrase-final "stuck" across addressees is puzzling: "stuck" was unique in this regard. In general, then, the magnitude of lengthening of phrase-final vowels in child-directed speech is equal to or greater than that present in adult-directed speech.

With respect to the pause data, there were again three hypotheses of interest: (1) whether pauses are more likely to occur at phrase boundaries than at nonboundary locations, (2) whether pauses are more likely to occur in speech to children than in speech to adults, and (3) whether pause length in child-directed speech tends to be greater than in adult-directed speech. It has been noted previously that pauses tend to occur between phrases (for example, Streeter 1978), and this tendency was apparent in the data from this study, where, of 138 total pauses following target words, 136 followed phrase-final targets. Thus, the presence of a pause was a high likelihood indicator of a phrase boundary. In instances where mothers paused after a given word only when speaking either to an adult (8 of 34) or to a child (26 of 34), pauses were more likely to occur in child-directed speech. In most instances (51 of 85), however, mothers who paused after a phrase-final target paused both when reading to an adult and when reading to a child. Overall, only a fraction of phrase boundaries were marked by pauses in either child-directed speech (32%) or adult-directed speech (25%).

The pauses that did occur were not uniformly distributed across target words: most pauses occurred after either "stop" (N = 55, 31 to children, 24 to adults) or "big" (N = 50, 27 to children, 23 to adults). For these two targets, pauses were reliable markers of phrase boundaries, occurring in 91% and 79% of all possible child-directed sentences, respectively, and occurring in 71% and 68% of all adult-directed sentences, respectively. Pauses occurring after "stop" were significantly longer in speech to children than in speech to adults, but this was not the case for pauses occurring after "big."

Note that there was an effect of pause lengthening following "stop" in speech to children, though there was no significant vowel-lengthening interaction for this word. In general, these data are compatible with the possibility that at least one of the possible prosodic cues to phrase boundaries is exaggerated in child-directed speech for each target. For further details of the results and analyses of additional prosodic cues, see Morgan 1986.

In sum, the results of this study indicate that phrase boundaries tend to be reliably marked in speech by either vowel lengthening, or pauses, or both, and that in certain cases these cues may be exaggerated in speech to children. The interpretation of these results is subject to certain limitations and caveats. First, prosodic phenomena occurring at only a fraction of possible phrase boundaries were examined, and all these boundaries occurred at the ends of major sentence constituents. Data cited in Cooper and Paccia-Cooper 1980 indicate that prosodic cues to the ends of minor sentence constituents generally tend to be rather weak. Second, although all mothers in the study reported that they regularly read to their children, none of them typically read stories verbatim. Moreover, it is quite clear that the prosody of reading speech is not identical to that of spontaneous speech, though it is difficult to identify the exact differences. Several mothers seemed to read to their children at a faster rate and with flatter intonation than they used in simply speaking to them. If this is generally the case, then only reduced versions of the prosodic exaggerations normally present in speech to children may have been examined here. Further examination of spontaneous speech is required to resolve this question.

The demonstration that aspects of surface phrase structure are reliably encoded by prosodic cues does not imply that these cues can be decoded by the listener; difficulties here are readily apparent. For example, even if phrase-final vowels were always exaggeratedly lengthened in speech to children, and even if vowel lengthening were conditioned only by structural factors, it is not immediately clear how useful a cue to phrase structure this might be. Individual speakers may display substantial variability in vowel durations in different words, and there may be great variability in vowel durations across speakers for individual words. Thus, in order to tell whether a word in a particular sentence spoken by a particular person is followed by a phrase boundary, one would have to compare the duration of the vowel in that token of the word to some known reference value calculated for that word and for that speaker. But this reference value could have been calculated only if the structural position of a previous token of the word spoken by this speaker were known. In short, although vowel duration may effectively encode the presence or absence of subsequent phrase boundaries, the decoding of structural information on the basis of vowel durations alone will present serious difficulties. A different problem arises in conjunction with the use of pauses to identify phrase boundaries. Unlike relative vowel durations, the physical cue here is more or less constant, but it is also unreliable: as noted above, relatively few phrase boundaries tend to be marked with pauses.

In practice, however, the situation is probably not so dire. Prosodic cues to phrase boundaries do not occur in isolation; instead, they occur in correlation with one another. Though there is some evidence that adults can make structural judgments about sentences based on individual prosodic cues (see Collier and t'Hart 1975, Scott 1982, Scott and Cutler 1984, Streeter 1978), there is also evidence that infants may be most sensitive to multiple, correlated cues (Karzon 1985). Naturally, it must be demonstrated that those correlations that can be readily perceived are accurate and reliable indicators of phrase boundaries, but at present there is no reason in principle why this cannot be done.

Finally, prosody does not supply the only cues to surface phrase structure. After some initial syntactic analysis of input has been performed, other cues, such as function-word location, may be recruited as well. Perhaps the fundamental role of prosody in language input is to provide a basis for these initial analyses: prosodic cues may allow children to roughly segment their input into units that may then be submitted to lexical and (limited) distributional analyses. Further cues will emerge from these analyses, and these cues, in conjunction with the prosodic cues, may allow children to more accurately segment subsequent input. The resulting units may be submitted to further analysis, from which additional cues may emerge. Step by step, children may gain control over the complex set of cues to phrase structure that adults can use; in so doing, children should also gain the ability to accurately and completely represent the structure of the language they hear. The following study examines whether children can use prosodic cues to phrases, in the absence of any other type of cue, to represent the bracketing of speech they hear.

Children's Use of Prosody in Bracketing Input

Previous studies have suggested that children may rely on prosodic cues in parsing their input. Read and Schreiber (1982) had 7-year-olds play a game involving the repetitions of parts of sentences they heard. The children were first exposed to two experimenters modeling the task: one experimenter said a complete sentence, and the second experimenter repeated a particular part of it. After a few such examples the children took over the role of the second experimenter and continued the game. Several variations of the game were employed, depending upon which part of the sentence was repeated by the model. In one version the model repeated the subject phrases of the sentences. So long as the subject phrase contained multiple words, children performed quite accurately. However, when the subject phrase contained only a single word, their performance was much poorer. In a second version of the game the model repeated the last word of the subject phrase and the first word of the following phrase. In this version no children tested achieved the criterion of accuracy.

Read and Schreiber suspected that children might be relying on prosodic cues to identify which portions of the sentences to repeat, so they constructed a set of sentences (this time using recorded stimuli) with misleading prosody. For example, they spliced together the first three words of "Our dogs bark at neighborhood cats" with the last three words of "Our dog's bark sometimes frightens people." "Our dogs bark" does not constitute a prosodic phrase, whereas "Our dog's bark" does; thus, in the created sentence "Our dogs bark sometimes frightens people" the prosodic cues to segmentation are pitted against the syntactic and semantic cues. Again, Read and Schreiber had children play the repetition game, with the model repeating, for example, "Our dogs bark." Their child subjects tended to repeat the prosodically defined phrases (here, "Our dogs") rather than the syntactically or semantically defined phrases.

Tager-Flusberg (1985) has examined whether prosody may affect children's comprehension of sentences. She had 4- to 6-year-old children act out sentences with center-embedded relative clauses lacking complementizers (for example, "The boy the girl hit ran home"). Some of these sentences were recorded with normal prosody; others were recorded with list-like prosody. Children's comprehension of the former type of sentences was far superior to their comprehension of the latter type. Again, these results suggest that children may use prosody in parsing their input.

Neither of these studies, however, demonstrates that children are able to employ prosody to construct representations of surface sentence structure in the early stages of acquisition. To be sure, there is a substantial amount of evidence that very young children are sensitive to various aspects of prosody and can discriminate among utterances on the basis of prosodic cues (Fernald 1981, Fernald and Kuhl 1981, Jusczyk and Thompson 1978, Karzon 1985, Kuhl and Miller 1975, Morse 1972, Spring and Dale 1977, Sullivan and Horowitz 1983). But there is no evidence that young children use prosody to bracket their input. In each of the above-mentioned studies it is possible that children initially performed the relevant analyses on the basis of syntactic or semantic cues and only later discovered that prosodic cues are correlated with these analyses.

In the present study 3- to 5-year-old children's use of prosody in segmenting "sentences" in an unfamiliar language was examined. So that syntactic and semantic cues to bracketing could be eliminated, random strings of nonsense syllables were used as stimuli. An echoing task, similar to that used by Read and Schreiber but here involving recall of the final parts of sentences, was used to assess children's segmentation. The crucial question here was whether children could learn to echo the last few words of a sentence regardless of whether those words formed a prosodic phrase or not.

Method

Subjects Twenty 3- to 5-year-old children served as subjects in this study. Ten children were assigned on a random basis to each of two echoing conditions: Phrase Echo (mean age 4;8, range 3;10 to 5;4) and Nonphrase Echo (mean age 4;7, range 3;7 to 5;3). Data from five additional children were discarded, because of their failure to cooperate in performing the echoing task. All children were enrolled in the University of Minnesota Laboratory Nursery School during the school year 1983–1984.

Materials Twenty four-word strings were constructed on a random basis using a vocabulary of ten easily pronounceable nonsense syllables. Ten of these strings constituted a practice set; the remaining strings were the test set. A separate tape was prepared for each of the two echoing conditions. A male voice recorded on one track of the tape spoke the twenty complete strings, and a female voice serving as a model and recorded on the second track echoed the final two or three syllables of each of the practice strings. In the practice set complete strings occurred first, followed, approximately three seconds later, by their echoed portions; approximately ten seconds separated the string-echo pairs. In the test set complete strings occurred approximately at fifteen-second intervals.

The twenty strings in the Phrase Echo condition were pronounced so that a prosodically defined phrase boundary fell after the first syllable in half the strings (using the prosodic pattern of the sentence "Dogs [ate their bones]") and after the second syllable in the other half (using the prosodic pattern of the sentence "Feed her [dog bones]"). Thus, half of the strings had three-syllable final phrases, and half had two-syllable final phrases. In the practice set these final phrases were echoed by the model. The twenty strings in the Nonphrase Echo condition were pronounced so that a prosodically defined phrase boundary fell after the second syllable in half the strings (using the same prosodic pattern as above) and after the third syllable in the other half (using the prosodic pattern of the sentence "Feed her dog [bones]"). In the practice set for this condition the model echoed the syllable before the phrase boundary plus all syllables following the phrase boundary. Across the two conditions the same syllables were echoed for each string; the difference between the conditions was that these syllables formed a complete prosodic phrase in the Phrase Echo condition, whereas these syllables straddled a phrase boundary in the Nonphrase Echo condition.

Examples of strings used in the test set are given in (1) and (2). The phrase boundary in each string is denoted by "[", and the to-be-echoed syllables are italicized. Sentences (1a) and (2a) were presented in the Phrase Echo condition, and sentences (1b) and (2b) were presented in the Nonphrase Echo condition.

(1) a. HUN MIN [*DAT GOP*
    b. HUN MIN *DAT* [*GOP*
(2) a. NEP [*MIP BOT DEM*
    b. NEP *MIP* [*BOT DEM*

Procedure   Children were tested individually in an ordinary laboratory room. The echoing task was first introduced by means of a puppet show portraying the story of a child, Echo, whose gender matched that of the subject. In the story Echo encountered a number of animals who spoke to her; Echo replied by repeating the last part of what had been said to her. For example, a rooster said, "Cock-a-doodle-doo," to which Echo replied, "Doodle-doo"; a dog said, "Bow-wow-wow," to which Echo replied, "Wow"; and so forth. The puppet show first was given with the experimenter playing all roles and then was repeated with the child playing the role of Echo.

Following this, the child was introduced to two hand puppets, Ko-ko and Wak-wak, who spoke a funny language (via implanted speakers connected to a tape deck and amplifier) and liked to play a copying game, just like Echo. The child listened to Ko-ko say the first five complete strings of the practice set, while Wak-wak repeated the last part of each string. For the last five strings in the practice set, the tape deck was stopped after Wak-wak echoed the final portion of each string, and the child was asked to repeat what Wak-wak had just said. All children were able to imitate the echoed portions of all five strings, regardless of which condition they were in.

When these practice strings were successfully completed, the child was told that Wak-wak was very sleepy and had to take a nap. Ko-ko, however, wanted to continue playing and asked the child to play with him. The strings of the test set were then played, and the tape deck was stopped after each one, until the child made some response. If the child failed to respond, the tape was rewound, and the string was replayed. This procedure was continued for all ten strings of the test set. The child was then conducted back to the nursery school.

During the experimental sessions the children wore a remote microphone; their responses were recorded for later coding and analysis. In coding the data, the number of syllables the child uttered after each string in the test set was noted (it was not required that the child pronounce the syllables correctly or preserve the prosody of the original utterance, although children typically did both). Each response was then assigned to one of the following categories. A response was *correct* if the child echoed the same portion of the utterance the model (Wak-wak) would have (that is, in the Phrase Echo condition a correct response would be to echo all syllables in the final phrase; in the Nonphrase Echo condition a correct response would be to echo the syllable preceding the phrase boundary plus all syllables in the final phrase). A response was *partial-phrase* if the child echoed only the final phrase (this category applied only to subjects in the Nonphrase Echo condition). A response was *partial* if the child echoed some number of final syllables not constituting a phrase, *beginning* if the child echoed syllables from the beginning, rather than the end, of the string, *whole* if the child echoed the entire string, or *no response* if the child failed to respond after hearing a string three times.

Results and Discussion
Children's responses in the two conditions are shown in table 4.2. An inspection of these results indicates that children in the Phrase Echo condition were generally able to echo the strings they heard correctly, in conformance with the model to which they had been exposed. In contrast, only one child in the Nonphrase Echo condition ever echoed correctly, and this for only one string. The predominant response of children in this second condition was to echo the final phrase of each string, although this was not in conformance with the behavior of the model to which they had been exposed.

Table 4.2
Children's responses in the echoing study

	Correct	Partial-Phrase	Partial	Beginning	Whole	No Response
Phrase Echo	8.9	NA	0.5	0.0	0.5	0.1
Nonphrase Echo	0.1	8.2	0.2	0.4	0.6	0.5

Note: Mean values are given, based on a total of ten responses per child.

The difference in *correct* responses by children across the two conditions was highly significant, $t(18) = 21.00$, $p < .0001$. However, there was no difference between the *correct* responses of children in the Phrase Echo condition and the *partial-phrase* responses of the children in the Nonphrase Echo condition, $t(18) = 0.92$, NS. Thus, children in both conditions echoed prosodically defined phrases, whether or not their model had done so. As further indication that this was the preferred strategy, note that three of the four *beginning* responses by children in the Nonphrase Echo condition were complete initial phrases.

As a result of the presence of a prosodic boundary (which included vowel lengthening and pause cues) within the to-be-echoed portion of the strings in the Nonphrase Echo condition, these stimuli had greater duration than the corresponding stimuli in the Phrase Echo condition. For example, the Nonphrase Echo three-syllable to-be-echoed portions averaged 1524.1 msec, whereas the Phrase Echo three-syllable to-be-echoed portions averaged 1187.8 msec. Hence, it is possible that this additional length made the echoing task more difficult in the Nonphrase Echo condition. Perhaps if this confound were removed (which could not be done without distorting the stimuli), the preference for echoing phrases would disappear.

In fact, there is no evidence that duration played any role in determining the difficulty of the echoing task. Subjects in the Phrase Echo condition did perform better on two-syllable to-be-echoed stimuli than on three-syllable to-be-echoed stimuli, $t(9) = 3.25$, $p < .01$, and this result could be attributed to the difference in average duration between these stimuli. On the other hand, it seems more likely that this difference may have been due simply to the different numbers of syllables in these stimuli. Moreover, the average duration of three-syllable to-be-echoed stimuli in the Phrase Echo condition was greater than that of two-syllable to-be-echoed stimuli in the Nonphrase Echo condition; nevertheless, performance on the former was superior, $t(18) = 11.21$, $p < .001$. Finally, recall that children in both conditions imitated successfully during the modeling phase of the practice set.

The stimuli used in this experiment were random strings of nonsense syllables; thus, there were neither syntactic nor semantic cues to how these strings should be segmented. Hence, the difference in performance across the two conditions hinged solely on the prosodic characteristics of the stimuli. Insofar as the echoing task employed here provides a reasonable measure of how children segment the speech they hear, the results of this experiment strongly suggest that children can use prosody, in the absence of other cues, in performing such segmentations. It is unclear, however, whether these results reflect children's use of a particular strategy in listening to the stimuli, or whether they are indicative of the structure of the child's memorial representation of linguistic input. Therefore, these results do not indicate whether the representation of bracketing plays a role in the child's induction of syntax. The two studies described in the next chapter begin to address this question.

Chapter 5
Bracketed Input and the Outcome of Acquisition

With regard to the empirical validity of the Bracketed Input Hypothesis, the most important, yet most difficult, issue to address is whether bracketing information plays an identifiable role in the process of language acquisition. This issue is crucial because the demonstrations that bracketing information is readily available in language input and can be represented by children do not entail that such information is used to constrain the hypotheses children will consider. The obvious experiment to perform would be to remove all bracketing information from a child's input and to then observe how (and if) the child acquired language. Just as obviously, this experiment cannot ethically be performed.

Alternatively, it might be possible to observe naturally occurring instances of input deprivation. The deaf children examined by Goldin-Meadow and Mylander (1984) provide one such example. Although these children have apparently acquired certain aspects of language, their sign systems are clearly deficient compared to linguistic systems acquired by children under normal conditions of input. The problem here, though, is that Goldin-Meadow and Mylander's subjects have not suffered from an appropriately selective type of deprivation; rather, Goldin-Meadow and Mylander argue that these children have been deprived of any meaningful input whatsoever. So far as I am aware, there are no instances in which bracketing information is selectively removed from children's input through natural causes.[1] In sum, the role of bracketing information in acquisition must be observed through indirect means.

In chapter 3 I noted that two predictions concerning acquisition can be straightforwardly derived from the proof presented there. First, the assumption that children make use of bracketed input entails that they will not make errors of misadjunction, which would otherwise be possible. Second, this assumption entails that children will eventually acquire grammars that are strongly equivalent to the grammars underlying the languages they hear. In this chapter I will present a study bearing on the second prediction. This study examines the acquisition of two constructions in English for whose structure no distributional evidence exists. The central idea is that different learners could adopt consistent analyses of these constructions only if bracketing information indicating their structures is used in guiding these analyses.

The role of bracketing information may be somewhat more directly observed by experimentally manipulating input in the learning of miniature languages in the laboratory. I will present a second study in this chapter examining the contributions of prosodic cues to phrases in input to the acquisition of the syntax of such a language. However, there are obvious difficulties involved in interpreting the results of artificial language studies. First, the languages used necessarily lack much of the richness of natural languages, and it is simply not known how such impoverishment might change the nature of learning. Second, though the target languages are relatively simple, the learning task is still quite complex; thus, most artificial language studies have used adult subjects (as is the case in the study described below). It is certainly possible that adults use entirely different strategies in learning artificial languages than do children in acquiring natural languages. I will discuss these issues further in conjunction with the study.

Acquisition of Distributionally Nondetermined Constructions

In the absence of bracketed input, there are certain errors that the child may make that can never become detectable (and hence could never be corrected). Suppose that a child makes an error of misadjunction, formulating a transformation so that it produces correct derived strings but incorrect derived structures. Suppose further that no other transformations operate on the output of this rule. In this case the child could never discover and repair this mistake. On the other hand, given bracketed input, such errors should not occur. Thus, in order to test the strong equivalence prediction, we must find movement transformations in English such that no other transformations apply subsequently and such that there are multiple possible "landing sites" (Baltin 1982) for the moved phrase. In the absence of bracketed input, we should expect equal proportions of learners to adopt each of the possible landing site analyses; given bracketed input, we should expect learners to tend to adopt one analysis (perhaps subject to dialectal variations).

In English there appear to be a number of transformations producing derived structures for the details of which there is no distributional evidence. Among these are the rules of Topicalization and Prepositional Phrase Preposing (for verb phrase but not sentential prepositional phrases). These are illustrated in (1) and (2), respectively.

(1) Some vegetables, John likes to eat.

(2) With the Vegamatic, I can chop, slice, dice, peel, and puree.

In what form are these rules acquired? In the absence of bracketed input, these rules should be acquired in varying forms by different learners; given bracketed input, all learners should adopt the same analysis of these rules. I will argue that the preposed phrase in Topicalization and Prepositional Phrase Preposing constructions is moved to a distinct site and that that site is different from the one occupied by the preposed phrase in Left Dislocation and Preposed Adverbial Phrase constructions (see (3) and (4)).

(3) Some vegetables, John likes to eat them.

(4) After he gets home from school, John likes to eat candy.

Below I will describe how certain judgments of pronoun reference offer a method for diagnosing which landing site analysis individuals adopt for these constructions. This study will examine whether such judgments are consistent across individuals.

In linguistic theory it is generally accepted that embedded clauses form phrases both by themselves and in conjunction with their complementizers (for example, "that" or "which"). This entails that there be an additional syntactic category—termed *S-bar* (denoted by S')— that dominates both an embedded sentence and its complementizer. Since every embedded clause is dominated by S', it is most parsimonious to assume that matrix clauses are dominated by S' as well. (For further discussion concerning S', and X' theory in general, see Jackendoff 1977.) Thus, there are in general two possible landing sites for preposed phrases. Assuming that, for example, the Topicalized phrase is adjoined as a (perhaps nonimmediate) daughter of S, the derived structure of (1) would be represented as shown in tree 5.1; alternatively, if the phrase is adjoined as a (perhaps nonimmediate) daughter of S', tree 5.2 would illustrate the derived structure.

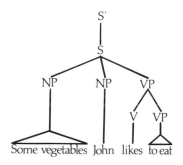

Tree 5.1

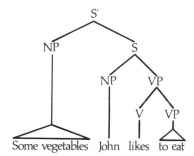

Tree 5.2

To reiterate, if the assumption of bracketed input is correct, it should be expected that individuals will tend to have acquired one of these structures rather than the other (I will argue below that this should be similar to the one in tree 5.1, at least in my dialect); if it is incorrect, then individuals should be evenly split between these two structures—some having acquired one, some the other.

It is simple to show that the preposed phrases in Left Dislocation (including "as-for" phrases) and Preposed Adverbial Phrase constructions must be attached to S' (or perhaps some higher node such as S''): in each case the preposed phrase can precede a *wh*-word, as shown in (5)–(7).

(5) Your father's watch, who did you give it to?

(6) As for John, what does he like to eat?

(7) After John eats dinner, where does he go?

Wh-words are in *COMP*(lementizer) and are daughters of S'; thus, any preceding phrases must also be daughters of S' (or S''). As illustration, the derived structure of (5) is given in tree 5.3.

In contrast, phrases moved by Topicalization and Prepositional Phrase Preposing generally cannot precede *wh*-words, as illustrated by (8) and (9).

(8) *Your father's watch, to whom did you give?

(9) ?With the Vegamatic, what can you chop?

This is one bit of evidence that preposed phrases in these constructions are not attached to S'. (The acceptability of (9) seems to be related to whether or not contrastive emphasis is present; without such emphasis (9) is clearly ungrammatical for me.)

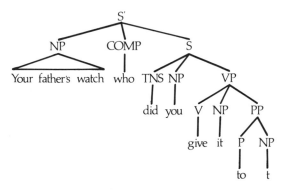

Tree 5.3

On the other hand, there is no straightforward indication that these preposed phrases must be attached to *S:* I know of no syntactic test (that is, distributional evidence) for *S*-constituency in English. The evidence concerning the derived structure of Topicalization and Prepositional Phrase Preposing constructions is confusing, and a number of analyses of these constructions have been offered in the linguistic literature. Below I will give a series of inferential arguments that offer converging support for an *S*-attachment analysis. The same facts are applicable to both Topicalization and Prepositional Phrase Preposing, so I will give arguments only for the former. The consensus among linguists seems to be that these two rules are in fact the same. However, that the same syntactic facts apply in both cases does not require that these two constructions are acquired simultaneously or have the same range of use: sentences with Prepositional Phrase Preposing seem to be both more common and more natural than sentences with Topicalization.

Topicalization and Prepositional Phrase Preposing are among the rules that Emonds (1970, 1976) termed *root transformations*. These rules have a limited range of application. According to Emonds, they can only apply in "root," or matrix, clauses. Hooper and Thompson (1973) noted counterevidence to this claim: Topicalization can apply in the complements of certain verbs (including "say," "believe," and "think") and in nonrestrictive relative clauses. These possibilities are illustrated in (10) and (11).

(10) I believe that Mary, John likes.

(11) The ASPCA is a worthwhile cause, to which my estate, I would gladly contribute.

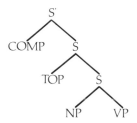

Tree 5.4

Hooper and Thompson suggested a pragmatic explanation for these facts: root transformations can apply in any clause that is asserted rather than presupposed. However, they offered no syntactic characterization of this property. I propose that the syntactic reflex of an asserted clause is that it contains a *TOP* node; such clauses have structures like that illustrated in tree 5.4. Given this structure, Topicalization and Prepositional Phrase Preposing are simply movement into *TOP*.

Both Ross (1967) and Chomsky (1977) have noted (again, contrary to Emonds's characterization) that Topicalization can pull phrases out of clauses that are arbitrarily deeply embedded. Thus, like *Wh*-Movement, Topicalization appears to violate Subjacency (= Binary Principle). Examples of such apparently unbounded movement are given in (12)–(15); in these examples the original location of the Topicalized phrase is denoted by "T."

(12) This book, I asked Bill to get his students to read T.

(13) Beans, I don't think you'll be able to convince me Harry has ever tasted T in his life.

(14) Mary, I want Bill to admit that he loves T.

(15) Mary, I heard that Bill wants to date T.

One way to get around this problem is to assume that Topicalization in sentences such as these results from a cyclic movement. Thus, the second key assumption in my analysis is that there is a TOP-to-TOP Raising rule, formally analogous to the COMP-to-COMP Raising that Chomsky (1973) proposed to account for *Wh*-Movement. To illustrate, consider the derivation of (15), whose deep structure is given schematically as tree 5.5.

In the lowest cycle "Mary" is moved into TOP_2 by Topicalization. "Mary" is then raised into TOP_1 and TOP_0 by successive applications

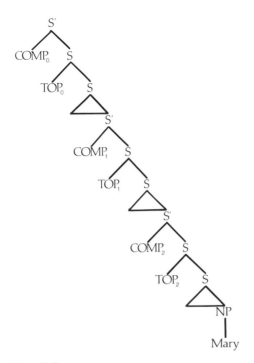

Tree 5.5

of TOP-to-TOP Raising. Since movement out of *TOP* can only be into another *TOP*, the impossibility of raising an embedded Topicalized *NP* to subject is accounted for. (Compare (16) and (17).)

(16)   It is believed that Mary, John loves.

(17)   *Mary is believed that John loves.

I will now consider other analyses of Topicalization that have been proposed and show that the present analysis accounts for data that escape the others. The first of these is the COMP Substitution analysis proposed by Emonds (1976). Under this analysis, Topicalization is considered to be movement into *COMP*. Given that, as is generally assumed, COMPs cannot be doubly filled, it follows that Topicalization should not be allowable in embedded clauses. However, as (10) and (11) show, this prediction is incorrect.

In addition, this analysis suggests that (15) should be ungrammatical, whereas (14) should be grammatical. Consider again tree 5.5. In (14) $COMP_2$ is filled with "that." Under the COMP Substitution analysis, "Mary" can be moved into $COMP_1$ and then raised into $COMP_0$ by

COMP-to-COMP Raising. In contrast, in (15) $COMP_1$ is filled with "that." By the COMP Substitution analysis, "Mary" can be moved into $COMP_2$, but it cannot be moved into $COMP_0$: this movement would cross two S' nodes and would thus violate Subjacency. (Here, and for the remainder of these arguments, I assume that S' is the bounding node for Subjacency in English.) However, I can detect no difference in the acceptability of these two sentences.

An argument against the generality of this analysis follows from facts concerning verb placement in Icelandic. Maling and Zaenen (1977, cited in Baltin 1982) have shown that there is a verb-second constraint that operates in all clauses, matrix or root. A topicalized *NP* can count as the first phrase in this constraint. Thus, (18), but not (19), is grammatical. However, a *wh*-word cannot count as a first phrase: (20) is acceptable, but (21) is not.

(18) Eg held ath smalann   muni troll   taka a morgun.
      I   think that the shepherd will   the trolls take tomorrow
      (= I think that the shepherd, the trolls will take tomorrow.)

(19) *Eg held ath smalann   troll   muni taka a morgun.
      I   think that the shepherd the trolls will   take tomorrow
      (= I think that the shepherd, the trolls will take tomorrow.)

(20) Hann spurthi hverjum   Olafur hefthi hjalpath.
      he   asked   who(dat.) Olaf   had   helped

(21) *Hann spurthi hverjum   hefthi Olafur hjalpath.
      he   asked   who(dat.) had   Olaf   helped

These facts indicate that the Topicalized *NP* is adjoined to a node within the domain of the verb-second constraint (namely, S), whereas *wh*-words are adjoined to a node outside this domain (namely, S'). Given the COMP Substitution analysis, it should be expected that either both Topicalized NPs and *wh*-words should count in this constraint, or neither should. On the other hand, these facts fall out neatly from the analysis I have proposed: all and only those phrases dominated by S count for purposes of this constraint.[2]

The second analysis I will consider here is the *Wh*-Movement analysis of Topicalization given by Chomsky (1977). Chomsky observes that Topicalization shares four crucial characteristics with *Wh*-Movement: it leaves a gap (a trace), it appears to violate Subjacency, it observes the Complex Noun Phrase Constraint (see (22)), and it observes the *Wh*-Island Constraint (see (23)).

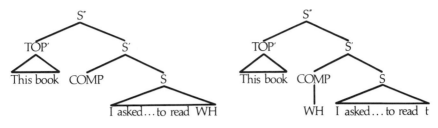

Tree 5.6   **Tree 5.7**

(22) *This book, I accept the argument that John should read.

(23) *This book, I wonder who read.

In his analysis Chomsky postulates the base rules given in (24) and (25).

(24) S″ ⇒ TOP′ S′

(25) S′ ⇒ {COMP S, S″}

The Topicalized *NP* is base-generated in the *TOP′* position, and a *wh*-word is generated in the position this *NP* binds. Thus, the base structure of (26) is as shown in tree 5.6. *Wh*-Movement applies to this structure to yield the structure shown in tree 5.7, to which a *Wh*-Phrase Deletion rule in turn applies to yield (26).

(26) This book, I asked Bill to get his students to read.

The appeal of this analysis is that it explains straightforwardly why Topicalization and *Wh*-Movement share the above four characteristics: they are the same rule. In addition, this analysis allows for a unified account of Topicalization and Left Dislocation: they are identical, except that a pronoun appears in place of the *wh*-word in the latter type of construction. However, a number of facts do not fit this analysis.

First, in sentences with both Left Dislocation and Topicalization the Left Dislocated phrase must occur before the Topicalized phrase (see (27)–(29)).

(27) John, your watch, I gave (to) him.

(28) Your watch, to John, I gave it.

(29) *John, your watch, I gave it (to).

This, of course, follows naturally if Left Dislocated phrases are adjoined to *S′* and Topicalized phrases are adjoined to *S*, as I have proposed. However, without additional assumptions, this fact does not follow from Chomsky's analysis. The deep structure of (29), under this

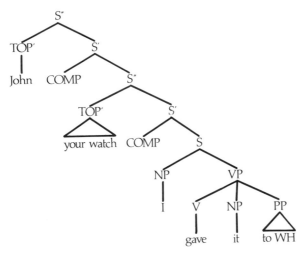

Tree 5.8

analysis, is given in tree 5.8. In the lower S' cycle "to who" is *Wh*-Moved into *COMP*. In the upper S' cycle COMP-to-COMP Raising takes place, followed by *Wh*-Phrase Deletion. Thus, this sentence is erroneously permitted.

There is a way to rule out this derivation, however: assume S'' to be a bounding node. Under this assumption, the COMP-to-COMP Raising in the upper S' cycle would violate Subjacency, and (29) could not be generated. In fact, this is the tack Chomsky pursues; as he notes, the assumption of S'' as a bounding node also correctly rules out Raising to Subject of embedded Topicalized *NP*s (see tree 5.5).

From the assumption that S'' is a bounding node it follows that neither Left Dislocation nor Topicalization should be possible in *wh*-clauses. In the case of Left Dislocation this prediction is correct, but for Topicalization it is in error. The relevant base structure for Left Dislocation and Topicalization in embedded clauses is given in tree 5.9. In a Left Dislocation sentence a *wh*-word can be moved into $COMP_1$ from S. But it cannot be moved into $COMP_0$. The movement from $COMP_1$ to $COMP_0$ would cross two bounding nodes and thus violate Subjacency. Thus, Left Dislocation in relative clauses should be ungrammatical. As (30) shows, this is correct.

(30) *The ASPCA is a worthy cause, to which my estate, I would gladly bequeath it.

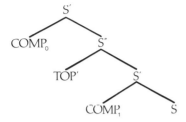

Tree 5.9

In a Topicalization sentence a bound *wh*-word is raised into $COMP_1$ (later to be deleted). The *wh*-word to be relativized cannot be moved into this position; rather, it must be raised into $COMP_0$ from S. However, this raising would violate Subjacency, because this movement must cross two bounding nodes (S' and S''). Thus, Topicalization in relative clauses should also be ungrammatical. As (31) shows, however, this is not always the case.

(31) The ASPCA is a worthy cause, to which my estate, I would gladly bequeath.

If S'' is not assumed to be a bounding node, then Topicalization is correctly permitted in relative clauses. But in this case it follows (incorrectly) that Left Dislocation should be permitted in relative clauses as well. In sum, whether S'' is taken as a bounding node for Subjacency or not, Chomsky's analysis fails on some data.

In addition, certain aspects of interpretations of sentences depend on surface structure configurations. On Chomsky's analysis, the same sets of readings should be possible for both Topicalization and Left Dislocation sentences, since both types of phrases are in the same surface structure position. However, this is not always the case.

First, in certain circumstances Topicalization sentences may have multiple readings, like simple declaratives, whereas Left Dislocation sentences are unambiguous. For example, consider sentences (32)–(34).

(32) Tom eats some vegetables, and so does Bill.

(33) Some vegetables, Tom eats, and so does Bill.

(34) Some vegetables, Tom eats them, and so does Bill.

(32) has two possible interpretations: first, that there are some vegetables such that Tom and Bill both eat them; second, that Tom and Bill each eat some vegetables, but the particular vegetables each one eats

may be different. These two readings differ in that the quantifier "some" has wide scope in the former and narrow scope in the latter. Sentence (33), with Topicalization, allows the same two readings. However, in (34), with Left Dislocation, only the wide scope interpretation is possible. This contrast may be clearer in sentences in which only the narrow scope reading is plausible, as in (35)–(37). (37) seems to be quite bizarre, because it means that both Sue and Mary had the same baby boy—a physical impossibility.

(35) Sue had a baby boy, and so did Mary.

(36) A baby boy, Sue had, and so did Mary.

(37) ?A baby boy, Sue had it, and so did Mary.

Quantifier scope is a function of surface syntactic structure, as evidenced by the contrast between (38) and (39)–(40) (these examples are from Baltin 1981).

(38) *I don't read many books, but I do read many books.

(39) Many books, I don't read, but many books, I do.

(40) ?Many books, I don't read them, but many books, I do (read them).

The fact that only the wide scope reading of "some" is possible in (34), whereas both readings are possible in (33), suggests that "some" must be "higher" in the surface structure of the former than in the surface structure of the latter. This would follow if preposed phrases are daughters of S' in Left Dislocation sentences and daughters of S in Topicalization sentences, as I have proposed, but this does not follow from Chomsky's analysis.

Finally, if, as I have argued, Prepositional Phrase Preposing and Topicalization result in S-attachment of the moved phrase, there is one additional contrast that should obtain between these constructions and the S'-attachment constructions. In the latter, but not in the former, a noun in the preposed phrase can be coreferential with a pronominal matrix subject. Thus, compare (41) with (42) and (43), and (44) with (45).

(41) For John, he bought a book.

(42) As for John, he bought a book.

(43) While John was on vacation, he bought a book.

(44) John's book, he found on the floor.

(45) John's book, he found it on the floor.

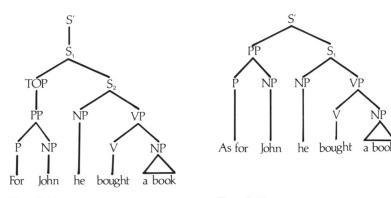

Tree 5.10   **Tree 5.11**

In (41) and (44) "he" must be someone other than "John"; in (42), (43), and (45) "he" and "John" can refer to the same person. These facts concerning coreference may offer a simple method for diagnosing the structures speakers have induced for sentence constructions with preposed phrases.

One explanation for this contrast is that phrases that are daughters of *S* are "c-commanded" by the matrix subject, whereas phrases that are daughters of *S'* are not; and a pronoun cannot c-command its antecedent (Reinhart 1976, 1981). As illustration, consider the structures of (41) and (42), given as trees 5.10 and 5.11, respectively. Reinhart (1981) gives the following definition for "c-command":

Node A c(onstituent)-commands node B iff the branching node α_1 most immediately dominating A either dominates B or is immediately dominated by a node α_2 which dominates B, and α_2 is of the same category type as α_1. (p. 612)

In tree 5.10 the node S_1 defines the c-command domain of the *NP* "he." This node also dominates "John"; therefore, "he" c-commands "John," and coreference is impossible. In tree 5.11 S_1 again defines the c-command domain of the *NP* "he." Here, however, S_1 does not dominate "John": "he" does not c-command "John," so these noun phrases can be either coreferential or noncoreferential.

The search for the proper characterization of structural constraints on nominal-pronominal coreference in linguistic theory has a long and tortuous history, aptly described by the title of Bach's (1970) paper, "Problominalization." Reinhart's C-Command Constraint, though not without its difficulties (see, for example, Solan 1983), seems to be more descriptively adequate than any of the alternatives. In recent linguistic theories the notion of c-command has been implicated in other grammatical phenomena as well; for example, in the theory developed in Chomsky 1981 a noun can bind a trace only if the noun c-commands it (as in tree 5.3, where "who" binds the trace *t*). This lends independent justification to Reinhart's constraint. For present purposes, I will simply assume that c-command correctly characterizes constraints on coreference.

One question concerning the syntax of pronominalization calls for discussion here: at which level does the C-Command Constraint apply? If it applies to base structures, then we would expect the pronouns in (41) and (44) to be noncoreferential with "John" regardless of the attachment of the moved phrases. This is because "he" c-commands "John" in the original position of these phrases. Thus, in (46) and (47) "he" and "John" are noncoreferential.

(46) He bought a book for John.

(47) He bought a book while John was on vacation.

(48) I saw him in John's room.

(49) In John's room, I saw him.

On this basis, however, we should expect mandatory noncoreference in (43) as well, since "John" is c-commanded by "he" in the base structure of this sentence, too. Compare (43) with (47). Note also the different possibilities for the interpretation of "him" in (48) and (49).

These facts suggest that instead Reinhart's C-Command Constraint must apply to surface structures. Thus, the fact that Topicalization and Left Dislocation sentences admit different possibilities for pronominal reference constitutes evidence that they must have different surface structures, along the lines I have suggested.

To summarize, there is no distributional evidence for the surface structures of sentences with Topicalization and Prepositional Phrase Preposing. In the absence of bracketed input, we should not expect all learners to adopt the same analysis of these constructions, whereas, given bracketed input, we should. I have given a number of arguments that indicate that Topicalization and Prepositional Phrase Preposing sentences do have a particular derived structure. If we can determine whether individuals have predominantly acquired this structure, this will constitute a test of the Bracketed Input Hypothesis.

Provided the c-command analysis of pronominalization is correct, as I have assumed here, judgments of pronoun interpretation will allow diagnosis of the derived structures that speakers assign to these sentences. That is, in sentences with pronominal subjects and potential antecedents in preposed phrases, given S-attachment analyses, speakers should offer only noncoreferential judgments; given S'-attachment analyses, they should offer either coreferential or noncoreferential judgments. Once again, the Bracketed Input Hypothesis predicts that speakers should have tended to acquire Prepositional Phrase Preposing and Topicalization as S-attachment constructions, whereas the null hypothesis predicts that they should be evenly split between analyzing them as S-attachment constructions and analyzing them as S'-attachment constructions. The study described here uses pronoun reference judgments to determine which of these predictions is correct.

Method

Subjects Solan (1983) has provided evidence indicating that children between the ages of seven and nine have typically acquired structure-based rules for interpreting pronouns, whereas younger children may not have. Accordingly, subjects in the present study fell into the older age range. Twenty second graders and twenty third graders from the Lincoln Trail School in Mahomet, Illinois, served as subjects. Ten children from each grade were assigned at random to each of two experimental groups. In one group coreference judgments were obtained for sentences with Prepositional Phrase Preposing or Left Dislocation (henceforth, PP-LD). In the second group these judgments were obtained for sentences with Topicalization or base-generated S'-attached phrases (henceforth, TOP-S'). The mean age of second graders was 8;4 in the PP-LD group and 8;3 in the TOP-S' group; the corresponding means for third graders were 9;4 and 9;3.

In addition, twenty-seven adults drawn from the psychology subject pool at the University of Illinois served as subjects. Twelve adults were assigned at random to each of the experimental conditions. Data from three adults were discarded: two because they were nonnative speakers of English, and the third because he gave coreferential judgments for all sentences presented.

Materials Four types of experimental sentences were employed, including sentences exemplifying Prepositional Phrase Preposing, S'-Phrases (including "as for" and preposed adverbial phrases), Topicalization, and Left Dislocation. Examples of these four types of sentences are given in (50)–(53), respectively.

(50) For the poodle, he turned on the TV.

(51) As for the poodle, he turned on the TV.

(52) The zebra's book, he dropped on his foot.

(53) The zebra's book, he dropped it on his foot.

As noted, each subject gave coreference judgments for only two types—either Prepositional Phrase Preposing and Left Dislocation, or Topicalization and S'-Phrases.

Subjects in both groups gave coreference judgments for eight types of control sentences, examples of which are given in (54)–(61).

(54) He broke the lion's chair when he sat down.

(55) The zebra turned his bed upside down.

(56) The girl put him on the hippo's bed.

(57) The girl put the zebra on his bed.

(58) He put the lamp in the hippo's room.

(59) The zebra put the lamp in his room.

(60) Some blocks which were in the lion's room made him trip.

(61) Some blocks which were in his room made the zebra trip.

Sentences (54)–(59) were chosen to exemplify a broad range of possible grammatical roles (subject, direct object, direct object–possessive, and prepositional object–possessive) and relative orderings for antecedents and pronouns in simple sentences. (60) and (61) exemplify different orderings of subordinate and superordinate antecedents and pronouns. These constructions were chosen so that the overall pattern of responses on these sentences would indicate whether particular subjects used structural criteria in making their judgments of pronoun reference.

All sentences referred to a set of toys. Among the toys were four main characters: a poodle, a lion, a zebra, and a hippo. Each animal had a set of possessions, including a room, a bed, a chair, a table, and a book. Each animal wore a "belt" of colored tape, and its possessions were painted the same color. For example, the zebra had a blue belt and a blue bed, chair, and so forth. There was a small number of miscellaneous toys, including a TV, a lamp, a block, and a female doll.

Pronoun reference judgments were collected through two experimental tasks: a comprehension task and a picture judgment task. In the comprehension task subjects were given sets of five toys and were asked to act out sentences with these. Four blocks of six sentences each were used in this task. Each block included one example of each of the two types of experimental sentences being tested for the particular group, as well as one example of each of four types of control sentences. Blocks 1 and 3 included control sentences like (54), (57), (58), and (61); blocks 2 and 4 included control sentences like (55), (56), (59), and (60). Identical control sentences were given to subjects in both groups. Sentences were randomized within each block; all subjects heard the blocks of sentences in nominal order, but half the subjects in each group heard the sentences within each block in forward order, and the remaining half heard them in reverse order. This counterbalancing was used to eliminate possible order effects but was not employed as a factor in analyses of the data. The sentences used in this task for each group, along with the sets of toys accompanying each of these, are given (in forward order) in the appendix.

In the picture judgment task subjects heard sentences and were then asked to judge whether photographs they were shown accurately portrayed these sentences. Eighteen sentences were employed in this task: three exemplars each of the two appropriate experimental sentences, and two exemplars each of six types of control sentences (corresponding to (54), (55), (56), (58), (60), and (61)). Two of the three exemplars of the experimental sentences were paired with pictures portraying pronoun-antecedent coreference. Thus, in order to consistently judge these sentences as being noncoreferential (as predicted for Prepositional Phrase Preposing and Topicalization sentences), subjects would have to reject the pictures presented to them as being inappropriate for the sentence they had heard two out of three times. Intuitively, this seems to bias this task against the experimental hypothesis. Of the two exemplars of control sentences, one was paired with a "coreferential" picture, and the other was paired with a "noncoreferential" picture. The set of eighteen sentences was randomized; all subjects received the same order of presentation. The sentences used in this task, along with descriptions of the paired photographs, are given in the appendix.

Procedure   The children were first addressed in groups of five to nine. Each group was brought into the experimental room and given a brief introduction to the task. The children were told that the experiment would concern understanding of language and that they would hear a number of sentences about a set of toys. Their role would be to act out each sentence using the toys. Names and birthdates were collected at this point. Assignment to conditions was made as described above;

within conditions assignment to orders was random. Later the children were brought from their classrooms and tested individually.

The procedure was administered in two sessions. In the first session, which generally lasted about twenty minutes, children were given detailed instructions and were tested over the first three blocks (eighteen sentences) of the comprehension trials. In the second session, which typically lasted about fifteen minutes, children were tested over the fourth block of the comprehension task and over the complete picture judgment task.

At the first session children were instructed that they would be given five toys before hearing each sentence; their task was to act out the sentence using those toys. The color-coding scheme was explained, and the task was demonstrated, giving examples of both coreferential and noncoreferential control sentences. Children were assured that there were no "right" or "wrong" answers in the task.

After being given three practice trials, children heard the eighteen sentences from the first three blocks and acted out each one. If a child appeared to be unduly hesitant about acting out a sentence, the experimenter repeated it. Aside from one type of sentence (Prepositional Phrase Preposing with an initial "for"), children rarely requested of their own accord that a sentence be repeated. It was originally intended that the toys would be placed in random order in front of the children. However, the first few children all dutifully rearranged the toys so that, for example, the poodle's chair was next to the poodle. Clearly, children had no difficulty in grasping the import of the color-coding scheme. Subsequently the toys were placed so that each animal and its possession were adjacent. After the eighteen sentences were completed, the child was escorted back to the classroom.

At the beginning of the second session the children received a brief reminder about the nature of the task and then acted out the six sentences of the fourth block. Children then received instructions for the picture judgment task. They were told that this task had been given to another, younger child (opposite gender of the subject) and that pictures had been taken of how this other child had acted out the sentences. The subject children's task was to say whether or not they agreed with the way the other child had acted out the sentences; children were further told that they would probably agree sometimes and disagree other times. When this task was completed, the child was again escorted back to the classroom.

The entire experiment was administered individually to the adult subjects. Instructions given to the adults were similar to those described above. The same procedure was used, except that adults completed the experiment in a single session, generally lasting about half an hour. Responses for all subjects on each sentence in both tasks were scored as "coreferential" or "noncoreferential," depending on how the pronoun was interpreted.

Results and Discussion

How can it be determined whether subjects in this study have acquired the predicted structures for Prepositional Phrase Preposing and Topicalization sentences? At a minimum, we need to know whether subjects gave different patterns of pronoun reference judgments for Prepositional Phrase Preposing and Topicalization sentences versus Left Dislocation and S'-Phrase sentences. This issue may be addressed in part by conducting within-subject analyses for Prepositional Phrase Preposing versus Left Dislocation sentences and for Topicalization versus S'-Phrase sentences, and in part by conducting between-subjects analyses for Prepositional Phrase Preposing versus S'-Phrase sentences and for Topicalization versus Left Dislocation sentences. Such analyses cannot form a complete basis for attributing particular structural representations of these sentence types to subjects, however. On the one hand, significant results might follow from subjects' consistently giving coreferential judgments for S'-Phrase and Left Dislocation sentences, while failing to give consistent noncoreferential judgments for the other two types of sentences (contrary to my hypothesis). On the other hand, nonsignificant results might ensue if subjects consistently give noncoreferential judgments for Prepositional Phrase Preposing and Topicalization sentences (in keeping with my hypothesis) but also give noncoreferential judgments for the other two types of sentences (recall that in certain structures pronouns and nouns must be noncoreferential, whereas in others they may be either coreferential or noncoreferential; coreference is never required).

If we can attribute S-attachment or S'-attachment representations to individual subjects for Prepositional Phrase Preposing and Topicalization sentences, then simple binomial tests may be used to determine whether one or the other of these representations is acquired more often than chance. The problem here is what criterion to use in attributing representations to individuals. A strict criterion might state: if subjects always give noncoreferential judgments for these types of sentences, they can be assigned to the S-attachment category; otherwise, they must be assigned to the S'-attachment category (seven of seven noncoreferential judgments would be required to attain within-subject significance, binomial $p = .008$). I will refer to this criterion as the "7-of-7 criterion." Performance on the tasks used in this study may not perfectly reflect subjects' underlying knowledge, however, particularly for the younger subjects. A slightly more lax criterion may be more appropriate. I will therefore also use the following, somewhat arbitrary, criterion: if subjects give at least three noncoreferential judgments for Prepositional Phrase Preposing and Topicalization sentences on the comprehension task and at least two noncoreferential judgments for these sentences on the picture judgment task, they can be assigned to the S-attachment category; otherwise, they must be assigned to the S'-attachment category (the binomial probability of five of seven noncoreferential judgments is .227). I will refer to this criterion as the "5-of-7 criterion."

The central question of this study is whether the ultimate outcome of acquisition reflects the use (at some point) of bracketing input. In this light, data from the adults is of primary importance and therefore will be discussed first. A secondary issue concerns how early the use of bracketed input may be revealed. Data from the children bear on this latter issue, and discussion of these data will follow. Given the complex nature of the crucial stimuli and of the tasks employed, one might expect the child data to be equivocal. Among adults, errors on control sentences for which noncoreferential judgments were required were extremely rare: one subject made one error on an item in the picture judgment task. Responses from the complete set of control sentences were examined to determine whether any subjects were using simple order-based judgment strategies (that is, noun first equals coreferential, pronoun first equals noncoreferential), but none of the adults fell into this category. Data from the adults are presented in table 5.1.

Within-subject analyses of variance revealed that subjects in both conditions differentiated between the two types of preposed-phrase sentences on both tasks. For subjects in the PP-LD group, on the comprehension task, $F(1,11) = 9.48$, $p < .025$; on the picture judgment task, $F(1,11) = 9.27$, $p < .025$. For subjects in the TOP-S' group, on the comprehension task, $F(1,11) = 201.14$, $p < .001$; on the picture judgment task, $F(1,11) = 85.80$, $p < .001$.

From inspection of the data in table 5.1 it should be apparent that subjects made quite different patterns of judgments for Prepositional

Table 5.1
Frequency of judgments by adult subjects (N = 12)

	Task			
	Comprehension		Picture Judgment	
Number of noncoreferential judgments	Prepositional Phrase Preposing	S'-Phrase	Prepositional Phrase Preposing	S'-Phrase
0	0	11	0	12
1	0	1	0	0
2	0	0	0	0
3	1	0	12	0
4	11	0	—	—
	Topicalization	Left Dislocation	Topicalization	Left Dislocation
0	1	1	0	1
1	0	1	1	1
2	1	3	2	5
3	2	3	9	5
4	8	4	—	—

Phrase Preposing and S'-Phrase sentences. Between-subjects analyses of variance confirm this impression: for the comprehension task, $F(1,22) = 1058.00$, $p < .001$; for the picture judgment task, no F ratio could be calculated because there was no within-group variance. Applying the 7-of-7 criterion discussed above, eleven out of twelve subjects had acquired the hypothesized structure for Prepositional Phrase Preposing; by the binomial test, $p = .0032$. Applying the 5-of-7 criterion, all subjects performed as predicted. Thus, we can safely conclude that the adults had learned the predicted structure for these sentences more often than chance.

A somewhat less striking picture emerges from the data on Topicalization sentences. Here neither of the between-subjects analyses of variance for judgments on Topicalization and Left Dislocation sentences attained significance: for the comprehension task, $F(1,22) = 1.66$, NS; for the picture judgment task, $F(1,22) = 2.30$, NS. An inspection of the data suggests that this may be due to the prevalence of noncoreferential judgments on Left Dislocation sentences. Employing the 7-of-7 criterion, eight of the subjects evidenced S-attachment, binomial $p = .1938$. However, employing the 5-of-7 criterion, ten of twelve subjects fell into this category, binomial $p = .0193$. Thus, we can tentatively conclude that subjects have acquired the predicted structure for Topicalization sentences more often than chance. That these results are somewhat weaker than those obtained with Preposi-

Table 5.2
Frequency of judgments by third grade subjects (N = 10)

| | Task | | | |
| Number of noncoreferential judgments | Comprehension | | Picture Judgment | |
	Prepositional Phrase Preposing	S′-Phrase	Prepositional Phrase Preposing	S′-Phrase
0	0	9	0	10
1	1	1	0	0
2	3	0	1	0
3	0	0	9	0
4	6	0	—	—
	(Without "for" sentences)			
0	0			
1	2			
2	8			
	Topicalization	Left Dislocation	Topicalization	Left Dislocation
0	2	4	1	2
1	2	3	4	3
2	2	2	1	2
3	4	1	4	3
4	0	0	—	—

tional Phrase Preposing may be due to the fact that subjects were rather unfamiliar with sentences with Topicalization; several subjects volunteered comments on their unusualness.

Errors on control sentences were somewhat more prevalent among third graders; however, only one subject (in the PP-LD group) made more than one error. In addition, one subject in the TOP-S′ group appeared to be using a simple order-based strategy (it was later discovered that this subject's first language was not English). Data from the entire group of third graders are presented in table 5.2; data from this group omitting these two subjects are presented in table 5.3. Separate analyses were performed including and excluding these two subjects. Since there were no differences in the results of these two analyses, only the results from the analysis including all subjects will be presented.

All within-subject analyses of variance were significant. For the PP-LD group, on the comprehension task, $F(1,9) = 30.38, p < .001$; on the picture judgment task, $F(1,9) = 12.57, p < .01$. For the TOP-S′ group, on the comprehension task, $F(1,9) = 16.15, p < .01$; on the

Table 5.3
Frequency of judgments by third grade subjects (excluding subjects making more than one error or using an order-based strategy) (N = 9)

Number of noncoreferential judgments	Task			
	Comprehension		Picture Judgment	
	Prepositional Phrase Preposing	S'-Phrase	Prepositional Phrase Preposing	S'-Phrase
0	0	8	0	9
1	1	1	0	0
2	3	0	1	0
3	0	0	8	0
4	5	0	—	—
	(Without "for" sentences)			
0	0			
1	2			
2	7			
	Topicalization	Left Dislocation	Topicalization	Left Dislocation
0	1	4	0	2
1	2	2	4	2
2	2	2	1	2
3	4	1	4	3
4	0	0	—	—

picture judgment task, $F(1,9) = 25.14$, $p < .001$. Third graders differentiated between different types of preposed-phrase sentences.

From inspection of the data in table 5.2 it seems that third grade subjects gave different patterns of judgments for Prepositional Phrase Preposing and S'-Phrase sentences. This is confirmed by between-subjects analyses of variance: for the comprehension task, $F(1,18) = 58.69$, $p < .001$; for the picture judgment task, $F(1,18) = 841.00$, $p < .001$. At least in the comprehension task, this may have simply been due to subjects' consistent coreferential judgments for S'-Phrase sentences. In fact, employing either criterion, only six of ten subjects can be assigned to the S-attachment category, and this is not significantly different from what would be expected by chance, binomial $p = .377$.

However, there is a striking discrepancy between judgments on Prepositional Phrase Preposing sentences across the two tasks: judgments were much less consistent on the comprehension task. On this task nine out of forty total judgments on these sentences were scored as coreferential. A closer inspection of the data reveals that seven of these nine coreferential judgments were given on sentences in which a "for" prepositional phrase was preposed. This was the one type of sentence for which children volunteered comments that they did not understand (the "for" in these sentences should be interpreted as meaning "on behalf of"). Thus, a further analysis was conducted, excluding these "for" sentences from the acting-out data. On the remaining sentences eight of ten subjects gave only noncoreferential judgments; the other two subjects split their judgments. By either criterion, these eight subjects can be assigned to the S-attachment category. This falls just short of significance, binomial $p = .0547$.

If we consider the picture judgment task alone, significant differences do emerge. Employing a criterion of 3 noncoreferential judgments on 3 trials, nine of ten subjects can be assigned to the S-attachment category, binomial $p = .0107$; employing a criterion of 2 noncoreferential judgments on 3 trials, all ten subjects can be assigned to this category, binomial $p = .0010$. The inclusion of only ten subjects severely restricts the power of the binomial test to reveal differences. Clearly, there seems to be a trend toward S-attachment in the data. Taking all this into consideration, we may tentatively conclude that a majority of third graders have acquired the S-attachment structure; more data will be required to confirm this.

The data in table 5.2 clearly do not support the contention that third graders have acquired the S-attachment structure for Topicalization sentences. Neither of the between-subjects analyses of variance is significant: for the comprehension task, $F(1,18) = 2.44$, $p > .05$; for the picture judgment task, $F(1,18) = 0.15$, $p > .05$. By the 7-of-7 criterion, no subjects can be assigned to the S-attachment category; by the 5-of-7 criterion, only four may be. In either case fewer than half the subjects demonstrated acquisition of the predicted structure. If adults are typically unfamiliar with Topicalization constructions, it is reasonable that children should be even more so. Thus, the most plausible interpretation of these results is that children have not yet acquired any particular structures for these sentences: Topicalization is a late acquisition.

Second graders were much more prone to make errors than adults or third graders, making twenty-one errors in total. Six subjects, four in the PP-LD group and two in the TOP-S' group, made multiple errors. Separate analyses, including and excluding these subjects, were conducted and are discussed below. The data for all second grade subjects are presented in table 5.4; the data for second graders excluding these six subjects are presented in table 5.5.

Table 5.4
Frequency of judgments by second grade subjects (N = 10)

	Task			
	Comprehension		Picture Judgment	
Number of noncoreferential judgments	Prepositional Phrase Preposing	S'-Phrase	Prepositional Phrase Preposing	S'-Phrase
0	1	10	1	8
1	1	0	1	2
2	3	0	3	0
3	3	0	5	0
4	2	0	—	—
	(Without "for" sentences)			
0	2			
1	3			
2	5			
	Topicalization	Left Dislocation	Topicalization	Left Dislocation
0	6	4	3	3
1	2	1	4	4
2	1	3	2	1
3	1	0	1	2
4	0	2	—	—

For the inclusive analysis, within-subject analyses of variance showed significant differences for both groups on the picture judgment task, but for neither group on the comprehension task. For the PP-LD group, on the comprehension task, $F(1,9) = 3.86$, NS; on the picture judgment task, $F(1,9) = 9.00$, $p < .025$. For the TOP-S' group, on the comprehension task, $F(1,9) = 4.36$, NS; on the picture judgment task, $F(1,9) = 6.69$, $p < .05$. Similar results were found in the exclusive analysis. Given these results, it is not clear whether second graders differentiated between different types of preposed-phrase sentences.

Between-subjects analyses of variance for Prepositional Phrase Preposing and S'-Phrase sentences showed significant differences: for the comprehension task, $F(1,18) = 36.00$, $p < .001$; for the picture judgment task, $F(1,18) = 32.14$, $p < .001$. An inspection of table 5.4 should make it clear that these differences, at least on the comprehension task, were primarily due to these subjects' consistent coreferential judgments for S'-Phrase sentences. There is little indication that second graders had learned the predicted attachment for Prepositional Phrase Preposing: even using the 5-of-7 criterion, only five of ten subjects

Table 5.5
Frequency of judgments by second grade subjects (excluding subjects making more than one error) (N(PP-LD) = 6; N(TOP-S') = 8)

| Number of noncoreferential judgments | Task | | | |
| | Comprehension | | Picture Judgment | |
	Prepositional Phrase Preposing	S'-Phrase	Prepositional Phrase Preposing	S'-Phrase
0	0	8	0	6
1	0	0	0	2
2	3	0	1	0
3	2	0	5	0
4	1	0	—	—
	(Without "for" sentences)			
0	0			
1	2			
2	4			
	Topicalization	Left Dislocation	Topicalization	Left Dislocation
0	5	1	2	1
1	1	1	3	2
2	1	2	2	1
3	1	0	1	2
4	0	2	—	—

could be assigned to the S-attachment category. This pattern does not change if we exclude the "for" phrase sentences from the acting-out task data: five children gave consistent noncoreferential judgments on the two remaining sentences, three children gave split judgments, and two children gave consistent coreferential judgments for these sentences.

However, if we consider only the picture judgment data for Prepositional Phrase Preposing sentences, employing a criterion of 2 noncoreferential judgments on 3 trials, eight of ten children might be assigned to the S-attachment category. This hints that second graders may have learned the predicted attachment, but there is no other supporting evidence for this conclusion in table 5.4. A slightly different picture emerges if we consider only the data from subjects who did not make multiple errors (see table 5.5). Applying the 2-of-3 criterion to the picture judgment data, all six of the remaining subjects in the PP-LD group could be assigned to the S-attachment category. If we consider the data from the complete set of comprehension Prepositional Phrase

Preposing sentences for these subjects, it appears that at most three could be assigned to the S-attachment category, but if we exclude the preposed "for" sentences, four of six could be assigned to this category. This result is not sufficiently extreme to support a significant result, binomial $p = .344$, but, given the small sample size, this is not surprising. A comparison of tables 5.4 and 5.5 suggests that subjects who made errors were most likely to give coreferential judgments for Prepositional Phrase Preposing sentences, whereas subjects not making errors tended to give noncoreferential judgments, as predicted. In turn, this suggests that second graders may have acquired the predicted attachment for these sentences by the time they have learned structure-based rules for interpreting pronouns, although additional data are clearly required to support this conjecture.

The second graders' data show no differences at all between Topicalization and Left Dislocation sentences. For the data in table 5.4, both between-subjects tests were nonsignificant: for the comprehension task, $F(1,18) = 1.77$, NS; for the picture judgment task, $F(1,18) = 0.04$, NS. Using the 5-of-7 criterion, only one subject can be assigned to the S-attachment category. Similar results were found in the analysis of the data in table 5.5. In short, there is no evidence that second graders have acquired the predicted structure for Topicalization sentences. This is hardly surprising: if older children have not yet learned this construction, one would not expect younger children to have, either.

The results of this study indicate that adults have learned the predicted S-attachment for both Prepositional Phrase Preposing and Topicalization sentences. Thus, the primary hypothesis of this study was confirmed. Third graders and perhaps second graders have also learned the predicted attachment for Prepositional Phrase Preposing sentences, but they appear to have not yet acquired any particular structure for Topicalization sentences. If only distributionally derived bracketing information were available in input, one would expect all three groups to be evenly split on acquired structures for these types of sentences. The results suggest instead that at some point in acquisition, for at least some types of structures, nondistributional bracketing information is available in input.

Certain limitations of these results should be noted. First, because of the nature of the experimental tasks, older subjects were used; furthermore, the particular constructions tested may be relatively late acquisitions. Therefore, it is not clear from this study whether bracketing information is necessarily employed in early stages of acquisition. On the other hand, the results of the second experiment in chapter 4 do indicate that children younger than those tested here can reliably bracket sentences they hear, at least when clear prosodic cues to the bracketing are present. Thus, the earlier use of bracketing information is certainly plausible.

Second, only one structural contrast was tested (attachment to S versus attachment to S'); thus, it is not necessarily the case that bracketing information is available for all structural positions. In a sense, however, this particular contrast is the least likely to be distinguished by such evidence: of all the possible sources of bracketing information, in English only prosody may distinguish between these two possible attachments. For other structural positions, additional potential sources of information are available (for example, function words, fragments, expansions, and partial-plus repetitions). Thus, it may be possible to generalize the present findings to different types of sentence structures as well.

Third, in arguing that distributional evidence alone cannot distinguish the attachments for the types of sentences considered here, I ignored certain other possibilities. One such possibility is that constructions like Topicalization and Prepositional Phrase Preposing are universally (that is, biologically determined to be) S-attachments. However, if this were the case, one should expect little, if any, variance in obtained judgments. This is clearly not the case with respect to (for instance) second and third graders' judgments on Topicalization sentences. A second possibility is that distributional evidence, coupled with a theory restricting possible points of attachment, might suffice. Such a theory—a "landing site" theory of movement rules—has been proposed by Baltin (1982). If correct, Baltin's theory might undercut the conclusions I have made here. However, I shall argue that this theory is inadequate.

In Baltin's theory movement transformations are restricted to the form "Move α to *," where α is a variable ranging over grammatical categories, and * is a point of adjunction drawn from a universal set of potential landing sites. There are six possible landing sites, defined by a category feature plus a location feature: possible categories are VP, S, and S', and possible locations are left periphery or right periphery. For example, in this theory Topicalization could be formulated as "Move NP to left periphery of S," and Left Dislocation could be formulated as "Move NP to left periphery of S'."

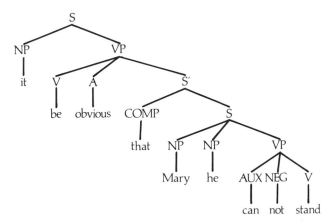

Tree 5.12

Assuming that movements to particular positions cannot be iterated and that *COMP* cannot be doubly filled, then in order to learn the correct point of attachment for Topicalization or Prepositional Phrase Preposing, it suffices merely to have input that indicates that the preposed phrase cannot be moved to the left periphery of *S'* (since the only remaining possibility is left periphery of *S*). (62) exemplifies one possible datum; the derived structure of this sentence is given as tree 5.12.

(62) It is obvious that Mary, he can't stand.

Here, because the *COMP* position is already filled (with "that"), "Mary" cannot be moved to the left periphery of *S'*. By process of elimination, only attachment to *S* is possible.

However, evidence exists suggesting that Baltin's inventory of landing sites may be incomplete. As a case in point, consider the movement of adverbial prepositional phrases (for example, "although" and "if" phrases). In matrix clauses adverbial prepositional phrases can be moved to the left periphery of *S'*. This follows from the fact that they may precede *wh*-words, as in (63). Note also that nouns in such phrases can be coreferential with pronominal matrix subjects, as in (64).

(63) If she really has a crush on John, why does Susan bad-mouth him?

(64) If Susan did like him, she would have nice things to say.

Baltin asserts that preposed adverbial prepositional phrases can also be adjoined to *S;* as evidence, he notes that such phrases can be preposed in embedded clauses, as in (65).

(65) Susan thinks that because John wears loafers, he is a nerd.

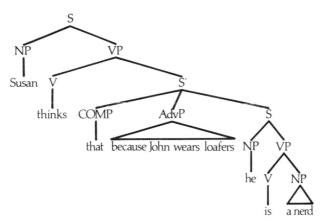

Tree 5.13

However, the only basis for considering the "because" phrase to be adjoined to *S* here is the landing site theory itself. Otherwise, there is no reason to argue that preposed adverbial prepositional phrases should be attached to different nodes in matrix and embedded clauses. Moreover, "he" can be coreferential with "John" in (65); if the "because" clauses were attached to *S*, this should not be possible. This suggests that the derived structure of (65) is best represented as shown in tree 5.13. (Alternatively, the prepositional phrase could be a daughter of *COMP*.)

Since preposed adverbial phrases can apparently be attached to *S'* in embedded clauses, there is no reason why this should not be possible for preposed noun or prepositional phrases. Consider again (62). Given the additional landing site illustrated in tree 5.13, this datum can no longer unambiguously indicate whether the topicalized "Mary" is attached to *S* or *S'*. Therefore, even granting a restriction on possible landing sites, distributional evidence alone will not suffice to indicate the correct point of attachment for Topicalization or Prepositional Phrase Preposing.

In sum, the results of this study indicate that bracketing information is available at some point in acquisition and is used in acquiring at least certain constructions. Of course, Topicalization and Prepositional Phrase Preposing are hardly central to the syntax of English; these results do not indicate the extent to which such information is employed, particularly in early stages of acquisition. The following study suggests that bracketing information may be required for the acquisition of fundamental aspects of syntax.

Bracketed Input and Acquisition of a Miniature Language

One of the early suggestions for the use of miniature languages as a tool in discovering properties of natural languages crucial for acquisition came from Chomsky (1965):

Systems can certainly be invented that fail the conditions, formal and substantive, that have been proposed as tentative linguistic universals. . . . In principle, one might try to determine whether invented systems that fail these conditions do pose inordinately difficult problems for language learning, and do fall beyond the domain for which the language-acquisition system is designed. (p. 55)

The study described here (Morgan, Meier, and Newport 1986, Experiment 1) investigated whether phrase-bracketing information in input is required for the acquisition of certain aspects of syntax. Acquisition of a language when input included such information was contrasted with acquisition of the same language when input was identical except for the absence of nondistributional cues to bracketing.

Our concern here was not with the acquisition of transformational rules, but rather with the acquisition of rules concerning cooccurrence relations among word classes. To be sure, transformations form but one aspect of natural language grammars. In addition to defining relations among sentences, the syntax of a language must define several other characteristics of sentence structure. Perhaps the most obvious of these are rules concerning the linear structures of sentences: all languages have constraints on what words can and must occur in sentences, and most languages have constraints on the orders in which words can appear. Though some of these rules can be expressed in unconditional terms—in English every sentence must have a main verb—most must be expressed conditionally—an article may appear in a sentence only if there is an associated noun. These dependencies—cooccurrence relations—hold between classes of words, rather than individual words. Typically, the domain of such dependencies is the phrase; indeed, networks of cooccurrence relations supply the primary internal justification for the phrase structure analysis of natural languages. Our hypothesis was that cues in input to the domains within which dependencies hold may be necessary for the learning of the dependencies themselves.

Early artificial language studies using semantically empty, stripped-down linguistic systems showed that subjects were able to learn both the absolute positions of classes of words (actually, nonsense syllables)

(Braine 1963, Smith 1963, 1966) and the positions of classes of words relative to single marker elements (Braine 1966). However, subjects exposed to this type of system did not learn dependencies holding between classes. Smith (1969), for example, found that subjects presented with strings of the form MN or PQ (where M, N, P, and Q denote word classes) produced at recall a high proportion of ungrammatical MQ and PN strings. Thus, even very simple dependencies apparently could not be learned on the basis of distributional analyses alone.

Moeser and Bregman (1972) hypothesized that the learning of dependent relations in syntax might be possible only when these relations reflected properties of the world to which the language referred. Consequently, they created a miniature linguistic system that incorporated a reference world; subjects in their study were exposed to a sample of the language under differing conditions of reference world organization. In one condition the reference world contained information only about the class membership of the words of the language. In a second condition the reference world was organized so that linguistic dependencies were represented as conceptual dependencies between referents. For example, the referent of one word might be a rectangle, whereas the referent of another word, dependent on the first, might be a sort of border variation. Moeser and Bregman found that subjects in both conditions mastered the simplest linear aspects of the syntax, but only subjects in the second condition learned the dependencies.

In Morgan and Newport 1981 we hypothesized that Moeser and Bregman's results were due not to the conceptual portrayal of syntactic dependencies in the reference world, but rather to the cues to phrase structure that were provided by depicting referents of dependent words as single, complex figures. We tested our hypothesis by replicating Moeser and Bregman's two conditions and introducing a third condition in which the referents of words were simple, independent figures spatially grouped in correspondence with the phrasal groupings of words in the input sentences. Subjects in this new condition performed just as well as did subjects in the conceptual dependency condition.

The essential idea of Morgan and Newport 1981 was that bracketed input might be required for the acquisition of dependencies. But the way in which bracketing information was encoded in that study—via the spatial arrangement of referents—did not correspond to any of the cues to bracketing normally available in the input to natural language learning. In subsequent studies we have been interested in investigating whether alternative cues to phrase bracketing might be equally effective in promoting the learning of syntax. The study described below examined whether the learning of syntactic dependencies would be facilitated when the input to language learning included bracketing information encoded by prosody (see the first experiment in chapter 4 for a description of prosodic cues to phrase bracketing in natural language).

Method

College students enrolled in a general psychology course served as subjects in this experiment. Thirteen subjects were assigned to each of three intonation conditions.

In all conditions the same target language was employed. This was a finite (nonrecursive) language including about 10,000 possible strings. The strings of this language could be generated by a simple set of phrase structure rules, including in part the following:

$$S \Rightarrow AP + BP + (CP)$$

$$BP \Rightarrow \begin{Bmatrix} E \\ CP + F \end{Bmatrix}$$

AP, BP, and *CP* were three types of phrases, and *E* and *F* were among the lexical categories of the language. Each of these lexical categories contained several nonsense syllable words, and each of the words in the vocabulary of the language was paired with a particular nonsense shape referent, so that the referents of words in a particular category shared some characteristic (for example, referents of one category of words were rectangles of various colors).

The strings of the language possessed both unconditional and conditional characteristics. As an example of the former, all strings had to include either a word from class *E* or a word from class *F*. As an example of the latter, if a string contained a word from class *F*, that word had to be preceded by the words constituting a *C* phrase. We expected that only those subjects who received an overt phrase-bracketing cue in their input would be entirely successful in acquiring the conditional aspects of the syntax.

A small set of sentences was chosen to be the language input, and these sentences were presented to subjects one at a time. The words of a sentence and their accompanying referents appeared on a slide; simultaneously, the sentence was spoken by a recorded voice. Input in all three conditions included the same set of sentences; the conditions differed from one another only in the prosodic patterns that were used in pronouncing the sentences.

In the first condition, *Monotone Intonation,* each sentence was spoken as if the words of the sentence formed a simple list. This condition tested whether purely linear information is sufficient to support learning of syntax. In the second condition, *Arbitrary Intonation,* sentences were spoken with an English-like intonation, using prosody to group words into units. These units were consistent across the input but did not conform to the units of the phrase structure grammar. This condition was included as a control for purely memorial effects of grouping. In the third condition, *Phrase Intonation,* sentences were spoken with an English-like intonation, using prosody to group words into units conforming to the constituents of the phrase structure grammar. This was the experimental condition, testing whether phrase-bracketing information is required to promote learning of syntax.

Subjects were exposed to the entire input set four times; after each exposure they were given a battery of tests. Each presentation of input with accompanying tests constituted a trial. One type of test, the *Rules Tests,* was designed to measure subjects' knowledge of the unconditional and conditional aspects of the syntax. Items on this type of test each included two novel strings that were identical except for the presence of a single error in the incorrect alternative. Subjects were required to judge which of the two alternatives was a grammatical string in the language.

A second type of test, the *Constituent Tests,* was designed to measure subjects' knowledge of the phrase structure of the language. These tests required subjects either to judge which of two sentence fragments, each consisting of two or three words in grammatical order, formed a better group (the *Fragment Constituent Tests*) or to judge which of two permuted versions of a grammatical string was preferable (the *Transformational Constituent Test*). As was the case with input strings, subjects in all conditions received identical sets of tests. For further details of the basic language, the input set of sentences, the tests, and the general procedure, see Morgan, Meier, and Newport 1986.

Results and Discussion

We divided the data from the Rules Tests into two sets, one comprising items testing unconditional aspects of the syntax and the other comprising items testing conditional aspects of the syntax. The mean per-

Table 5.6
Artificial language experiment Rules Test scores—mean percentage correct

	Unconditional rules				
	Trial 1	Trial 2	Trial 3	Trial 4	Total
Monotone Intonation	69.7	73.6	69.7	75.0	72.0
Arbitrary Intonation	71.6	77.4	80.3	81.8	77.8
Phrase Intonation	71.6	78.9	88.4	90.4	82.3
	Conditional rules				
	Trial 1	Trial 2	Trial 3	Trial 4	Total
Monotone Intonation	53.2	60.3	57.7	65.4	59.1
Arbitrary Intonation	51.9	53.2	59.6	68.6	58.3
Phrase Intonation	65.4	69.8	77.6	84.6	74.3

centage correct for each group on each set of items is shown in table 5.6. Each of the data sets was analyzed using two planned comparisons, the first contrasting the Phrase Intonation and Arbitrary Intonation conditions (isolating the contribution to syntax learning of phrase-bracketing information in input) and the second contrasting the Arbitrary Intonation and Monotone Intonation conditions (isolating the general contribution to syntax learning of grouping information in input).

On the items testing unconditional rules, across the entire set of trials, performance of the Phrase Intonation and Arbitrary Intonation conditions did not differ. On the final trial alone, however, Phrase Intonation subjects were significantly superior to Arbitrary Intonation subjects. Differences in learning of unconditional rules between the Arbitrary Intonation and Monotone Intonation conditions were not significant either across all trials or for the final trial alone. As table 5.6 shows, subjects in all conditions performed well above chance on the unconditional rules, scoring 75% correct or better by the final trial.

In contrast, as we expected, performance on items testing conditional rules of the syntax was sharply different across the three conditions. Subjects whose input included prosodic phrase-bracketing cues showed a consistent superiority in the acquisition of these rules, as revealed by the data in table 5.6. Across all trials and for the final trial alone, the Phrase Intonation and Arbitrary Intonation conditions were significantly different. However, the presence of nonphrasal grouping cues in input made no contribution to the learning of conditional rules: performance of the Arbitrary Intonation and Monotone Intonation conditions did not differ. By the final trial the Phrase Intonation condi-

Table 5.7
Artificial language experiment Constituent Tests scores—mean percentage correct

	Fragment Test 1	Fragment Test 2	Transformational Test
Monotone Intonation	60.0	49.7	50.6
Arbitrary Intonation	39.1	33.0	48.7
Phrase Intonation	76.0	83.7	74.4

tion averaged almost 85% correct on the conditional rules; several subjects were at ceiling. In contrast, no subject in either of the other two conditions was ever at ceiling. In fact, the performance of the Arbitrary Intonation and Monotone Intonation groups on the final trial was similar to the Phrase Intonation group's performance on the first trial.

Mean percentage correct for each group on the Fragment Constituent Tests and the Transformational Constituent Test is given in table 5.7. The results of the Constituent Tests were analyzed with the same planned comparisons used for analyzing the Rules Test data. On all three tests the Phrase Intonation condition was significantly better than the Arbitrary Intonation condition. On the Transformational Constituent Test the Arbitrary Intonation and Monotone Intonation conditions did not differ. Interestingly, however, the Arbitrary Intonation condition performed significantly worse than the Monotone Intonation condition on the two Fragment Constituent Tests. A fine-grained analysis of these data revealed that subjects in the Arbitrary Intonation condition had learned the consistent, but arbitrary, groups cued in their input.

Summary and Conclusions   This experiment demonstrates that the presence in the input to language learning of prosodic cues to phrase structure can significantly enhance the acquisition of syntax. Subjects in all three input conditions learned the word-referent pairings and at least some aspects of the linear structure of the miniature language. However, subjects in the Phrase Intonation input condition showed somewhat better learning of the unconditional aspects of syntax and markedly superior acquisition of the more complex, conditional rules of the grammar.

Furthermore, results from the Constituent Tests indicate that subjects in the Phrase Intonation condition succeeded in learning the phrases of the language. Subjects in the Arbitrary Intonation condition also learned the groupings of words evident in their input, though these did not correspond to phrases. However, this knowledge availed them little: these subjects did not differ in rule learning from those in the Monotone Intonation condition, who failed to learn any consistent groupings whatsoever. This pattern of results indicates that it is not the induction of grouping per se, but rather a particular type of induced grouping—the grouping of words into phrases—that is critically related to the acquisition of syntactic rules. Moreover, the induction of phrases appears to be dependent on the presence of bracketing information in input.

The results of this study are similar to those reported in Morgan and Newport 1981. Morgan, Meier, and Newport 1986, presents two additional studies examining the efficacy of other types of phrase-bracketing cues. In the experimental condition of one study bracketing information was encoded by the addition of function-word-like elements to input (single-letter words without referents). In the second study bracketing information was encoded by the introduction of concord morphology, in which the elements of each phrase received identical, rhyming suffixes. The results of these two studies parallel those described above: subjects receiving bracketing information were most successful in learning the syntax of the language. The similarities in the results of these studies suggest that the particular way in which bracketing information is cued is relatively unimportant, so long as some such cue is present in input. Moreover, these last two studies suggest that bracketing information enhances acquisition even when the cue used to encode it adds objective complexity to input.

At the beginning of this chapter I noted that there are two major obstacles to the straightforward generalization from artificial language study results to natural language learning. The first problem is that the linguistic systems used in such studies are quite impoverished in comparison with natural systems, and this impoverishment may change the nature of the learning task. The second problem is that adults may approach the artificial language learning task in a quite different way than children approach natural language learning. I will discuss each of these in turn.

First of all, extreme impoverishment of a linguistic system may have strikingly adverse effects on learning: this conclusion follows from the early negative results concerning dependency learning in artificial languages (see Smith 1969). In a sense, our argument amounts to the claim that bracketing information supplies the dimension of richness required for such learning to succeed. Beyond this, the linguistic system we have used is much less rich than any natural language. In contrast to natural languages, our language was nonrecursive and therefore finite. In most studies our language lacked morphological and phonological systems. The lexicon was extremely simple and had no sort of internal structure. Syntactically, our language was much simpler than any natural language: there were no pronominal forms, no transformations, no case or tense/aspect marking (note that many of these omitted syntactic devices would supply additional cues to phrase bracketing). Finally, the world to which the language made reference was entirely static, and the language was not used communicatively.

It appears to me that there are two ways in which increased richness might affect the nature of learning. First, such richness might supply additional information for the induction of aspects of syntax. With regard to the learning of dependencies among word classes, on which our studies focused, there are three sorts of relevant information. First, there is bracketing information, whose relevance to the acquisition of dependencies we have clearly demonstrated. Natural languages typically possess multiple, correlated cues to bracketing, rather than single cues such as we investigated. However, one would hardly expect multiple cues to make weaker contributions to learning; on these grounds, our results must be generalizable. The second sort of relevant information is distributional evidence. In all conditions in all our studies sufficient distributional evidence was available to support the induction of both phrases and dependencies among word classes. Yet such induction succeeded only when the distributional evidence was supplemented with cues to bracketing. This suggests that unaided distributional analysis presented too complex a task to our subjects, so it is unlikely that simply providing more evidence (additional input sentences), which would make the task even more complex, would enhance learning. Natural languages do include different types of evidence relevant to distributional analyses—patterns of pronominalization and transformational relations among sentences, to name two—but these types of evidence primarily supply additional cues to phrase bracketing. If it were discovered that, for example, the inclusion of pro-forms in language input enhanced acquisition of dependencies, this would certainly be consistent with our claims. Third, dependencies in natural language syntax often reflect semantic dependencies. Here the results of Morgan and Newport 1981 are most relevant: there we showed that the cuing of dependencies in the conceptual organization of a reference world supplies no enhancement to the learning of syntactic dependencies beyond that provided by the cuing of phrase boundaries. In sum, there is no reason to believe that the presence of additional, nonbracketing information in natural languages lessens the need for phrase-bracketing information in the acquisition of linguistic dependencies.

Second, it is possible that the increased richness of natural languages and natural language input causes more powerful learning abilities to be recruited. Such learning abilities might not require bracketing information. This is certainly possible, but there is absolutely no evidence to support this contention. In the absence of such evidence, it is most parsimonious to assume that similar learning abilities are recruited in both the natural and the artificial language learning situations.

The issue of learning abilities brings us back to the second difficulty in interpreting the results of artificial language studies: adults and children generally have different learning abilities, so that the discovery of factors affecting adults' learning may not be applicable to children's learning. With regard to most sorts of problem-solving tasks, adults' abilities are more powerful than children's; therefore, if we find that the absence of some sort of information inhibits adults' success, we might expect this finding to apply a fortiori to children.

However, it is also possible that the abilities adults used in our artificial language learning task are qualitatively different from those used by children in language acquisition. Most obviously, it is unlikely that children approach language learning as a conscious problem-solving task. In an effort to discover how adults had gone about learning our language, we interviewed many of our subjects at the end of our experimental sessions. Such self-reports are of course not completely reliable, but they indicated that adults did not successfully apply conscious problem-solving strategies to artificial language learning, either. Many subjects reported that they had initially attempted to formulate and test specific hypotheses about the language, but that they found this too difficult to do. In their descriptions of what they did on the tests subjects typically reported that they had either guessed or chosen alternatives on some vague intuitive basis. Finally, even those subjects who had learned all the dependency rules of the language (as measured by their performance) often could not state what those rules were.

In short, adults, like children learning natural languages, may have learned our language intuitively; whatever the nature of these intuitive learning abilities, they appear to thrive on bracketed input.

Chapter 6
Open Questions

In this chapter I wish to comment briefly on several unresolved issues relating to the Bracketed Input Hypothesis. First, the learnability proof in chapter 3 was based on a specific grammatical model—standard transformational grammar—and the results of this proof conceivably could be limited to this model. Whether bracketed input is required for the acquisition of nontransformational grammars is an open question, but there may be reason to believe that such information will be relevant, if not necessary, for acquisition in other grammatical theories as well. Second, the Bracketed Input Hypothesis entails that children be able to reconstruct some of the bracketing of some of the sentences they hear. I will discuss how this hypothesis might be further specified, with an eye on restricting the amount of information required. Third, learnability is but one condition that a successful theory of language acquisition must satisfy. In addition, such a theory must provide an accurate developmental account. At this point, we should work toward developing accounts that satisfy both requirements. To this end, I will discuss the prospects for deriving predictions concerning sequences of acquisition and errors in acquisition from learnability models.

The Bracketed Input Hypothesis and Nontransformational Grammars

The Degree 2 and Degree 1 Learnability proofs both bear on the acquisition of standard transformational grammars. There is an excellent chance that in reality children acquire some quite different grammatical system. It is possible that many of the assumptions incorporated in these proofs will turn out to be irrelevant for the acquisition of nontransformational grammars. Here I wish to argue that the Bracketed Input Hypothesis will not be one such assumption.

The past fifteen years have witnessed a substantial proliferation of grammatical theories. I cannot hope to discuss all of these here; rather, I will confine my remarks to the two currently most prominent non-transformational theories of grammar: Gazdar's (1982) context-free grammar, known as Generalized Phrase Structure Grammar (GPSG), and Bresnan's (1978, 1982) Lexical-Functional Grammar (LFG).

First, though, note that all present grammatical theories require that speakers have acquired syntactic knowledge of surface structures. If we grant that speakers can use nonlinguistic context to construct accurate representations of the meanings encoded by input sentences (and may construct base structures or the equivalent therefrom), then in one sense transformational grammars generating such surface structures should be the easiest to acquire, because they admit the richest definition of distributional evidence. (That is, in transformational grammars different types of sentences are explicitly related, whereas this is not always true in other types of grammars.) Thus, if we find that the inclusion of some type of information in language input simplifies the acquisition of transformational grammars, this should hold true, a fortiori, for nontransformational grammars. At this point, I cannot show that bracketing information is necessary for the acquisition of nontransformational grammars, but I will argue that the availability of information revealing details of surface structure must at least simplify such acquisition.

In GPSG surface structures are generated directly. The rules of this grammar have two parts: the first is a standard context-free phrase structure expansion rule, and the second is a Montague Grammar interpretation rule. Thus, each surface structure phrase is associated with a certain type of interpretation. In arguing for his theory, Gazdar noted that one benefit of context-free grammars is that they may easily be shown to be "learnable." As evidence for this claim, he cited work by Thatcher (1967, 1973). The key assumption that Thatcher made that allows identifiability of context-free grammars was that input must consist of surface structures rather than simple strings; Levy and Joshi (1978) demonstrated that the crucial aspect of Thatcher's assumption was that input contain bracketing information. In fact, other assumptions incorporated in both Thatcher's and Levy and Joshi's work remove their models from the realm of learnability; so far as I know, there currently exists no learning theory for GPSG. It appears to me, however, that with regard to GPSG there is only one possible alternative to bracketed input as a basis for induction of context-free rules:

namely, correspondences between semantic interpretations and syntactic structures.

A learning theory incorporating a "semantic bootstrapping hypothesis" for the induction of phrase structure rules has been developed for lexical-functional grammars.[1] The core of LFG is the lexicon, which contains in part information about the thematic arguments required by each predicative entry, along with the grammatical role filled by each argument. For example, the verb "hit" takes agent and patient arguments, which are canonically realized as subject and object of the verb. In conjunction with the constraints of X' theory (see Jackendoff 1977), grammatical information in the lexicon specifies the nature of c(onstituent)-structures of sentences; the thematic information contributes to the specification of f(unctional)-structures, which receive semantic interpretation. Pinker (1982) presented a proof showing that lexical-functional grammars are function learnable (see chapter 2). However, this proof failed to show either what complexity of input is required for learning of such grammars or how particular c-structure (surface structure) rules are acquired. Pinker did sketch a model of how some c-structure rules might be acquired, but this was not incorporated in any way in his proof. Pinker 1984 extends and elaborates this earlier work but provides no rigorous proof. Nevertheless, it is interesting to consider the status of the Bracketed Input Hypothesis in relation to Pinker's learning model for LFG.

Pinker's model conceptualizes acquisition of particular rules as occurring in two stages. The first of these incorporates the Semantic Bootstrapping Hypothesis (SBH) and the second involves what Pinker terms "structure-dependent distributional learning." The function of semantic bootstrapping is to provide the child with a means of analyzing unknown syntactic constructions. With regard to the induction of phrase structure rules, Pinker proposes bootstrapping strategies by which the child can guess the syntactic category of unfamiliar words, construct surface structure trees for unfamiliar constructions, and infer the phrase structure rules involved in generating such trees. These strategies are given below.[2]

P1. (a) Build as complete a tree for the string as possible by parsing it with existing phrase structure rules and existing lexical entries, if there are any. (b) For parts of the sentence that do not yet subtend branches of the tree, label the words with the lexical categories that are the canonical grammaticizations of the semantic properties of the word meaning (e.g., noun for thing, verb for action). Build a branch extending each lexical category upward to its maximal projection (i.e., X'' according to the version of X-bar theory adopted here). S is the maximal projection of the head of the sentence. The head of the sentence is the V″ encoding tense, aspect, and modality if there is one among the major constituents in the string; otherwise it is X″, where X is the major predicate of the proposition encoded in the sentence.

P2. (a) Connect the SUBJ noun phrase as the daughter of the root S-node. (b) Connect the remaining branches according to the information in the uncommitted f-structure and the X-bar principles (e.g., functional argument = sister of X, [restrictive] modifier = sister of X′ [nonrestrictive modifier = sister of X″]), and the analogous conditions for specifiers. (c) If the connections mandated by (a) and (b) are impossible without crossing branches, connect the complement one node higher than the specified node. Apply this procedure recursively if necessary.

P3. Create annotated phrase structure rules [see note 1] corresponding to the tree fit onto the sentence by P1-P[2], according to the conventions relating trees to rewrite rules. . . . (pp. 67–68)

Once phrase structure rules have been induced for a novel construction by means of semantic bootstrapping, they can be applied in parsing subsequent input. If the once-novel construction appears in the child's input again, this time incorporating an unknown word, the child can now use these previously induced rules to infer the grammatical category of the new word. This process constitutes Pinker's structure-dependent distributional learning component,

"structure-dependent" because it is the distribution of words within constituent or inflectional structures already acquired that triggers learning. This is in contrast to learning procedures based on the distribution of entities in particular serial positions or in particular adjacency or co-occurrence relations with other words. . . . (p. 42)

Note that semantic bootstrapping is recruited only in the initial learning of constructions, whereas the brunt of acquisition is borne by distributional learning. An example of one of the strategies involved in structure-dependent distributional learning is given below.

L1. Add entries to the lexicon corresponding to the categorizations of input words defined by the tree [constructed by previously induced phrase structure rules, supplemented when necessary by the bootstrapping strategies noted above], or strengthen any existing lexical categorizations that are identical to the ones defined by the tree. Add subcategorization information to the lexical entries of the argument-taking predicates by examining the functions encoding its arguments in the tree. . . . (p. 68)

Pinker's notion that much of acquisition depends on structured representations of input is nearly equivalent to the Bracketed Input Hypothesis.[3] To be sure, Pinker does not demonstrate that structure-dependency is a necessary aspect of distributional learning. Nevertheless, the (implicit) inclusion of the Bracketed Input Hypothesis in a fairly well worked out learning theory for LFG suggests that bracketed input may indeed contribute to the induction of at least certain types of nontransformational grammars.

Pinker and I do differ in the assumptions we make concerning the original source of bracketing information. In Pinker's model bracketing information is originally recovered from input by means of the child's implicit knowledge of X′ constraints acting in conjunction with the child's apprehension of the semantic functions encoded in input. My assumption throughout has been that surface bracketing information is supplied by a variety of nonsemantic devices, including prosody, phonology, and morphology. This was the only assumption compatible with acquisition of standard transformational grammars, because one of the key assumptions of this grammatical theory is that semantic interpretation relates only to the underlying structure of sentences. If a broader range of possible grammatical theories is considered, however, it becomes possible to formulate both strong and weak versions of the Bracketed Input Hypothesis depending upon whether semantic information is considered to contribute to the child's representation of bracketing. These are stated below.

Bracketed Input Hypothesis—Strong Version (BIH-S): The successful acquisition of syntax on the basis of simple input depends crucially on the child's construction of representations of the surface bracketing of input sentences. Such representations are constructed by means of the child's knowledge of surface structure rules acting in concert with bracketing cues encoded in input. These cues include various prosodic, phonological, and morphological devices but exclude any aspects of the semantic interpretation of input sentences.

Bracketed Input Hypothesis—Weak Version (BIH-W): The successful acquisition of syntax on the basis of simple input depends crucially on the child's construction of representations of the surface bracketing of input sentences. Such representations are constructed by means of the child's knowledge of surface structure rules acting in concert with bracketing cues encoded in input. These cues include various prosodic, phonological, and morphological devices; bracketing information may also be derived from the semantic interpretation of input sentences.

In essence, the weak version of the Bracketed Input Hypothesis allows semantic information to constitute one source of input bracketing cues. The strong version does not allow this possibility. SBH rounds out the picture by claiming that semantic information is the only source of input bracketing cues. How can we decide among these possibilities? There appear to be three possible methods. First, it could be shown that learning theories incorporating one or the other of the stronger hypotheses are inadequate in principle. Second, it could be shown that one or both of the stronger hypotheses entail implausible assumptions. Third, the status of each of these hypotheses could be empirically investigated.

Granting for the moment that both BIH-S and SBH entail plausible assumptions, it is doubtful whether learning theories incorporating one or the other of these hypotheses could be shown in general to be inadequate. This is because such theories incorporate large numbers of additional assumptions; given so many degrees of freedom, it would be truly surprising if theories providing for learnability on the basis of simple data could not be worked out.

On the other hand, questions concerning the plausibility of either of these hypotheses may surely be raised. I have been at some pains throughout to note difficulties with the Bracketed Input Hypothesis. Pinker also provides some pessimistic comments concerning what he calls a " 'prosodic bootstrapping' model":

First of all, it is not clear whether Cooper and Paccia-Cooper's correlations between syntax and prosody are universal, as opposed to being rules of English phonology, and they would have to be universal for the child to be able to exploit them in learning an arbitrary natural language. Furthermore, . . . the effects they sought are quite small in comparison with the effects of intrinsic word length, syllable structure, phonetic composition, sentence length, word frequency, word-finding difficulties, and other confounding factors. Thus the child must have some way of mentally subtracting the effects of all these factors before he or she can invert the syntax-to-speech encoding function and recover the syntactic analyses of sentences. I think it is fairly unlikely that a universally valid subtraction-and-inversion procedure of this sort exists, let alone that it is available to a child who has not yet learned anything about his or her language. (pp. 51–52)

I should point out that I have *not* proposed a "prosodic bootstrapping" hypothesis. First, I have not suggested that syntactic rules can be directly read off the representations created with the aid of bracketing information (as is the case with semantic bootstrapping in Pinker's procedures P1–P3) but more simply that bracketing information allows children to isolate the domains within which their distributional learning strategies operate optimally. Second, I have suggested that bracketing information is typically encoded by the conjunction of several devices, only one of which is prosody. Third, I have not claimed that bracketing information "is available to a child who has not yet learned anything about his or her language"; rather, I assume that children must first make some headway in segmenting speech that they hear into linguistically relevant units before they can begin to analyze the syntax of their language (Pinker makes the same assumption) and that bracketing cues become available as a result of this segmental analysis. Nevertheless, Pinker's remarks are well taken: much work remains to be done in specifying how children may extract nonsemantic bracketing cues from their input.

Close examination of SBH raises similar questions. One problem is that this hypothesis requires that the child be able to map very accurately between input sentences and real-world events. The difficulty is that sentences provide discrete and partial descriptions of events, whereas complete events themselves flow seamlessly into one another. Hence, such mapping depends crucially either on the child's perspicacity in determining which predicates relate to which events or on the sensitivity of the child's interlocutor in providing sentences that correspond to the *exact* focus of the child's attention. This mapping process is extremely complex (see Gleitman 1981 for further discussion of this), and Pinker provides no explicit model of how it may be accomplished. Moreover, it seems unlikely that all necessary aspects of semantic information can be recovered from nonlinguistic context and individual word meanings. For example, the bootstrapping procedure P2(b) requires that the child be able to distinguish between arguments and modifiers of predicates and between restrictive and nonrestrictive modifiers. In a sentence like (1),

(1) Everyone hates the picture of John which is hanging in my living room.

the phrase "which is hanging in my living room" may be taken to be either a restrictive or a nonrestrictive modifier of "picture," depending upon the presuppositions of the speaker and the hearer. (Note that there typically are *prosodic* cues that indicate the status of such modifiers.) Lacking access to the intentions of the speaker, there appears to be no way for the child to accurately determine the attachment of the relative clause on the basis of semantic information alone; it is implausible to attribute to children the unfailing ability to assess the intentions of those who speak to them. In sum, both BIH-S and SBH entail certain implausibilities. The weaknesses of these hypotheses may prove to be largely complementary, suggesting that BIH-W may provide a more satisfactory alternative.

Ultimately, all of these hypotheses must stand or fall on the basis of their empirical support. I have noted that there are three criteria that any input hypothesis must satisfy: the hypothesized input must be adequately available in the child's environment, it must be adequately represented by children learning language, and it must play a demonstrable role in shaping the outcome of acquisition. In chapters 4 and 5 I presented studies bearing on each of these criteria, all of whose results were consistent with at least BIH-W. Pinker (1984) appears to take a somewhat narrower view on what sort of empirical evidence might be relevant to the testing of SBH:

. . . it can be tested empirically only by manipulating the inputs to the child and by ascertaining the nature of the rule system induced. (p. 54)

Pinker notes, however, that such studies can only be carried out in principle, but *gedanken* experiments are an unsatisfactory source of evidence here. The criteria I have proposed are applicable to SBH as well, and there are several approaches that could supply evidence disconfirming this hypothesis. In addition, it seems to me that miniature language studies, despite the difficulties associated with their interpretation, offer an interesting means of testing input hypotheses. The studies that I have carried out provide evidence suggesting that both BIH-S and SBH are incorrect: the results of Morgan and Newport 1981 indicate that bracketing information encoded by means of semantic reference is sufficient to facilitate acquisition of syntax, whereas the studies in Morgan, Meier, and Newport, in preparation, indicate that similar results may obtain given only nonsemantically encoded bracketing information. These results are compatible, however, with BIH-W.

In conclusion, learning theories that have been developed to account for the acquisition of nontransformational grammars or that have been claimed to provide support for certain types of nontransformational grammatical theories uniformly incorporate some variant of the Bracketed Input Hypothesis. The determination of whether bracketed input is necessary for the acquisition of nontransformational grammars (either in principle or for learnability from simple data) must await the development of more rigorous learning models of such grammars. In the interim, however, the fact that BIH (or some close relation) has been included in learning theories for several grammars offers a measure of general support for this hypothesis. The sources of bracketing information in language input have yet to be fully identified, but at this point I suspect that we will discover that the child is designed to take advantage of as many sources of such information as possible.

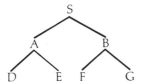

Tree 6.1

On Restricting Assumptions Concerning Input

In this section I will briefly discuss some ways in which the assumptions incorporated in the learnability work discussed above might be restricted. First, with regard to the Bracketed Input Hypothesis, one might ask how much bracketing is required. This will depend in part, of course, on what aspects of grammar bracketed input is considered to contribute to the learning of. So far as the acquisition of transformations alone is concerned, it is not necessary that the child ever construct a complete bracketing for any utterance. Rather, the child must only be able to identify the structural positions to which phrases have been moved; the assumption that children can in fact do so is all that is required for the Degree 1 proof. Typically, this will entail constructing only a partial bracketing; characteristics of surface structure that do not bear on the derived positions of moved phrases will be irrelevant. To illustrate, suppose that in tree 6.1 D is moved so that it becomes a left sister of F (rather than a right sister of E). In this case, in order to formulate a correct movement transformation, the learner must know the location of only two brackets: is the derived string $[E - D] F - G$ or $E [D - F] G$? In the worst case, considering all possible sentences in a language, this means that for every grammatical category that can occur either at the beginning of a phrase or at the end of a preceding phrase, the child must be able to identify where the phrase boundary falls with respect to that category. But this is much less stringent than requiring that children be able to identify the locations of all phrase boundaries. In general, children need not fully parse their input, and this restriction may result in some savings in processing resources.

If attempts to theoretically restrict the points to which phrases may be moved, such as Baltin's (1982) landing site theory, are on the right track, then it may be possible to further restrict the amount of surface structure bracketing the child must construct. That is, as the inventory of possible landing sites is restricted, so too is the number of structural contrasts the child must ever need to identify. In fact, it may turn out that very little surface bracketing information is needed—perhaps only enough (in English) to distinguish between S'- and S-attachment for preposed phrases and S'-, S-, and VP-attachment for postposed phrases. Notice that these contrasts occur toward the beginnings and ends of sentences—positions that, on memorial grounds, we might expect to be salient. Alternatively, it is possible that landing sites are restricted to those whose bracketing can be unambiguously determined on the basis of nondistributional evidence. If potential landing sites are restricted by perceptual considerations, this suggests that different languages may employ different inventories of landing sites.

On the other hand, it may turn out that the processing costs associated with constructing complete parses are not prohibitive. If the possibilities for details of surface structures are sufficiently constrained (for example, by X' theory; see Jackendoff 1977), and if children have knowledge of these constraints (this assumption has been incorporated in Pinker's learnability models), then it is possible that most aspects of surface structure can be reconstructed automatically. Clearly, for mature language users, parsing must be automatized. This has been elegantly demonstrated by Lackner and Garrett (1973), who showed that in a dichotic listening task the content of a sentence presented to the unattended ear can bias the interpretation of an ambiguous sentence presented to the attended ear. Thus, for the language learner, performing a complete parse may result in few costs beyond those incurred by partial parses of less familiar aspects of surface structure, as discussed above.

X' theory and restrictions on movement transformations can do nothing, however, to mitigate the need for base structure (or, in LFG, f-structure) representations. If children are learning a transformational grammar, they need some fully specified structure to which they can apply their derivations. There are two possibilities for what this structure might be: it could be a base structure, as has been assumed throughout, or it could be a surface structure. I believe it would be interesting to investigate whether it might be possible to construct a theory accounting for the acquisition of a parser—that is, a theory in which derivations run "backward" from surface to base structures. Such a theory would require that children be able to construct a more complete bracketing of surface strings in their input than that suggested above, and it would require that there be certain constraints on the form of possible base structures. The child would derive and interpret a permissible base structure for each input string and would check this interpretation against the environment for plausibility. Thus, the construction of base structures would be a function of the child's grammar, rather than of other, presently ill-specified processes. Another difference between this sort of theory and the ones discussed previously is that deterministic generative theories allow structural ambiguity and prohibit paraphrase, whereas the opposite is true for deterministic parsing theories. However, so many details of such a parsing theory remain to be worked out that for the present it seems that in order to allow work to proceed we must accept the base structure assumption (or its equivalent) as necessary for feasible models of language acquisition.

On Deriving Developmental Predictions

One desirable property of a theory of acquisition would be the ability to provide predictions of acquisition sequences and errors. We can define three levels of detail for developmental predictions. At the broadest (and arguably the most important) level a theory should accurately account for the fact that children succeed in acquiring language. At present learnability theories can uniquely lay claim to succeeding in this regard. At an intermediate level we might want to predict the relative order in which constructions or rules are acquired. At the most detailed level we might want to be able to predict how the child's grammar, given that it is in some particular state, will change, given some particular input.

However, the possible explanations at the latter two levels that can be accommodated by the learnability theory I have presented are at present quite restricted. In chapter 1 I presented two models of syntax acquisition: a real-time model (see figure 1.3) and a simplified model underlying learnability theory (see figure 1.4). The difference between these two models is that most of the sources of nonstationarity were removed from the former to produce the latter. The problem here is that it is precisely these sources of nonstationarity that may explain the developmental course of language acquisition. One can imagine a large number of factors that might underlie developmental change, of which I will list but a few: First, the nature of the child's language input may change across time. Second, children's ability to represent the information available in such input will change across time. Third, the child's learning mechanism may be inherently structured in such a way as to produce different developmental stages; for example, the output of analysis of one aspect of syntax may be required as input to the analysis of some other aspect. Fourth, across time, limitations on the child's learning system may change, as, for instance, the child becomes increasingly able to integrate multiple sources of information. Fifth, the constraints on the child's grammatical hypotheses may change with maturation, thus producing developmental change. Sixth, the grammatical system the child is acquiring may have intrinsic constraints on the order in which its rules may be acquired. The first and last of these possibilities apply most directly to present conceptions of learnability theory (although see Pinker 1984 for extensive discussion of the third possibility and Borer and Wexler 1984 for an example of the fifth possibility), but there is little reason to believe that either of these factors has much influence on development.

First, though "fine-tuning" hypotheses have been proposed (for example, by Snow (1972)), there is little evidence to support the contention that children's language development is guided by changes in their input. Newport, Gleitman, and Gleitman (1977), for example, found that when the child's age is controlled for there is no relation between the complexity of the mother's speech and the level of the child's language development. Further discussion of this issue may be found in Wexler and Culicover 1980; let it suffice here to say that explanations for patterns of development must likely be sought elsewhere.

Second, to date most syntactically based predictions of relative order of acquisition have not fared well. A substantial amount of data, from investigations of both development and sentence processing, has been amassed against the Derivational Theory of Complexity (for a review, see Fodor, Bever, and Garrett 1974). Brown and Hanlon's (1970) theory of Cumulative Derivational Complexity has not fared much better: this theory offers few syntactically based predictions that would not be made on other grounds (for example, relative sentence length), and the available evidence appears to be equivocal for instances in which clearly divergent predictions are made (for details, see Maratsos 1983).

Two general difficulties beset syntactically based predictions of acquisition order. First, such predictions are necessarily tied to particular grammatical models. If the underlying model is incorrect, specific predictions must also be incorrect, even if this general strategy is on the right track. To take an example, Smith (1961) proposed that adjectives should be derived from relative clauses. On this view, the phrase in (2) is derived from the phrase in (3).

(2) the red dog

(3) the dog which is red

Smith's proposal was incorporated in Chomsky's (1965) grammar, but shortly thereafter passed out of linguistic favor. The developmental prediction following from this proposal is clear, and clearly wrong: children should use phrases like (3) before they use prenominal adjectives. On the other hand, if this proposal is not in the theory of grammar, no such prediction follows. Nevertheless, psycholinguists have continued to point to this incorrect prediction as providing evidence against syntax-based predictions of acquisition in general. For the most part, the theories generating predictions for which contradicting evidence has been found have long ago been superseded. However, there is still no general consensus among linguists as to what constitutes a correct descriptive theory of syntax; moreover, as theories of grammar have tended to become less abstract, predictions following uniquely from syntactic considerations have become fewer and fewer.

The second difficulty is perhaps even more intractable than the first. Predictions based on models of mature syntactic competence can be expected to hold for children only insofar as the generalizations incorporated in children's grammars correspond to those in the mature grammar. Through the last decade or more, controversy has raged around the question of how to correctly characterize the rules of children's grammars. The evidence does not seem to be sufficient to support the contention that children's early rules are syntactic in nature (see Maratsos 1983 for a review). On the other hand, if we grant that adults' rules are syntactic whereas children's are not, it is not clear how to account for the required transition (see Gleitman and Wanner 1982; Pinker (1984) also discusses this problem under the rubric of the *continuity hypothesis*). But even if we know that, say, the child's rules are syntactic in nature, this does not guarantee that the particular rules in the child's grammar will correspond to those in the mature grammar. For example, Brown and Hanlon's theory predicts that passive questions should appear later than either declarative passives or active questions, but this prediction holds only if the child forms passive questions by iterating the operations of question formation and passive formation. On the other hand, if the child formulates a single operation producing passive questions, there is no reason why this prediction should hold.

If these two factors present problems for predictions of acquisition orders, they present even greater difficulties for theories attempting detailed developmental predictions. In short, the problem is this: if we do not know the state of the child's grammar at time N, there is no way to predict what it will be at time $N+1$. It may be possible to make informed assumptions about the nature of mature grammars and of the child's grammar (that is, that the child's grammar includes rules corresponding to those of the mature grammar). Ideally, learnability theories should serve as instruments for generating fine-grained developmental predictions, yet, even granting these assumptions, serious obstacles remain. In order for a learning model to accurately predict changes, we must know when such changes are likely to ensue, what they are based on, and how they are made. At this point I would like to discuss these three problems with relation to the real-time syntax acquisition model described in figure 1.3.

First, when are modifications to internal grammars made? One reasonable general assumption is this: Children's immediate task is to understand and act on the language they hear. Thus, the problem of constructing a grammar has relatively low priority. This suggests that it is only when processing resources remain after the primary task of comprehension—that is, of forming a coherent internal representation—that grammatical modifications will be pursued. It is not a priori clear what sort of input will afford this situation. One problem is that, even when we find characteristics of input that facilitate language growth in general, we do not know why this should be so.

For example, several researchers have reported that the frequency of mothers' use of expansions and partial-plus repetitions is positively correlated with certain measures of language growth (Newport, Gleitman, and Gleitman 1977, Hoff-Ginsberg 1981). I can think of at least six explanations for this. First, clusters of repeated or slightly modified utterances ought to maximize the probability that the child will fully attend to at least one of the utterances in the cluster. Second, by providing the child with repeated opportunities to parse particular sentences, repetitions of utterances might facilitate acquisition by reducing the child's transient processing load. Third, clusters of utterances referring to a common topic may maximize the child's comprehension, allowing additional time to understand the context to which the utterances refer, and thereby reduce processing load. Fourth, sequences of expansions and partial-plus repetitions may broaden the range of constructions addressed to the child, thus increasing the likelihood that constructions minimally different from those the child is familiar with will occur (that is, there is an effect of moderate novelty in language acquisition). Fifth, sequences of expansions and partial-plus repetitions may increase the likelihood that novel syntactic material (or syntactic material that the child is currently acquiring) is salient (is stressed, occurs in sentence-initial position, and so forth). Sixth, partial-plus repetitions and/or expansions may provide pairs of utterances with minimal syntactic differences, thereby facilitating distributional analysis. One could imagine other possibilities as well.

The first two possibilities suggest that the incidence of exact repetitions should be positively correlated with language growth. However, Newport, Gleitman, and Gleitman (1977) report a significant *negative* correlation. They report that this negative effect is due to the fact that such sequences are generally composed of imperatives, which independently have a negative effect on language growth. Even when imperative sequences are discarded, however, a small (not significant) negative effect of exact repetitions remains. Thus, we can tentatively discard the first two explanations. It is less clear how to determine whether the remaining possibilities obtain. Given presently available evidence, any, or perhaps all, of these explanations may have a role in acquisition. But until we know which of these are operative, it will be impossible to predict in detail which input will provoke changes in the child's grammar.

The second obstacle to deriving developmental predictions from learnability theories hinges on the fact that we do not know exactly *what* the child's process of hypothesization operates on. On one level we do not know which characteristics of the environment enter into the child's construction of grammar—whether they are utterances alone, or utterances and context, or these plus prosody, gestures, facial expressions, and so forth. At a deeper level we do not know how the child's internal representation of such characteristics corresponds to our own. It is possible, though not likely, that there is an exact correspondence—that is, the child's representation is veridical. More likely, the child forms only a partial representation of the relevant characteristics of the environment, and the nature of this representation changes over time. Lacking a description of the child's internal representation of input, it is difficult to see how to generate fine-grained predictions of acquisition.

The third obstacle to making such predictions stems from our lack of knowledge concerning how children modify their grammars. How exactly does the hypothesizer operate—what sorts of rules do children create? The answer to this question hinges partly on the type of grammar children are acquiring. If children are acquiring a lexical-functional grammar, the rules they acquire would be quite different from those they would acquire if they were learning a transformational grammar. Supposing that children are acquiring transformational grammars, what sorts of transformations can they hypothesize? In Wexler and Culicover's theory, and in my proof, it was assumed that learners hypothesize transformations that bridge the discrepancies between their grammar and their input. It is possible, depending on the degree of discrepancy, that some such transformations may be quite complex, involving multiple movements and/or deletions. It may in fact be the case that if children hypothesize transformations, they can only hypothesize those that perform a single operation (see Valian, Winzemer, and Erreich 1981). As far as I can see, a constraint of this sort would have no substantive effects on the learnability results, but it would quite certainly lead to different predictions of acquisition sequence. For example, at the intermediate level of relative acquisition order, if a theory allows learners to formulate complex transformations, there is no reason why "cumulative complexity" should characterize development. Conversely, if a theory restricts the learner to formulating simple transformations, the cumulative complexity prediction follows directly. However, granting this constraint still does not lead directly to particular predictions at any level of finer detail. Suppose that a child hypothesizes a single-operation transformation even when this does not remove all the discrepancy between grammar and input. Which discrepancy is chosen to be removed? Does the child perform a breadth-first or a depth-first comparison? Perhaps the child operates only on those discrepancies that are salient—but an independent theory of salience would need to be developed if this supposition is to have any meaning.

In painting this gloomy picture, I do not mean to imply that attempts to develop detailed theoretical predictions of acquisition sequence are not worthwhile. On the contrary, it seems to me that making contact between general acquisition theories and the wealth of descriptive evidence we now have is of primary importance. There are two general points that I hope this discussion has made. First, it is simple to criticize existing learnability theories on the grounds that they fail to make the sorts of predictions in question, but it is another, and a very much more complex, matter to formulate theories that succeed in this regard (although see Pinker 1984 for a valiant attempt to specify such a theory). Second, there are a host of problems that must be solved before any such theory can emerge, and I have attempted to point out some of the most obvious of these.

I believe that we are in a somewhat better position to make learnability-theoretic predictions concerning errors characteristic of acquisition, though here too there are difficulties. In chapters 2 and 3 I discussed the types of errors allowed in Wexler and Culicover's theory and the Degree 1 proof. Both models allow errors of over- and undergeneralization. In addition, Wexler and Culicover's theory allows order-preserving misadjunction errors. It is a reasonably straightforward matter to create a taxonomy of misadjunction errors and to check this against the errors that children actually make. So far as I know, there are no examples of such errors.

In fact, this matter is a bit more subtle than I have thus far made it out to be. Suppose that we create such a taxonomy and find that few if any of these errors are evidenced by children. Provided that children assign the same structural descriptions to utterances as do their target grammars, we may conclude that they do not make misadjunction errors. But if this assumption is not correct, the conclusion is unwarranted. The point is that the types of errors children make are a function of the nature of their current grammars: errors that do not seem to be misadjunctions may nevertheless be just that, and vice versa. Nevertheless, if we never find any obvious examples of such errors, it may be reasonable to tentatively conclude both that children do not make misadjunction errors and that children do make accurate assignments of structural descriptions, lacking other evidence to the contrary.

There is a third type of error that is ruled out by both learnability models that may nonetheless actually occur. This is the so-called Basic Operation error, discussed by Valian and her colleagues (see, for example, Valian, Winzemer, and Erreich 1981). An example of such an error is "What did you did?" In the derivation of this sentence the tense marker (here lexicalized as "did") should be inverted with the subject. The Basic Operation Hypothesis states that all movement transformations comprise copying and deletion operations; this error arises because tense inversion has been formulated as a simple copying operation, with no deletion, so that the tense also surfaces in its original position (hence the second "did," which should be "do"). These types of errors cannot occur in either of the learnability models because they require that the learner derive an exact match to input.

However, suppose that, as suggested above, we require only that the learner repair a single discrepancy between its derived structure and its input. For example, the learner might receive as input "What did you do?," whereas its grammar derives "What you did?" There are two discrepancies here: the initial "did" is missing, and the "do" is a "did." If the learner can only repair one discrepancy, it will derive either "What did you did?" or "What you do?"

With no constraints on which discrepancy the learner will choose to repair, this partial matching to sample hypothesis seems to generate exactly the same set of predictions as the Basic Operation Hypothesis. However, certain of these predicted errors never appear. For example, instead of "What did you do?," we never hear "What did you do what?" or "Did you do?" Thus, we might try another tack. Suppose now that we require the learner to repair only salient discrepancies. Obviously, we will need an independent theory of "salience," but, as a first approximation, we might assume that stressed and/or sentence-initial discrepancies are preferentially repaired. On this view, Basic Operation errors will occur only on unstressed, noninitial items. Thus, we do not get "Did you do?" because the initial "what" is missing, and we do not get "What did you do what?" because "what" in final position is invariably stressed: "You did what?" I am not certain whether this last proposal is entirely correct, but it seems to be more accurate than the alternatives discussed above.

In summary, deriving error predictions from learnability models may be reasonably straightforward. The inclusion of bracketed input eliminates the possibility of misadjunction errors; modification of the learning procedure so that partial matches to input are allowed in turn allows Basic Operation errors. Still, there appear to be certain types of errors that are not handled gracefully by learnability models. For example, Karmiloff-Smith (1979) and Bowerman (1982) have discussed errors appearing relatively late in acquisition that seem to result from general reorganizations of internal grammars, prompted by functional considerations. Acquisition in current learnability theories is driven solely by the learner's matching its grammar to the target grammar, and at present it is not clear how the possibility of internally prompted grammatical reorganizations can be integrated into these models.

Conclusion

In this monograph I have explored some of the implications of the Bracketed Input Hypothesis for theories of language acquisition. I have presented a learnability proof incorporating this hypothesis as a basic assumption, which demonstrates learnability of transformational grammars from exceedingly simple input. This model has other benefits over previous models: in particular, it makes only modest processing demands on the language learner, allows learnability from a smaller amount of input (and hence over a shorter period of time) than other models, and disallows types of syntactic errors that do not seem to occur in actual acquisition. I have also presented studies that corroborate some of the predictions bearing on the Bracketed Input Hypothesis: there may reliably be prosodically encoded bracketing information in children's input; children appear to be able to represent at least some aspects of bracketing; speakers appear to have predominantly acquired particular structural analyses of constructions for which there is no distributional evidence; and the presence of bracketing information in input can be shown to significantly alter the learning of a miniature language by adults.

In closing, I would like to return briefly to the question I posed at the outset: How are we to explain the fact that children reliably succeed in inducing correct grammars for their languages? Elsewhere it has been argued cogently that part of this explanation must be that children come to the task of language acquisition with a biological endowment that constrains the sorts of grammars, and grammatical rules, that they can entertain as possibilities. In this monograph I have argued that certain features of children's language input—in particular, information that acts in concert with children's budding grammatical knowledge to allow bracketing of sentences into their constituent phrases—conspire with these constraints to fully determine children's grammatical induction; these features may play a somewhat more extensive role in this conspiracy than has previously been considered to be the case. Much work remains to be done in formulating a detailed developmental explanation of the child's rapid, accurate, and relatively effortless acquisition of language.

Appendix
Stimuli for Comprehension and Picture Judgment Tasks, Coreference Study

Comprehension Task

Experimental sentences were Prepositional Phrase Preposing and Left Dislocation for Group 1 and Topicalization and S'-Phrases for Group 2. Objects presented to the subjects are noted parenthetically below each sentence. For Randomization B, the sentences in each block were presented in the reverse of the order given here.

Block 1
The girl put the zebra on his bed.
    (zebra, hippo, zebra's bed, hippo's bed, girl)
A table that he moved fell on the lion.
    (lion, poodle, lion's table, poodle's table, block)
He put the lamp in the hippo's room.
    (hippo, zebra, hippo's room, zebra's room, lamp)

For the poodle, he turned on the TV.	(Group 1)
As for the poodle, he turned on the TV.	(Group 2)

    (poodle, lion, poodle's room, lion's room, TV)

The zebra's book, he dropped it on his foot.	(Group 1)
The zebra's book, he dropped on his foot.	(Group 2)

    (zebra, lion, zebra's book, lion's book, lamp)
He broke the lion's chair when he sat down.
    (lion, zebra, lion's chair, zebra's chair, TV)

Block 2
The girl found him next to the lion's table.
    (lion, hippo, lion's table, hippo's table, girl)

The lion's book, he carried it on his head.   (Group 1)
The lion's book, he carried on his head.   (Group 2)
   (lion, poodle, lion's book, poodle's book, TV)
On the hippo's chair, he sat down.   (Group 1)
After the hippo moved the block, he sat down.   (Group 2)
   (hippo, zebra, hippo's chair, zebra's chair, block)
The poodle turned his table upside down.
   (poodle, lion, poodle's table, lion's table, TV)
The hippo took his lamp from his room.
   (hippo, zebra, hippo's room, zebra's room, lamp)
A block that the poodle moved fell on him.
   (poodle, lion, poodle's bed, lion's bed, block)

Block 3
With the lion's book, he knocked over the lamp.   (Group 1)
When the lion shook, he knocked over the lamp.   (Group 2)
   (lion, poodle, lion's book, poodle's book, lamp)
The hippo's bed, he turned it upside down.   (Group 1)
The hippo's bed, he turned upside down.   (Group 2)
   (hippo, poodle, hippo's bed, poodle's bed, TV)
The girl found the zebra next to his chair.
   (zebra, lion, zebra's chair, lion's chair, girl)
Some blocks which were in his room made the zebra trip.
   (zebra, hippo, zebra's room, hippo's room, block)
He found the TV on the lion's bed.
   (lion, hippo, lion's bed, hippo's bed, TV)
He carried the poodle's book on his head.
   (poodle, zebra, poodle's book, zebra's book, block)

Block 4
The poodle found the TV on his table.
   (poodle, zebra, poodle's table, zebra's table, TV)
The girl put him on the hippo's bed.
   (hippo, lion, hippo's bed, lion's bed, girl)
For the zebra, he found the lamp.   (Group 1)
As for the zebra, he found the lamp.   (Group 2)
   (zebra, poodle, zebra's room, poodle's room, lamp)
Some blocks which were in the hippo's room made him trip.
   (hippo, poodle, hippo's room, poodle's room, block)

The poodle's chair, he broke it when he sat down.   (Group 1)
The poodle's chair, he broke when he sat down.   (Group 2)
   (poodle, hippo, poodle's chair, hippo's chair, lamp)
The zebra turned his bed upside down.
   (zebra, hippo, zebra's bed, hippo's bed, block)

Picture Judgment Task

Experimental sentences included Prepositional Phrase Preposing and
Left Dislocation for Group 1 and Topicalization and S'-Phrases for
Group 2. The contents of the associated photograph are noted paren-
thetically below each sentence.

He dropped the hippo's book on his foot.
   (Hippo has hippo's book on foot.)
On the poodle's table, he found a block.   (Group 1)
As for the poodle, he found a block on the table.   (Group 2)
   (Zebra sees block on poodle's table.)
A table that he knocked over hurt the hippo.
   (Lion's table on upside-down hippo, lion looking on.)
On the hippo's bed, he went to sleep.   (Group 1)
After the hippo got into bed, he went to sleep.   (Group 2)
   (Hippo lying on hippo's bed.)
The girl chased him under the lion's bed.
   (Girl chasing lion under lion's bed.)
The lion's chair, he sat down on it.   (Group 1)
The lion's chair, he sat down on.   (Group 2)
   (Lion sitting on lion's chair.)
With the zebra's book, he hit the girl.   (Group 1)
As for the zebra, he hit the girl with a book.   (Group 2)
   (Zebra hitting girl with zebra's book.)
He sat down on the poodle's chair.
   (Poodle sitting on poodle's chair.)
The girl followed him to the poodle's room.
   (Girl following zebra into poodle's room.)
He took the bed from the zebra's room.
   (Poodle taking zebra's bed from zebra's room.)
A book which was by his table belonged to the poodle.
   (Poodle by poodle's table, looking at poodle's book.)

The hippo carried his book on his head.
  (Hippo with hippo's book on head.)
A book which was by the hippo's table belonged to him.
  (Hippo looking at lion's book by hippo's table.)
The hippo's book, he threw it at the girl.   (Group 1)
The hippo's book, he threw at the girl.   (Group 2)
  (Hippo throwing hippo's book at girl.)
The lion dropped his book on his foot.
  (Lion with lion's book on foot.)
A table that the zebra knocked over hurt him.
  (Zebra's table on upside-down zebra.)
The zebra's table, he moved it.   (Group 1)
The zebra's table, he moved.   (Group 2)
  (Hippo pushing zebra's table.)
He turned the zebra's bed upside-down.
  (Zebra pushing over zebra's bed.)

Notes

Chapter 1

1. The particular way in which some type of information is manifested need not be universal, so long as all languages include some means of encoding that information. Below I will indicate a number of devices through which phrase-bracketing information may be encoded in language input, but it is unlikely either that any particular language employs all of these or that all languages employ the same set of devices. For example, certain types of phrase boundaries may be indicated in English by a pattern of falling and rising pitch; in tonal languages, which use pitch for lexical purposes, this means of encoding bracketing information is probably unavailable. However, if every language incorporates some subset drawn from a finite set of these devices, then the correlations among these will universally provide bracketing information.

"Universal" should be construed in a rather constrained sense here, as William Merriman has pointed out to me. Suppose, for example, that there is a certain type of construction that occurs only in a subset of possible languages and can be acquired only if some particular type of information is available in input. Further, such information does not occur in the input drawn from languages lacking this construction. Even though this information is not universal in the usual sense, it could still be judged necessary if it is present in all language-learning situations in which the construction for which it is required occurs.

2. Doubtless, these do not exhaust all the possibilities. For example, it is possible that, lacking some type of information in input, a learner could acquire complete structural knowledge of any language but would systematically assign anomalous interpretations to some set of sentences. Alternatively, it might be possible for some aspect of input to be necessary only for a particular stage of acquisition, perhaps to bootstrap the child into a more complex analysis of grammar. However, any one of the criteria described in the text may provide a sufficient basis for positively determining the necessity of some aspect of input. Note further that these criteria are not mutually exclusive: the absence of some type of information may completely block the acquisition of some languages and may prevent acquisition of complete structural knowledge of other lan-

guages. In such a case the information in question would be both extensionally and intensionally necessary.

Formal demonstrations that, other things being equal, some aspect of input meets one or more of these criteria of necessity establish only that there is a sufficient basis for believing such input to be necessary. We are in the uncomfortable position of being unable to perform the sort of empirical manipulations that might rule out alternative explanations. I suspect that it may always be possible to construct a formal model in which putative native constraints on grammatical hypotheses perform the same functions as does input in a model lacking such constraints. However, Occam's razor clearly favors the latter sort of model. In addition, input-based explanations are likely to be more easily falsifiable than nativistic explanations and should be preferred on this basis as well.

3. In previous times it was widely believed that children who were not exposed to any language input would acquire the true, universal language of humankind. Feldman, Goldin-Meadow, and Gleitman (1978) cite an account from Herodotus concerning an Egyptian pharaoh who caused two children to be raised without exposure to language; these children began spontaneously to use words from a language called Phrygian. Similarly, King James I is supposed to have had a child raised in isolation; this child began speaking Hebrew. The sign systems invented by deaf children of hearing parents do not appear to be equivalent to any particular language acquired with input but do appear to incorporate certain universal aspects of language (see Goldin-Meadow 1982 and Goldin-Meadow and Mylander 1984 for further discussion).

4. No matter how complex, distributional analyses alone will not be sufficient to reveal all aspects of syntactic structure, as Chomsky (1965) has argued. For example, syntactic rules may be subject to general constraints on the form of human grammars; the data on which a distributional analysis is based may reflect the operation of such constraints, but the constraints themselves will not be directly revealed therein. Certainly, the linguistic argumentation typical of recent years is not based solely on distributional analysis of corpora of sentences but in addition takes into consideration both patterns of interpretations and distributions of ungrammatical versus grammatical sentences. The latter two types of data together severely limit the possibilities for inductive generalizations. It is unlikely that children have access to the last type of data (see Brown and Hanlon 1970; also Wexler and Culicover 1980 for discussion), so that the distributional analyses that children perform must be constrained in some manner.

5. Such representations have been termed "skeletal structures" by Levy and Joshi (1978).

6. All recent linguistic theories—Standard Theory (Chomsky 1965), Government and Binding Theory (Chomsky 1981), Lexical-Functional Theory (Bresnan 1982), and Generalized Phrase Structure Grammar (Gazdar 1982)—attempt to capture the relations among sentences (or, more precisely, the structures underlying sentences) in some manner. I do not seek to champion any one of these theories here. My point is simply that whatever means is employed to explain these relations must be structure-dependent.

7. It is not always the case that expansions will supply information about phrases. For example, if the mother expanded "Red block" as "The red block," this should not be taken as evidence that "The" and "Red block" are both phrases. Thus, expansions will be useful in general for revealing phrase structure only if there are additional constraints on the child's structural analyses of input.

8. There are two potential difficulties with closed class words as a source of information for phrase bracketing. First, if the child is to use closed class words to identify phrases, the words in this class must have been previously identified. It might seem that the child could accomplish this only by performing some prior distributional analysis of input. There is an alternative possibility, though. Kean (1980) has argued that, unlike open class words, closed class words do not receive normal sentence stress. Thus, there may be an acoustic basis for distinguishing between these two classes of words. This account is somewhat complicated by the fact that some closed class words may receive contrastive stress (as in "*In* the truck"), but it is not clear how often such stress occurs in the child's input.

A second potential difficulty with using closed class words to identify phrases is that although such items typically occur at the beginnings of phrases in (for example) English and mark phrase boundaries, this is not always the case. In English, particles (such as "on" in "Put your clothes on") can occur in phrase-final position, but they are otherwise indistinguishable from prepositions. In addition, objects of prepositions may be relativized or *wh*-questioned, with the result that the prepositions are stranded in phrase-final position. Thus, sequences of closed class items may occur in such a way that phrase boundaries are not perspicuously indicated, as in the sentence "What did you give the stuff that John took *off with up for?*" It is probably safe to assume that the incidence of sentences such as this in the child's input is vanishingly rare. Moreover, in situations where closed class words do not supply reliable cues to phrase structure, other (normally correlated) cues may be available.

9. As discussed in note 4, such distributional analyses must be subject to certain constraints. With regard to the interpretation of studies of adult language learning, the problem is whether adults' analyses are subject to the same constraints. If they are not, then it is possible that adults may require richer data to arrive at a particular analysis than would be the case for children. This is certainly not true for most types of problem-solving situations.

10. More precisely, such automata are finite state *tree* automata—structurally identical to the more usual finite state *string* automata, but capable of utilizing more complex input.

11. The proviso that the number of possible states is known is a very powerful assumption. This is (very) roughly equivalent to requiring that the number of possible rules in a grammar be known in advance, an unlikely assumption with regard to natural language acquisition. Note that the framework developed by Levy and Joshi is *not* equivalent to that of learnability theory as discussed in chapter 2. In particular, the Superfinite Theorem (see chapter 2) does not hold

for Levy and Joshi's system. I thank Scott Weinstein for pointing this out to me.

12. This letter series completion problem underestimates the complexity of induction in language acquisition in several ways. For one, there is apparently no particular ordering of input that holds across different children.

13. This can be demonstrated using Cantor's method of diagonalization (see Boolos and Jeffrey 1980), which reveals that the number of possible solutions to this simple letter series completion problem is equivalent to the number of real numbers.

14. I have given this letter series completion problem to over 1,000 students in the last few years. The "triples" solution noted in the text is the most common one given. A slightly less common, though similar, solution involves bracketing the input as (ABC) E (Gxx), so that the next two letters are H and I. Two or three students have come up with the prime number solution noted in the text. No student has ever suggested any other solution, suggesting that, indeed, some sorts of constraints are operating here.

15. This is not to imply that noisy and noise-free inputs are equivalent for noninstantaneous learning models. Osherson and Weinstein (1982) provide a proof that the languages that can be acquired on the basis of noisy input are in general a subset of the languages that can be acquired on the basis of noise-free input.

16. Scott Weinstein (personal communication, 1984) has pointed out to me that it is not necessary for the learner to be constrained from the beginning of acquisition, so long as at some point in acquisition the learner's hypotheses do become subject to certain constraints. Such a learner should evidence many errors in the early phase of acquisition. In a similar vein, the set of constraints under which a learner operates need not be constant across acquisition. See Borer and Wexler (1984) for discussion of one such possibility.

Chapter 2

1. Other criteria of learning are possible. For example, one might require that a learner converge on a correct grammar with some probability of $1 - e$; this is the criterion of learning adopted in work by Wexler and his colleagues discussed below and in the learnability proof presented in chapter 3. See also Osherson and Weinstein 1982 for alternative learning criteria.

2. Gold's learning procedure involved an "enumeration procedure" in which the learner is conceived of as possessing an ordered list of all possible grammars. The learner tests each successive grammar in the list until one is found that is compatible with all previous input. The grammar is then adopted as the learner's current hypothesis. When an input is received that is not compatible with this current hypothesis, the process is repeated: each succeeding grammar is tested until a compatible one is found. In this model complete grammars are hypothesized or rejected. Other learning procedures are possible; one of these is discussed below in conjunction with the work of Wexler et al. See also

Osherson, Stob, and Weinstein 1982 for a discussion of alternative learning procedures.

3. Languages may be formally defined as consisting of quadruples {S, V_N, V_T, R}, where S is the start symbol, V_N is a set of nonterminal symbols (symbols that may be rewritten as strings of other symbols), V_T is a set of terminal symbols (symbols that may not be rewritten), and R is a set of rewrite rules. In an *unrestricted rewrite system* any string of symbols drawn from V_N may be rewritten as a string of nonterminal and/or terminal symbols that may be of greater, equal, or lesser length than the original string. *Context-sensitive* rules have the additional stipulation that the resulting string of symbols must be greater or equal in length to the original set of symbols. *Context-free* rules have the further stipulation that the original string of symbols must be exactly one symbol long. *Finite state* rules have the added stipulation that there may be at most one nonterminal symbol in the resulting string. See Hopcroft and Ullman 1979 for a complete discussion of formal language types.

4. Given the sorts of augmentations proposed by Gazdar, in particular metarules that allow for the generalization of phrase structure rules via variables, it is unclear whether generalized phrase structure grammars are truly context-free. These augmentations would appear to permit a set of grammars that is (weakly) equivalent to the set of grammars allowed in standard transformational theory.

5. Hirsh-Pasek, Treiman, and Schneiderman (1984) have suggested that there may be subtle cues in the structure of parent-child discourse that provide feedback on the ungrammaticality of child utterances: parental repetitions are more likely to occur following ungrammatical child utterances than grammatical child utterances. Demetras and Post (1985) and Penner (1985) have observed similar discourse patterns and have also observed that conversational topic continuations by the parent are more likely to occur following grammatical child utterances. However, the distribution of parental responses is not a unique function of the grammaticality of the preceding child utterance. Thus, it is an open question whether children can utilize this feedback as providing negative information. Moreover, Gold's definition of negative information required that all ungrammatical sentences potentially be so labeled in input; clearly, this is not the case for children learning language. A more restricted definition of negative information may be formulated, so that only *diagnostic* negative examples need be provided the learner. That is, for a class of languages to be learnable, there must be a finite amount of input that will serve to distinguish any given language from all other languages. Thus, determining what constitutes diagnostic information with respect to the class of natural languages depends in part on ascertaining how this class is constituted. In short, the finding that some corrections are available in the child's language input in itself does not provide a sufficient basis for the conclusion that input includes negative information.

6. Suppose that such an ordering of input were imposed on the class of languages given in the proof of the Superfinite Theorem. In the simplest case input might be ordered so that sentences of increasing length are presented, with no

repetitions allowed until all possible sentences have been presented. In this case this class of languages is identifiable if the learner begins with the hypothesis that L_0 is the language being presented. This hypothesis may be maintained so long as the sentence *"a"* is never presented for a second time. However, if a finite language is presented, there is some finite time at which *"a"* will be represented. At this point the learner can (correctly) change its hypothesis to be the smallest language that allows the string immediately preceding the second presentation of *"a."*

7. The enumeration procedure is a brute force algorithm. Gold (1967) provides a proof that, at least for the classes of languages in the Chomsky hierarchy, there is no alternative learning procedure that is uniformly faster than the enumeration procedure. As noted in the text, such a procedure makes massive demands on memory and processing resources. In addition, this procedure requires that grammars that are not even remotely correct be considered if such grammars intervene in the enumeration between pairs of possibly correct grammars. Finally, since the ordering of grammars in an enumeration is arbitrary, no predictions concerning the relations between successive hypothesized grammars may be made. Intuitively, it seems most likely that children modify their internal grammars on some principled basis, changing one rule (or a small set of rules) at a time, rather than hypothesizing and discarding entire grammars.

8. Gazdar (1982 and elsewhere) has claimed that theories (such as Generalized Phrase Structure Grammar) defining natural languages as a subset of the context-free languages are to be preferred in principle because there are results showing that the class of context-free languages is "learnable." For reasons noted in the text, this claim is incorrect: such results are irrelevant to the determination of the nature of the class of natural languages. Moreover, Gazdar's claim appears to be based on the result proven in Levy and Joshi 1978, and, as noted in note 11, chapter 1, the framework employed there does not correspond to learnability.

9. This restriction on the domains within which transformations could operate was at odds with the then prevalent view that unbounded movements were possible. The basic observation on which this view was based was that *wh*-question words can be extracted from arbitrarily deeply embedded clauses, as in "Who did John report that Mary claimed that Bill said that Susan kissed?" See Ross 1967 for proposals concerning constraints on such unbounded movement. Chomsky (1977) has provided an account of *Wh*-Movement that reconciles such data with a cyclic (bounded) version of this rule.

10. Note that if all strings of type A are eliminated from each of the languages under consideration in this example, the resulting set of languages is exactly equal to that discussed in the proof of the Superfinite Theorem. The languages in the present example are infinite only because each contains a^* (that is, all strings consisting of any number of a's).

11. Suppose that some set of categories N_1, N_2, N_3, ..., is defined as the set of cyclic nodes. Then the cyclic domain of any node N will consist of all those

nodes dominated by N (this includes N itself, since domination is a reflexive relation) that are not dominated by any other N' that is subordinate to N.

12. The following conventions will be used throughout: The root (highest) S node of a sentence is denoted by S_0. The first embedded S node is denoted by S_1, the second embedded S node is denoted by S_2, and so forth. It is assumed in the examples that any clause can have at most one embedding, though this is not crucial for any of the following arguments. Individual nodes are in italics: A. Cycles are referred to by their dominating S node given in roman type. Thus, S_0 denotes the cycle dominated by the node S_0.

13. An implicit assumption here is that learners do not make deliberate errors; that is, any rule that the learner hypothesizes must be consistent with the present datum. If in fact the hypothesized rule is in error, this can only be revealed by some subsequent datum. Thus, the learner will make errors in hypothesizing incorrect rules, but these errors will become apparent—detectable—only in light of further data. In Wexler and Culicover's theory, however, the distinction between "errors" and "detectable errors" is more narrowly defined. In their theory the learner makes an error when it hypothesizes a transformation that adjoins a constituent incorrectly. Thus, errors produce the correct linear structure but an incorrect hierarchical structure. An error becomes detectable only when the erroneous rule (in conjunction with other rules) produces a derivation resulting in incorrect linear structure. In the text "detectable error" is used in this more restricted sense.

14. The criterion of learnability assumes that after some amount of time the learner will settle on a particular grammar. Further, it is only when the learner realizes that its grammar is in error that this grammar is modified. Thus, errors that do not come to the learner's attention will not cause any changes in the learner's hypotheses: the learner's grammar could be rife with errors, but so long as none of these errors is detectable, the criterion of learnability can be attained. In short, errors in general are irrelevant to the attainment of learnability; what is crucial is that any errors that can ever become detectable will become detectable on data of finite complexity.

15. There is no requirement, of course, that all constraints on natural language syntax must be explicable on the basis of considerations of learnability.

Chapter 3

1. Culicover (1984) provides a succinct account of the difference between "error" and "detectable error":

When the learner's transformational component and the adult's do not agree in the structures that they generate, we may say that there is an ERROR in the learner's component. When the error shows up as a difference between the strings that the two components generate, then we say that there is a DETECTABLE ERROR in the learner's component. Detectable errors serve as the cue to the learner that there is a discrepancy between the components, and thus indicate to the learner that it must revise its hypothesis about the grammar. (p. 79)

These particular senses of "error" and "detectable error" are not distinguished in the Degree 1 proof. Instead, disagreements in either derived structures or derived strings will motivate modifications to the learner's grammar.

This is not to say that the errors that a learner may make will be immediately apparent. On the contrary, I assume that they will not, for the learner will never make deliberate errors. Rather, an overgeneral or undergeneral transformation may be hypothesized, but the hypothesized rule will apply correctly to the datum by which it was motivated. Some later datum will be required to reveal the incorrect generality of the rule. In this sense, there is an error on the original datum that becomes a detectable error in light of the later datum. This distinction between "error" and "detectable error" is quite different from that intended by Wexler and Culicover, who did not consider generality errors in their proof.

2. In these examples I am assuming that Wexler and Culicover's set of assumptions, in particular the Freezing Principle, holds. Many of these assumptions will be discarded in the Degree 1 proof given below. Here, however, the point is simply to illustrate that by using a different method of proof, while maintaining the same assumptions about input, several of the grammatical constraints posited by Wexler and Culicover are no longer necessary.

3. Wexler and Culicover (1980) define the Principle of Transparency of Untransformable Base Structures as follows:

Let P be a partially derived 0-degree base p-m [phrase marker]. If no transformations in an adult transformational component A apply to P (that is, none of the S.D.s [structural descriptions] fits P), then there exists a 0-extension of P to a fully-derived base p-m P', such that P' is untransformable by A. (p. 168)

Suppose that in a Degree 0 phrase marker a transformation has applied that freezes some constituent C. After this transformation no further transformations can apply. By TUBS, there must be an alternative expansion of C that can be substituted for the frozen version of C and will not allow any transformations to apply. In other words, there must exist in every language a set of untransformable Degree 0 base structures, and there must be one such base structure corresponding to every fully derived Degree 0 phrase marker. However, there is no independent reason why any language should include any untransformable base structures at all. Nor, if there are such base structures, is there any independent reason why these should have any correspondence to derived structures. In short, there is simply no justification for TUBS outside of Wexler and Culicover's learnability system.

4. Standard linguistic notation is used: parentheses denote optionality; curly brackets enclose mutually exclusive options.

5. This constraint was in fact incorporated in Wexler and Culicover's proof under the rubric of "Ordering of S-Essential Transformations" (OSET).

6. I am assuming that there are no implicit end variables; rather, it is implicit that the symbol "#", denoting "sentence boundary," occurs at the beginning and end of structural descriptions throughout. T_3 explicitly should be interpreted as $\# - C - D - E - \# \Rightarrow \# - C + E - D - \#$. If T_3 were reformu-

lated to read $X - C - D - E \Rightarrow X - C + E - D$, then it would apply both to 3.12 and to 3.13: the variables X, Y, and Z may be fit by null or nonnull subtrees.

7. Several caveats are in order here. First, both Wexler and Culicover's proof and my proof assume that grammars will be of the general form described in the Standard Theory of transformational grammar. It is possible that the effects of bracketing information in input that are evident in a comparison of these two proofs are confined to grammars of this sort. That is, a pair of similar proofs based on, say, Generalized Phrase Structure Grammar might not show the same differences. Insofar as constraints on grammars are concerned, this is undoubtedly true. Whether bracketing information allows learnability from simpler data for Generalized Phrase Structure Grammars is an open question. I will return to this issue briefly in chapter 6, but I will not be able to resolve it in this work.

Second, as Wexler and Culicover note, it might be possible to attain Degree 1 Learnability in their system by assuming more stringent constraints on raising transformations. More generally, it is likely that any effects of particular aspects of input can always be mimicked by assuming appropriate constraints on grammatical hypotheses. The issue here is whether there should be any a priori preference for input-based hypotheses over constraint-based hypotheses. I believe that there should be, simply because the former are susceptible to falsification by a wider range of data than are the latter.

In a somewhat different vein, note that the comparison between the Degree 1 and Degree 2 proofs is not completely straightforward, because different methods of proof are employed in each. I will discuss this issue in the final section of this chapter.

8. In an earlier version of this proof a ninth assumption, the Freezing Principle, was included. An example demonstrating the relative necessity of this assumption follows.

If we consider only completed derivations, the Freezing Principle does not entail the existence of any error that can be revealed only by Degree 2 or greater data. However, errors can also be revealed by incomplete, aborted derivations caused by violations of the Principle of Determinism. Lacking the Freezing Principle, it is possible to construct an example in which such an error is revealed only by Degree 2 or greater data.

In this example both the target grammar and the learner's grammar include the rule $C - X - E - G \Rightarrow C - X - G + E$. This is a non-structure-preserving raising. In addition, the target grammar includes the rule $G - X - G \Rightarrow X - G$, whereas the learner's grammar includes the rule $F - X - G \Rightarrow X - G$. There is one possible Degree 1 phrase marker, shown as tree 1. No relevant transformations apply in the S_1 cycle of this phrase marker. In the S_0 cycle both grammars raise G and adjoin it as a left sister of E. The target grammar then deletes the leftmost G, whereas the learner's grammar deletes the leftmost F. The derived phrase markers are different, yet there is no error. This is because G is a nonlexical category, and its presence does not affect the learner's derived string in any way.

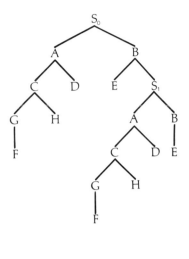

Tree 1

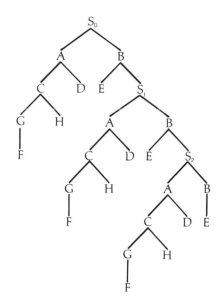

Tree 2

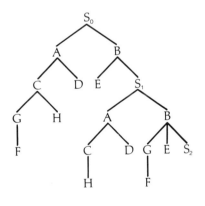

Tree 3

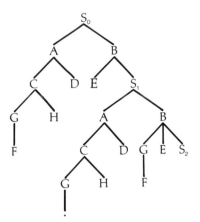

Tree 4

In tree 2 no relevant transformations apply in S_2 in either grammar. In the S_1 cycle both grammars raise G and adjoin it as a left sister of E. Now the target grammar deletes the leftmost G, whereas the learner's grammar deletes the leftmost F. The resulting trees (with the S_2 cycle omitted) are shown as trees 3 and 4. Note that in the tree derived by the target grammar there is only one G node in the S_1 cycle, whereas there are two G nodes in the tree derived by the learner's grammar. In the S_0 cycle of phrase marker 3 node G can again be raised. However, in the S_0 cycle of phrase marker 4 the raising transformation can fit the tree in two ways: both of the G nodes in the S_1 cycle are eligible. This is a violation of Determinism. The learner's grammar is in error, but this error can only be revealed on a Degree 2 or greater datum.

If the raising of G were structure-preserving, there would exist a Degree 1 phrase marker that would reveal this error. This would be equivalent to tree 4 (without, of course, the embedded S_2). Thus, this problem arises only if there is a non-structure-preserving raising that interacts with subsequent transformations.

Given the Freezing Principle, this example is impossible. After G is raised in the S_1 cycle of tree 2, no further transformations can apply: neither the leftmost G nor the leftmost F can be deleted. Thus, there remain two G nodes in the S_1 cycle for both grammars. However, only one of these is eligible for raising: the previous non-structure-preserving raising of G freezes B, and this raised G cannot be raised again. In the S_0 cycle of tree 2, then, the leftmost G in the S_1 cycle can be raised, and there can be no violation of Determinism.

There are simpler ways to rule out this problem. One possibility is to adopt a "tree-pruning" convention to the effect that any nonterminal node that does not dominate any other nodes is automatically deleted. Alternatively, it could be assumed that moved or deleted constituents leave behind a phonologically null trace (this assumption was adopted in Wexler and Culicover's proof). Given that there is linguistic counterevidence to the Freezing Principle (see Wexler and Culicover 1980) and that at least the pruning convention noted above has much less drastic ramifications, it seems best to discard this principle as a constraint on possible grammars.

9. Determinism, Precedence of Intracyclic Transformations, and Single Application of Transformations are also all necessary, as will become apparent in the discussion of the remaining five assumptions and in the proof itself. I will not, however, provide formal demonstrations of this. I thank Dan Osherson (personal communication, 1982) for pointing out the importance of effectiveness (which is the motivation for SAT) to me.

10. Certain theories of transformational grammar (see, for example, Ross 1967) have assumed that there are two types of transformations: cyclic transformations, which are subject to a particular set of constraints, and last-cyclic transformations, which are subject to an independent set of constraints. Since several rules originally considered to be last-cyclic (Wh-Movement, for example) have subsequently been reanalyzed as being cyclic (see Chomsky 1977), I assume here that all transformations are cyclic.

11. Wexler and Culicover originally defined the Principle of No Bottom Context (NBC) in such a way that nonraised (or nondeleted) nodes in bottom context had to be fit by variables. This has the effect of allowing nodes at the periphery of an embedded S to be uniquely identified. This is not allowed by TLC. In fact, for their proof, Wexler and Culicover assumed a version of NBC that is equivalent to TLC.

12. Specifically, there are three types of modifications of transformations that result in overgeneralization errors. First, a variable may be substituted for a specified node. Thus, T_i' will apply more generally than will T_i, for the variable X may be fit by A, any other node (or string of nodes), or by a null string of nodes. Second, a spurious variable may be inserted. Thus, T_{ii}' will apply more generally than will T_{ii}, for the variable X may be fit by a null string of nodes (in which case T_{ii} would also apply) or by a nonnull string of nodes (in which case T_{ii} would not apply). Third, a dominating node may be substituted for a string of dominated nodes. Suppose that there is a base rule of the form $A \Rightarrow B\,(C)$. In this case T_{iii}' would apply more generally than would T_{iii}, for it would apply to phrase markers in which A was expanded as $B - C$, as well as to phrase markers in which A was expanded simply as B.

T_i: $A - B - C \Rightarrow A - C + B$
T_i': $X - B - C \Rightarrow X - C + B$
T_{ii}: $A - B - C \Rightarrow A - C + B$
T_{ii}': $A - X - B - C \Rightarrow A - X - C + B$
T_{iii}: $B - C - D - E \Rightarrow B - C - D$
T_{iii}': $A - D - E \Rightarrow A - D$

Errors of undergeneralization can be constructed by reversing these processes.

13. The symbol "E_0" is used for expository purposes only, so that the node E that is generated in the S_0 cycle can be unambiguously denoted. This notation is not meant to imply that this node is categorically distinguishable from any other nodes of type E.

14. In fact, given the present formulation of IRN, without TLC there would be no limit to the number of possible transformations. In each cycle in an arbitrarily large phrase marker, increasingly large subtrees could be raised. Implicitly raised nodes are not eligible with respect to intracyclic transformations, but they are eligible for subsequent-cycle extracyclic transformations. Thus, without TLC any (or all) of these nodes could be used to fit transformations; but there is no limit on the number of such nodes or, more precisely, on the number of possible structural analyses of such sets of nodes.

15. The symbol "C_{1a}" is used to denote the leftmost node of type C generated in the S_0 cycle. As in note 13, this symbol is employed for expository purposes only.

16. There would be a violation of Determinism because the "NP" in the structural description of the Raising to Subject rule could be fit by either "John" or "Mary." One way around this difficulty would be to adopt a constraint allowing only subject NPs to be extracted from tensed clauses. In fact,

this is one effect of the Specified Subject Condition proposed by Chomsky (1977).

17. Nodes that are dominated by an explicitly raised node are implicitly raised.

18. Suppose, for example, that two raisings per cycle are allowed. In the S_1 cycle of some Degree 2 phrase marker some node A is raised; this raising is non-structure-preserving. Then in the S_0 cycle A is raised again in the same fashion. A second raising applies, raising some node B. But since the original raising of A was non-structure-preserving, it is possible that A and B cannot be base-generated within the same clause. In this case there could be no Degree 1 phrase marker such that both A and B could be raised in the S_0 cycle. Lemma 1 below demonstrates that any single node can be raised in both Degree 1 and Degree 2 phrase markers, but this result cannot be extended to multiple nodes.

19. Here "t" stands for "trace"—a phonologically empty marker left behind in the original site of a moved constituent.

20. S' ("S-bar") is a category that dominates both a clause and its complementizer. In the sentence "It seems that John loves Mary," for example, "John loves Mary" is dominated by S, whereas "that John loves Mary" is dominated by S'. For a more complete description of X' categories, see Jackendoff 1977.

21. That is, structural errors are always revealed in the Degree 1 system. Theorem 4 (No Degree 1 Error Concealing) allows for the possibility that there are errors of overgenerality or undergenerality that will never be revealed, but it is unclear what sense "overgenerality" and "undergenerality" would have in such cases.

22. I believe that the Principle of Single Application of Transformations is implicit in Wexler and Culicover's proof. Certainly, their Assumption against String Preservation would rule out the sorts of iterative applications of transformations discussed above with respect to SAT.

23. Three additional assumptions must be adopted to allow the generation of this language. First, if a nonterminal node does not dominate anything, that node is erased ("pruned"). This possibility was discussed in note 8 of this chapter. Second, if a node A dominates another node A, only the higher A may be analyzed by any transformation. This "A-over-A" constraint was proposed in Chomsky 1965. Third, if a node A dominates only another node A, then one of these nodes is pruned, and the tree is "telescoped."

24. Some grammatical theories may allow for null expansions of certain nonterminal nodes, but, so far as I know, no theory would allow for the base generation of null trees such as this grammar generates.

25. One transcript from each child at each of Brown's (1973) five stages of early language acquisition was used in this tabulation. From the information given in Brown 1973 it was not possible to identify any Adam Stage III transcripts, so only 14 transcripts were examined in total. The transcripts used were as follows: Stage I: Adam 6, Eve 5, Sarah 18; Stage II: Adam 13, Eve 7, Sarah 34; Stage III: Eve 13, Sarah 46; Stage IV: Adam 20, Eve 17, Sarah 75; Stage V: Adam 55, Eve 20, Sarah 89. I thank Roger Brown and the Child Language Data

Exchange System (MacWhinney and Snow 1985) for providing access to these transcripts.

In performing the tabulation, catenative verbs such as "going to" ("gonna"), "want to" ("wanna"), "have to" ("hafta"), and "got to" ("gotta") were not counted as main verbs. Thus, the sentence "I know you want to go" was counted as a Degree 1, rather than a Degree 2, sentence. This follows the convention established by Newport (1977), who discusses linguistic justification for this treatment of catenatives.

If these catenative verbs were to be considered as main verbs, there would be an additional 22 Degree 2 input sentences, for a total of 39. Ten of these 22 sentences were followed by child sequiturs. This high proportion of comprehension indicates that such sentences were treated differently from full-fledged Degree 2 input by the children, providing further justification for the distinction made in the tabulation.

26. There are two senses in which Degree 2 input might be required. The first, embodied in Wexler and Culicover's work, is that Degree 2 data may be needed for the detection and correction of specific errors the learner might make. This view entails that a substantial amount of Degree 2 data be available in input, to ensure that the likelihood of the appearance of particular Degree 2 phrase markers will be sufficiently high. It is this view to which the argument in the text is addressed.

Fodor (1984) has proposed an alternative argument for the necessity of Degree 2 input. Given that certain grammatical operations (for example, "root" transformations; see Emonds 1976) apply only in matrix clauses, it may be argued that the syntactic category dominating matrix clauses (S_M) is distinct from the category dominating embedded clauses (S_E). Degree 1 input suffices to indicate to the learner that S_M may dominate S_E, but Degree 2 input is required to inform the learner that S_E may also dominate S_E (that is, that multiple levels of embedding are allowed). This view entails only that some (at least one instance of) Degree 2 data occur in input. The language input data noted in the text are consistent with this view, which might be called "Degree 1+."

Chapter 4

1. This work could not have been completed without the assistance of several other people. I gratefully acknowledge the contributions of Jan Goodsitt in collecting the data and LuAnne Gunderson, Gina Kuecks-Morgan, and Heidi Patz in digitizing and measuring the key sentences.

2. To assess reliability of the measurements, approximately 20% of the keyword tokens were chosen on a random basis and remeasured by the author. Exact intercoder agreement was extremely rare, but intercoder duration disagreements in excess of 5 msec occurred on less than 15% of the selected tokens. In general, there was very good agreement on placement of the initial boundary, coinciding with the onset of a consonantal burst, but poorer agreement on placement of the final boundary.

Chapter 5

1. It is conceivable that aspects of bracketing information may be filtered from input under certain circumstances. For example, Broca's aphasics may selectively omit function words from their speech ("agrammatism"); or children suffering from chronic otitis media may have difficulties in perceiving some facets of prosodic information. In such circumstances, however, deficiencies of input are unlikely to be confined to the lack of bracketing information, and the redundant cuing of phrase bracketing typical of natural languages makes it unlikely that all such information will be absent. In short, all indications are that phrase-bracketing information is a highly robust aspect of language input.

2. Baltin uses these data from Icelandic to argue for a structural analysis of Topicalization similar to that which I propose here. However, he accounts for this analysis on the basis of putative constraints on possible "landing sites" for moved constituents (Baltin's theory is discussed further in the text below). Implicit in Baltin's use of these data is the notion that the structure resulting from Topicalization is uniform across all languages. By making use of these data, I do not wish to embrace this claim but more simply wish to argue that the COMP Substitution analysis of Topicalization cannot be correct in general.

Chapter 6

1. Both GPSG and LFG incorporate notations expanding the functions of phrase structure rules, though in somewhat different ways. In GPSG the vocabulary of grammatical categories is expanded to include complex symbols of the form XP/YP, denoting a phrase of type X containing a gap of type YP (that is, a YP node that dominates a trace). For example, a topicalized sentence such as *Beans, I like* would be generated in part by the phrase structure rule $S \Rightarrow NP + NP + VP/NP$. In LFG grammatical categories receive functional annotations indicating their grammatical roles in sentences. Thus, a sentence such as "John kissed Mary" would be generated by the annotated phrase structure rules $S \Rightarrow NP_{SUBJ} + VP$ and $VP \Rightarrow V + NP_{OBJ}$. For further details, see Gazdar 1982 and Bresnan 1982.

2. For simplicity of reference, I have renumbered Pinker's procedures. My P1(a) corresponds to his P1, my P1(b) corresponds to his P2, my P2 corresponds to his P4, and my P3 corresponds to his P5. Pinker's procedure P3, which specifies how nodes of the constructed tree should be annotated, is not relevant to the discussion here and has been omitted.

3. The input to Pinker's structure-dependent distributional learning component consists of trees whose nodes have been labeled and functionally annotated. This entails a significantly richer representation than that entailed by the Bracketed Input Hypothesis: in the latter case trees are assumed to encode bracketing information but to lack labeled nodes. Hence, Pinker's input assumptions subsume the Bracketed Input Hypothesis.

References

Anderson, J. A. (1976). *Language, memory, and thought*. Hillsdale, N.J.: Lawrence Erlbaum Associates.

Bach, E. (1970). Problominalization. *Linguistic Inquiry* 1, 121–122.

Baker, C. L. (1977). Comments on the paper by Culicover and Wexler. In P. W. Culicover, T. Wasow, and A. Akmajian, eds., *Formal syntax*. New York: Academic Press.

Baker, C. L. (1979). Syntactic theory and the projection problem. *Linguistic Inquiry* 10, 533–582.

Baker, C. L., and J. J. McCarthy, eds. (1981). *The logical problem of language acquisition*. Cambridge, Mass.: MIT Press.

Baltin, M. R. (1981). Strict bounding. In C. L. Baker and J. J. McCarthy, eds., *The logical problem of language acquisition*. Cambridge, Mass.: MIT Press.

Baltin, M. R. (1982). A landing site theory of movement rules. *Linguistic Inquiry* 13, 1–38.

Boolos, G., and R. Jeffrey (1980). *Computability and logic*. Cambridge: Cambridge University Press.

Borer, H., and K. Wexler (1984). The maturation of syntax. Paper presented at the Conference on Parameter Setting, University of Massachusetts, Amherst.

Bowerman, M. (1973). Structural relationships in children's utterances: Syntactic or semantic? In T. E. Moore, ed., *Cognitive development and the acquisition of language*. New York: Academic Press.

Bowerman, M. (1982). Starting to talk worse: Clues to language acquisition from children's late speech errors. In S. Strauss, ed., *U-shaped behavioral growth*. New York: Academic Press.

Braine, M. D. S. (1963). On learning the grammatical order of words. *Psychological Review* 70, 323–348.

Braine, M. D. S. (1966). Learning the positions of words relative to a marker element. *Journal of Experimental Psychology* 72(4), 532–540.

Braine, M. D. S. (1971). Two models of the internalization of grammars. In D. I. Slobin, ed., *The ontogenesis of grammar*. New York: Academic Press.

Bresnan, J. W. (1978). A realistic transformational grammar. In M. Halle, J. W. Bresnan, and G. A. Miller, eds., *Linguistic theory and psychological reality*. Cambridge, Mass.: MIT Press.

Bresnan, J. W. (1982). The representation of grammatical relations in syntactic theory. In J. W. Bresnan, ed., *The mental representation of grammatical relations*. Cambridge, Mass.: MIT Press.

Broen, P. A. (1972). The verbal environment of the language-learning child. *Monograph of American Speech and Hearing Association* no. 17.

Brown, A. L., J. D. Bransford, R. A. Ferrara, and J. C. Campione (1983). Learning, remembering, and understanding. In J. H. Flavell and E. M. Markman, eds., P. H. Mussen, series ed., *Handbook of child psychology*. Vol. 3: *Cognitive development*. New York: Wiley.

Brown, R. (1973). *A first language*. Cambridge, Mass.: Harvard University Press.

Brown, R. (1977). Introduction. In C. E. Snow and C. A. Ferguson, eds., *Talking to children*. Cambridge: Cambridge University Press.

Brown, R., and U. Bellugi (1964). Three processes in the child's acquisition of syntax. *Harvard Educational Review* 34, 133–151.

Brown, R., and C. Hanlon (1970). Derivational complexity and the order of acquisition of child speech. In J. R. Hayes, ed., *Cognition and the development of language*. New York: Wiley.

Chomsky, N. (1957). *Syntactic structures*. The Hague: Mouton.

Chomsky, N. (1965). *Aspects of the theory of syntax*. Cambridge, Mass.: MIT Press.

Chomsky, N. (1973). Conditions on transformations. In S. R. Anderson and P. Kiparsky, eds., *Festschrift for Morris Halle*. New York: Holt, Rinehart & Winston.

Chomsky, N. (1975). *Reflections on language*. New York: Pantheon Press.

Chomsky, N. (1977). On Wh-movement. In P. W. Culicover, T. Wasow, and A. Akmajian, eds., *Formal syntax*. New York: Academic Press.

Chomsky, N. (1980). *Rules and representations*. New York: Columbia University Press.

Chomsky, N. (1981). *Lectures on government and binding*. Dordrecht: Foris Publications.

Chomsky, N., and M. Halle (1968). *The sound pattern of English*. New York: Harper & Row.

Collier, R., and J. t'Hart (1975). The role of intonation in speech perception. In A. Cohen and S. G. Nooteboom, eds., *Structure and process in speech perception*. Heidelberg: Springer-Verlag.

Cooper, W. E., and J. Paccia-Cooper (1980). *Syntax and speech*. Cambridge, Mass.: Harvard University Press.

Cooper, W. E., J. Paccia, and S. Lapointe (1978). Hierarchical coding in speech timing. *Cognitive Psychology* 10, 154–177.

Cooper, W. E., and J. M. Sorensen (1981). *Fundamental frequency in sentence production*. New York: Springer-Verlag.

Crystal, D. (1969). *Prosodic systems and intonation in English*. London: Cambridge University Press.

Culicover, P. W. (1984). Learnability explanations and processing explanations. *Natural Language and Linguistic Theory* 2, 77–104.

Culicover, P. W., and K. Wexler (1977). Some syntactic implications of a theory of language learnability. In P. W. Culicover, T. Wasow, and A. Akmajian, eds., *Formal syntax*. New York: Academic Press.

Demetras, M. J., and K. N. Post (1985). An analysis of negative feedback in mother-child dialogues. Paper presented at the Biennial Meeting of the Society for Research in Child Development, Toronto.

Emonds, J. (1970). *Root and structure-preserving transformations*. Doctoral dissertation, MIT.

Emonds, J. (1976). *A transformational approach to English syntax*. New York: Academic Press.

Feldman, H., S. Goldin-Meadow, and L. Gleitman (1978). Beyond Herodotus: The creation of language by linguistically deprived deaf children. In A. Lock, ed., *Action, symbol, and gesture: The emergence of language*. New York: Academic Press.

Ferguson, C. A. (1964). Baby talk in six languages. *American Anthropologist* 66, 103–114.

Fernald, A. (1981). Four-month-olds prefer to listen to "motherese." Paper presented at the Biennial Meeting of the Society for Research in Child Development, Boston.

Fernald, A., and P. K. Kuhl (1981). Fundamental frequency as an acoustic determinant of infant preference for motherese. Paper presented at the Biennial Meeting of the Society for Research in Child Development, Boston.

Fodor, J. A. (1966). How to learn to talk: Some simple ways. In F. Smith and G. A. Miller, eds., *The genesis of language*. Cambridge, Mass.: MIT Press.

Fodor, J. A., T. G. Bever, and M. F. Garrett (1974). *The psychology of language*. New York: McGraw-Hill.

Fodor, J. D. (1984). Learnability and parsability: A reply to Culicover. *Natural Language and Linguistic Theory* 2, 105–150.

Furrow, D., K. Nelson, and H. Benedict (1979). Mother's speech to children and syntactic development: Some simple relationships. *Journal of Child Language* 6, 423–442.

Garnica, O. K. (1977). Some prosodic and paralinguistic features of speech to young children. In C. E. Snow and C. A. Ferguson, eds., *Talking to children*. Cambridge: Cambridge University Press.

Gazdar, G. (1982). Phrase structure grammar. In G. K. Pullum and P. Jacobson, eds., *The nature of syntactic representation*. Boston: D. Reidel.

Gazdar, G., G. K. Pullum, and I. A. Sag (1982). Auxiliaries and related phenomena in a restrictive theory of grammar. *Language* 58, 591–638.

Gleitman, L. R. (1981). Maturational determinants of language growth. *Cognition* 10, 103–114.

Gleitman, L. R., E. L. Newport, and H. Gleitman (1984). The current status of the motherese hypothesis. *Journal of Child Language* 11, 43–79.

Gleitman, L. R., and E. Wanner (1982). Language learning: State of the art. In E. Wanner and L. R. Gleitman, eds., *Language acquisition: The state of the art*. Cambridge, Mass.: Harvard University Press.

Gold, E. M. (1967). Language identification in the limit. *Information and Control* 10, 447–474.

Goldin-Meadow, S. (1982). The resilience of recursion: A study of a communication system developed without a conventional language model. In E. Wanner and L. R. Gleitman, eds., *Language acquisition: The state of the art*. Cambridge, Mass.: Harvard University Press.

Goldin-Meadow, S., and C. Mylander (1984). Gestural communication in deaf children: The effects and noneffects of parental input on early language development. *Monographs of the Society for Research in Child Development*, Serial No. 207, 49, Nos. 3–4.

Greenberg, J. H. (1963). Some universals of grammar with particular reference to the order of meaningful elements. In J. H. Greenberg, ed., *Universals of language*. Cambridge, Mass.: MIT Press.

Hamburger, H., and K. Wexler (1973). Identifiability of a class of transformational grammars. In K. J. J. Hintikka, J. M. E. Moravcsik, and P. Suppes, eds., *Approaches to natural language*. Boston: D. Reidel.

Hamburger, H., and K. Wexler (1975). A mathematical theory of learning transformational grammar. *Journal of Mathematical Psychology* 12, 137–177.

Hirsh-Pasek, K., R. Treiman, and M. Schneiderman (1984). Brown & Hanlon revisited: Mother's sensitivity to ungrammatical forms. *Journal of Child Language* 11, 81–88.

Hoff-Ginsberg, E. C. (1981). The role of linguistic experience in the child's acquisition of syntax. Doctoral dissertation, University of Michigan.

Hoff-Ginsberg, E., and M. Shatz (1982). Linguistic input and the child's acquisition of language. *Psychological Bulletin* 92, 3–26.

Hooper, J. B., and S. A. Thompson (1973). On the applicability of root transformations. *Linguistic Inquiry* 4, 465–497.

Hopcroft, J. E., and J. D. Ullman (1979). *Introduction to automata theory, languages, and computation*. Reading, Mass.: Addison-Wesley.

Hume, T. (1919). *An enquiry concerning human understanding*. New York: P. F. Collier & Son.

Huttenlocher, J., and D. Burke (1976). Why does memory span increase with age? *Cognitive Psychology* 8, 1–31.

Jackendoff, R. S. (1977). $\bar{X}$ *syntax: A study of phrase structure*. Linguistic Inquiry Monograph 2. Cambridge, Mass.: MIT Press.

Jusczyk, P. W., and E. J. Thompson (1978). Perception of a phonetic contrast in multisyllabic utterances by two-month-old infants. *Perception & Psychophysics* 23, 105–109.

Karmiloff-Smith, A. (1979). Language as a formal problem space for children. Paper presented at the MPG-NIAS Conference on Beyond Description in Child Language, Nijmegen, Holland.

Karzon, R. G. (1985). Discrimination of polysyllabic sequences by one- to four-month-old infants. *Journal of Experimental Child Psychology* 39, 326–342.

Kean, M. -L. (1980). Grammatical representations and the description of language processing. In D. Caplan, ed., *Biological studies of mental processes*. Cambridge, Mass.: MIT Press.

Kuhl, P., and J. D. Miller (1975). Speech perception in early infancy: Discrimination of speech-sound categories. *Journal of the Acoustical Society of America* 58, Suppl. 1, S56.

Lackner, J. R., and M. Garrett (1973). Resolving ambiguity: Effects of biasing context in the unattended ear. *Cognition* 2, 359–372.

Lehiste, I. (1970). *Suprasegmentals*. Cambridge, Mass.: MIT Press.

Levelt, W. J. M. (1974). *Psycholinguistic applications*. Vol. 3 of *Formal grammars in linguistics and psycholinguistics*. The Hague: Mouton.

Levelt, W. J. M. (1975). *What became of LAD?* Lisse, Netherlands: Peter de Ridder Press.

Levy, L. S., and A. K. Joshi (1978). Skeletal structural descriptions. *Information and Control* 39, 192–211.

MacWhinney, B., and C. Snow (1985). The child language data exchange system. *Journal of Child Language* 12, 271–296.

Maling, J., and A. Zaenen (1977). TOP-position. Paper presented at the Annual Meeting of the Linguistic Society of America, Philadelphia.

Mandler, J. (1983). Representation. In J. H. Flavell and E. M. Markman, eds., P. H. Mussen, series ed., *Handbook of child psychology*. Vol. 3: *Cognitive development*. New York: Wiley.

Maratsos, M. (1983). Some current issues in the study of the acquisition of grammar. In J. H. Flavell and E. M. Markman, eds., P. H. Mussen, series ed., *Handbook of child psychology*. Vol. 3: *Cognitive development*. New York: Wiley.

Maratsos, M., and M. Chalkley (1980). The internal language of children's syntax: The ontogenesis and representation of syntactic categories. In K. Nelson, ed., *Children's language*. Vol. 2. New York: Gardner Press.

McNeill, D. (1966). Developmental psycholinguistics. In F. Smith and G. A. Miller, eds., *The genesis of language*. Cambridge, Mass.: MIT Press.

Miller, G. A., and N. Chomsky (1963). Finitary models of language users. In R. D. Luce, R. R. Bush, and E. Galanter, eds., *Handbook of mathematical psychology*. Vol. 2. New York: Wiley.

Moeser, S. D., and A. S. Bregman (1972). The role of reference in the acquisition of a miniature artificial language. *Journal of Verbal Learning and Verbal Behavior* 11, 759–769.

Morgan, J. L. (1983). Learning a complex grammar from simple input. Doctoral dissertation, University of Illinois.

Morgan, J. L. (1984). Some concepts and consequences of Degree 1 learnability. *Papers and Reports in Child Language Development* 23, 98–106.

Morgan, J. L. (1985). Prosodic encoding of syntactic information in speech to young children. Paper presented at the Biennial Meeting of the Society for Research in Child Development, Toronto.

Morgan, J. L. (1986). Prosody and syntax in language input. Unpublished manuscript.

Morgan, J. L., R. P. Meier, and E. L. Newport (1986). Structural packaging in the input to language learning: Contributions of intonational and morphological marking of phrases to the acquisition of language. Unpublished manuscript.

Morgan, J. L., and E. L. Newport (1981). The role of constituent structure in the induction of an artificial language. *Journal of Verbal Learning and Verbal Behavior* 20, 67–85.

Morse, P. A. (1972). The discrimination of speech and nonspeech stimuli in early infancy. *Journal of Experimental Child Psychology* 14, 477–492.

Newport, E. L. (1977). Motherese: The speech of mothers to young children. In N. Castellan, D. Pisoni, and G. Potts, eds., *Cognitive theory*. Vol. 2. Hillsdale, N.J.: Lawrence Erlbaum Associates.

Newport, E. L., H. Gleitman, and L. R. Gleitman (1977). Mother, I'd rather do it myself: Some effects and non-effects of maternal speech style. In C. E. Snow and C. A. Ferguson, eds., *Talking to children*. Cambridge: Cambridge University Press.

Osherson, D., and S. Weinstein (1982). Criteria of language learning. *Information and Control* 52, 123–138.

Osherson, D., M. Stob, and S. Weinstein (1982). Learning strategies. *Information and Control* 53, 32–51.

Osherson, D., M. Stob, and S. Weinstein (1986). *Systems that learn: An introduction to learning theory for cognitive and computer scientists*. Cambridge, Mass.: MIT Press.

Penner, S. G. (1985). Parental responses to grammatically correct and incorrect child utterances. Doctoral dissertation, University of Minnesota.

Peters, S. (1972). The projection problem: How is a grammar to be selected? In S. Peters, ed., *Goals of linguistic theory*. Englewood Cliffs, N.J.: Prentice-Hall.

Piattelli-Palmarini, M., ed. (1980). *Language and learning: The debate between Jean Piaget and Noam Chomsky*. Cambridge, Mass.: Harvard University Press.

Pinker, S. (1979). Formal models of language learning. *Cognition* 7, 217–283.

Pinker, S. (1981). Comments on the paper by Wexler. In C. L. Baker and J. J. McCarthy, eds., *The logical problem of language acquisition*. Cambridge, Mass.: MIT Press.

Pinker, S. (1982). A theory of the acquisition of lexical-interpretive grammars. In J. W. Bresnan, ed., *The mental representation of grammatical relations*. Cambridge, Mass.: MIT Press.

Pinker, S. (1984). *Language learnability and language development*. Cambridge, Mass.: Harvard University Press.

Pye, C. (1981). Children's first verb forms in Quiche Mayan. Paper presented at the Sixth Annual Boston University Conference on Language Development, Boston.

Read, C., and P. Schreiber (1982). Why short subjects are hard to find. In E. Wanner and L. R. Gleitman, eds., *Language acquisition: The state of the art*. Cambridge, Mass.: Harvard University Press.

Reinhart, T. (1976). The syntactic domain of anaphora. Doctoral dissertation, MIT.

Reinhart, T. (1981). Definite NP anaphora and c-command domains. *Linguistic Inquiry* 12, 605–635.

Remick, H. (1971). The maternal environment of linguistic development. Doctoral dissertation, University of California at Davis.

Rizzi, L. (1978). Violations of the WH island constraint in Italian and the subjacency condition. *Montreal Working Papers in Linguistics* 11, 155–190.

Rochemont, M. S. (1982). On the empirical motivation of the raising principle. *Linguistic Inquiry* 13, 150–154.

Ross, J. R. (1967). *Constraints on variables in syntax*. Doctoral dissertation, MIT. (Distributed by the Indiana University Linguistics Club, Bloomington.)

Schlesinger, I. M. (1982). *Steps to language: Toward a theory of native language acquisition*. Hillsdale, N.J.: Lawrence Erlbaum Associates.

Scott, D. R. (1982). Duration as a cue to the perception of a phrase boundary. *Journal of the Acoustical Society of America* 71, 996–1007.

Scott, D. R., and A. Cutler (1984). Segmental phonology and the perception of syntactic structure. *Journal of Verbal Learning and Verbal Behavior* 23, 450–466.

Selkirk, E. O. (1980). On prosodic structure and its relation to syntactic structure. Mimeograph, Indiana University Linguistics Club.

Slobin, D. I. (1973). Cognitive prerequisites for the development of grammar. In C. A. Ferguson and D. I. Slobin, eds., *Studies of child language development*. New York: Holt, Rinehart & Winston.

Smith, C. S. (1961). A class of complex modifiers in English. *Language* 37, 342–365.

Smith, K. H. (1963). Recall of paired verbal units under various conditions of organization. Doctoral dissertation, University of Minnesota.

Smith, K. H. (1966). Grammatical intrusions in the free recall of structured letter pairs. *Journal of Verbal Learning and Verbal Behavior* 5, 447–454.

Smith, K. H. (1969). Learning co-occurrence restrictions: Rule learning or rote learning? *Journal of Verbal Learning and Verbal Behavior* 8, 319–321.

Snow, C. E. (1972). Mothers' speech to children learning language. *Child Development* 43, 549–565.

Solan, L. (1983). *Pronominal reference: Child language and the theory of grammar*. Dordrecht: D. Reidel.

Sorensen, J., W. Cooper, and J. Paccia (1978). Speech timing of grammatical categories. *Cognition* 6, 135–153.

Spring, D. R., and P. S. Dale (1977). Discrimination of linguistic stress in early infancy. *Journal of Speech and Hearing Research* 20, 224–232.

Streeter, L. A. (1978). Acoustic determinants of phrase boundary perception. *Journal of the Acoustical Society of America* 64, 1582–1592.

Sullivan, J. W., and F. D. Horowitz (1983). The effects of intonation on infant attention: The role of the rising intonation contour. *Journal of Child Language* 10, 521–534.

Tager-Flusberg, H. (1985). How children acquire complex syntax: The interaction of prosodic features and grammatical structure. Paper presented at the Biennial Meeting of the Society for Research in Child Development, Toronto.

Thatcher, J. W. (1967). Characterizing derivation trees of context-free grammars through a generalization of finite automata theory. *Journal of Computer and Systems Sciences* 1, 317–322.

Thatcher, J. W. (1973). Tree automata: An informal survey. In A. V. Aho, ed., *Currents in the theory of computing*. Englewood Cliffs, N.J.: Prentice-Hall.

Valian, V. (1981). Linguistic knowledge and language acquisition. *Cognition* 10, 323–329.

Valian, V., J. Winzemer, and A. Erreich (1981). A "little linguist" model of syntax learning. In S. L. Tavakolian, ed., *Language acquisition and linguistic theory*. Cambridge, Mass.: MIT Press.

Wexler, K. (1981). Some issues in the theory of learnability. In C. L. Baker and J. J. McCarthy, eds., *The logical problem of language acquisition*. Cambridge, Mass.: MIT Press.

Wexler, K., and P. W. Culicover (1980). *Formal principles of language acquisition*. Cambridge, Mass.: MIT Press.

Wexler, K., P. W. Culicover, and H. Hamburger (1975). Learning-theoretic foundations of linguistic universals. *Theoretical Linguistics* 2, 213–253.

Wexler, K., and H. Hamburger (1973). On the insufficiency of surface data for the learning of transformational languages. In K. J. J. Hintikka, J. M. E. Moravcsik, and P. Suppes, eds., *Approaches to natural language*. Boston: D. Reidel.

Williams, E. S. (1981). A readjustment in the learnability assumptions. In C. L. Baker and J. J. McCarthy, eds., *The logical problem of language acquisition*. Cambridge, Mass.: MIT Press.

Index

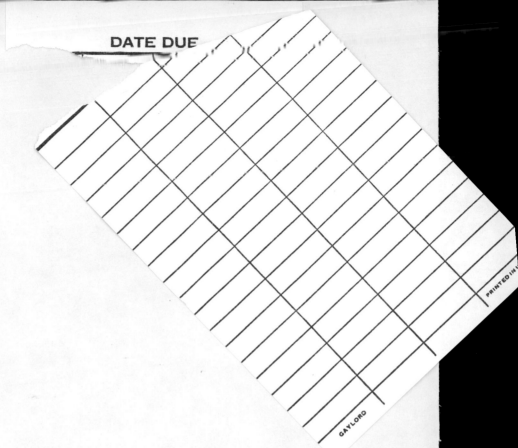